Mobile IP Technology and Applications

Stefan Raab

Madhavi W. Chandra, Ph.D.

Contributing Author: Kent Leung

Foreword by Fred Baker

Cisco Press

800 East 96th Street
Indianapolis, IN 46240 USA

Mobile IP Technology and Applications

Stefan Raab

Madhavi W. Chandra, Ph.D.

Contributing Author: Kent Leung

Copyright© 2005 Cisco Systems, Inc.

Published by:
Cisco Press
800 East 96th Street
Indianapolis, IN 46240 USA

Printed in the United States of America   1 2 3 4 5 6 7 8 9 0

First Printing June 2005

Library of Congress Cataloging-in-Publication Number: 2002116861

ISBN: 158705132X

Warning and Disclaimer

This book is designed to provide information about Mobile IP technology and applications. Every effort has been made to make this book as complete and as accurate as possible, but no warranty or fitness is implied.

The information is provided on an "as is" basis. The author, Cisco Press, and Cisco Systems, Inc. shall have neither liability nor responsibility to any person or entity with respect to any loss or damages arising from the information contained in this book or from the use of the discs or programs that may accompany it.

The opinions expressed in this book belong to the authors and are not necessarily those of Cisco Systems, Inc.

Trademark Acknowledgments

All terms mentioned in this book that are known to be trademarks or service marks have been appropriately capitalized. Cisco Press or Cisco Systems, Inc. cannot attest to the accuracy of this information. Use of a term in this book should not be regarded as affecting the validity of any trademark or service mark.

Corporate and Government Sales

Cisco Press offers excellent discounts on this book when ordered in quantity for bulk purchases or special sales.

For more information please contact: U.S. Corporate and Government Sales 1-800-382-3419 corpsales@pearsontechgroup.com

For sales outside the U.S. please contact: International Sales international@pearsoned.com

621.384

Feedback Information

At Cisco Press, our goal is to create in-depth technical books of the highest quality and value. Each book is crafted with care and precision, undergoing rigorous development that involves the unique expertise of members from the professional technical community.

Readers' feedback is a natural continuation of this process. If you have any comments regarding how we could improve the quality of this book, or otherwise alter it to better suit your needs, you can contact us through e-mail at feedback@ciscopress.com. Please make sure to include the book title and ISBN in your message.

We greatly appreciate your assistance.

Publisher	John Wait
Editor-in-Chief	John Kane
Executive Editor	Brett Bartow
Cisco Representative	Anthony Wolfenden
Cisco Press Program Manager	Jeff Brady
Production Manager	Patrick Kanouse
Development Editor	Sheri Cain
Project Editor	Marc Fowler
Copy Editor	John Edwards
Technical Editors	Steve Glass, Richard Shao, Kevin Turek
Team Coordinator	Tammi Barnett
Cover Designer	Louisa Adair
Composition	Mark Shirar
Indexer	Christine Karpeles

CISCO SYSTEMS

Corporate Headquarters
Cisco Systems, Inc.
170 West Tasman Drive
San Jose, CA 95134-1706
USA
www.cisco.com
Tel: 408 526-4000
    800 553-NETS (6387)
Fax: 408 526-4100

European Headquarters
Cisco Systems International BV
Haarlerbergpark
Haarlerbergweg 13-19
1101 CH Amsterdam
The Netherlands
www-europe.cisco.com
Tel: 31 0 20 357 1000
Fax: 31 0 20 357 1100

Americas Headquarters
Cisco Systems, Inc.
170 West Tasman Drive
San Jose, CA 95134-1706
USA
www.cisco.com
Tel: 408 526-7660
Fax: 408 527-0883

Asia Pacific Headquarters
Cisco Systems, Inc.
Capital Tower
168 Robinson Road
#22-01 to #29-01
Singapore 068912
www.cisco.com
Tel: +65 6317 7777
Fax: +65 6317 7799

Cisco Systems has more than 200 offices in the following countries and regions. Addresses, phone numbers, and fax numbers are listed on the
Cisco.com Web site at www.cisco.com/go/offices.

Argentina • Australia • Austria • Belgium • Brazil • Bulgaria • Canada • Chile • China PRC • Colombia • Costa Rica • Croatia • Czech Republic
Denmark • Dubai, UAE • Finland • France • Germany • Greece • Hong Kong SAR • Hungary • India • Indonesia • Ireland • Israel • Italy
Japan • Korea • Luxembourg • Malaysia • Mexico • The Netherlands • New Zealand • Norway • Peru • Philippines • Poland • Portugal
Puerto Rico • Romania • Russia • Saudi Arabia • Scotland • Singapore • Slovakia • Slovenia • South Africa • Spain • Sweden
Switzerland • Taiwan • Thailand • Turkey • Ukraine • United Kingdom • United States • Venezuela • Vietnam • Zimbabwe

About the Authors

Stefan Raab joined Cisco Systems in January 2001 from Nextel Communications as a technical leader and deployment engineer for the IP Mobility group, IOS Technologies Division (ITD). He has over nine years of experience with IP mobility deployments and is an expert on real-life applications for the technology. Since joining Cisco, Mr. Raab has focused on bringing his real-world experience to the software engineering process and relating advanced technologies to customers. Presently, he is working with advanced mobility technologies, including Mobile IPv6, Ad Hoc Networking, and Mobile IPv4 optimizations. He is coinventor of numerous patents submitted to the United States Patent and Trademark Office. Mr. Raab holds his B.S. degree in computer science from the College of William and Mary. He currently resides in South Riding, Virginia, with his wife, Jennifer, and daughter, Katrina. He has innumerable hobbies, ranging from woodworking and photography to training for and competing in triathlons.

Madhavi W. Chandra joined Cisco Systems in May 2000 from the National Institute of Standards and Technology as a software engineer for the IP Mobility group, IOS Technologies Division (ITD). She holds a bachelor of science degree in computer engineering from the University of Miami, and master's and Ph.D. degrees in computer engineering from Johns Hopkins University. Madhavi is instrumental in designing advanced technologies in IOS mobility involving features for Mobile IP and Mobile Ad Hoc Networks, in which she is one of the lead architects. Madhavi has various publications, including technical IEEE journal papers, IEEE conference papers, white papers, Internet drafts, and RFCs. She is coinventor of numerous patents submitted to the United States Patent and Trademark Office. Above all, Madhavi feels blessed to have a loving and spirited brother, Manoj, and a supportive family. She resides in Cary, North Carolina, with her husband, Sanjai, and son, Kaveen. One of the driving sayings in her life is, "It is nice to be important, but it is far more important to be nice and maintain your integrity."

About the Contributing Author

Kent Leung is a Cisco Distinguished Engineer at Cisco Systems, where he joined in January 1994. As the original Cisco IOS developer for Mobile IP, he was instrumental to the success in the first commercial deployment of this technology. Kent has been the lead architect for many Mobile IP features in Cisco routers and switches. Numerous innovations were issued patents from the United States Patent and Trademark Office. His contributions to standards development organizations include IETF, 3GPP2, and WiMAX. Kent received his bachelor of science degree in electrical and computer engineering from the University of California, Davis. He cherishes family time with his wife, Lynn, and children, Amy and Austin. His hobbies include tennis, reading, watching movies, and traveling.

About the Technical Reviewers

Steven Glass has a decade-long history with Mobile IP, beginning with its early days as an IETF draft in 1994. While with FTP Software from 1992–1998, Steven developed the first commercially available Mobile Agents in 1994, participated in the first Mobile IP Testathon in 1995, became its lead engineer in 1996, and coordinated the second Mobile IP Testathon in 1997. Employed by Sun Microsystems in 1999, he was the senior staff technical lead for Sun Microsystems' Mobile IP project from 2001–2002. Beyond Mobile IP, Steven became the technical lead for the release of Solaris 9 update 3 from 2002–2003. Other contributions include RFCs 3543, 2989, 2977, 2504, 2290, and 2196 for the IETF; several technical book reviews for Prentice Hall and Addison-Wesley, magazine publications, white papers, architectures, and draft reviews too numerous to mention; and he has contributed to many technological innovations, including a U.S. Patent application through Sun Microsystems for his work with "Home Agents as DHCP Proxies." Also an Internet Security and Privacy expert, Steven contributed to several startup ventures as a network and security architect for distributed video-processing systems, his own home-network appliances, and he is currently working on his own publication in Geoelectrodynamics. Steven received his bachelor's degree in Physics and Mathematics in 1991 from Boston University, where he also did post-graduate work. He has spent time in 25 countries, and his hobbies include a passion for baseball, mountain biking, sea kayaking, scuba diving, tennis, and skiing.

Richard Shao, CCIE No. 5723, joined Cisco in 1999 and is currently working as a technical marketing engineer supporting IP mobility in the Cisco Internet Technology Division. Prior to working in this division, Richard was a technical lead dealing with Cisco Catalyst switches in the Cisco Technical Assistance Center (TAC). Richard earned his master of science degree in telecommunication from the University of Colorado at Boulder.

Kevin Turek, CCIE No. 7284, joined Cisco in 2000 and is currently working as a network consulting engineer supporting wireless/mobility on the Advanced Technology in Cisco's Federal Support Program. He has been involved with several Cisco Press projects, including coauthoring the Cisco Press book Cisco Catalyst QoS: Quality of Service in Campus Networks. Kevin earned his Bachelor of Science degree in business administration at the State University of New York, Stony Brook.

Dedications

To Jennifer, for supporting me in this process and in life. To Katrina, for giving up so much daddy time and for being my hope and joy. And to my family and friends for their encouragement and motivation.

—Stefan Raab

To my parents, Sunanda and Subbarao Wunnava, for being my unconditional pillars, and to Asha and Pravosh Gupta, for their love. To my husband, Sanjai, who is my entrusted beacon. And to my son, Kaveen, whose smile lights up my heart and who instantaneously became the essence of my life.

—Madhavi W. Chandra

Acknowledgments

We want to thank the IOS Mobile IP team for giving us support, answering questions, clarifying text, and most of all, building the product. We would also like to thank our manager, Read Bell, for supporting us during the process. We are grateful to our technical reviewers for taking the time to apply their expertise in reviewing the manuscript.

We are grateful to our technical reviewers, Steve Glass, Richard Shao, and Kevin Turek, for taking the time to apply their expertise in reviewing the manuscript, and to Fred Baker for stepping up to write the foreword for our book.

This Book Is Safari Enabled

The Safari® Enabled icon on the cover of your favorite technology book means the book is available through Safari Bookshelf. When you buy this book, you get free access to the online edition for 45 days.

Safari Bookshelf is an electronic reference library that lets you easily search thousands of technical books, find code samples, download chapters, and access technical information whenever and wherever you need it.

To gain 45-day Safari Enabled access to this book:

- Go to http://www.ciscopress.com/safarienabled

- Complete the brief registration form

- Enter the coupon code 51LT-1Z4M-3CKH-07N1-AT54

If you have difficulty registering on Safari Bookshelf or accessing the online edition, please e-mail customer-service@safaribooksonline.com.

Contents at a Glance

Contents

Icons Used in This Book

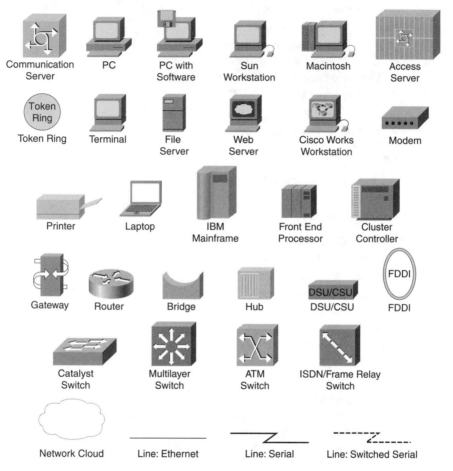

Communication Server   PC   PC with Software   Sun Workstation   Macintosh   Access Server

Token Ring   Terminal   File Server   Web Server   Cisco Works Workstation   Modem

Printer   Laptop   IBM Mainframe   Front End Processor   Cluster Controller

Gateway   Router   Bridge   Hub   DSU/CSU   FDDI

Catalyst Switch   Multilayer Switch   ATM Switch   ISDN/Frame Relay Switch

Network Cloud   Line: Ethernet   Line: Serial   Line: Switched Serial

Command Syntax Conventions

The conventions used to present command syntax in this book are the same conventions used in the IOS Command Reference. The Command Reference describes these conventions as follows:

- Boldface indicates commands and keywords that are entered literally as shown.

- Italics indicate arguments for which you supply actual values.

- Vertical bars (|) separate alternative, mutually exclusive elements.

- Square brackets [ ] indicate optional elements.

- Braces { } indicate a required choice.

- Braces within brackets [{ }] indicate a required choice within an optional element.

Foreword

In their opening sentences, the authors of this book, Madhavi W. Chandra and Stefan Rabb, span a gap in time of a few years and a few light-years. In 1943, the chief executive officer of what is now one of the world's largest information technology and computer manufacturing firms said, "I think there is a world market for maybe five computers." Twelve years later, the editor-in-charge of business books for Prentice Hall said: "I can assure you that data processing is a fad that won't last out the year." In 1990, I didn't normally tell people what I did for a living, because outside of a few geeks they had no idea what I was talking about. In 2000, I rhetorically asked a young coed whether she knew what the Internet was; she rolled her eyes and replied "that is SO condescending...."

For me, the Internet is all about mobility. Mobility means many things, though. I am mobile—at this instant, I am sitting in a hotel in Tokyo, talking on the telephone with people in Washington and Kabul, and preparing an email to a person from India who lives in North Carolina which I will send via a server in California. My computer is mobile—it moves around with me, and it is sometimes attached (with or without a wire) and sometimes not. In addition, we are finding ways to build networks that move as well.

The value of IP Mobility, the subject of this book, is for a fairly special aspect of this motion. If I connect from wherever I am, it is generally sufficient for me to be what Madhavi calls "nomadic"—to connect from where I am using a random IP address to a server. But if I need an address that someone else can predict (perhaps for Voice over IP, for a video exchange, or to use peer-to-peer software to exchange files of interest) then the address must follow me around as I wander through the fixed Internet. IP Mobility provides the ability not only for me to connect to the world at large but for it to find and connect to me.

Today, I'm told, Internet technology undergirds perhaps ten percent of the industrialized world. It is replacing traditional telephone technology as the way one carries voice or video, and mobile telephone technology is impacting the Internet as well, as service providers seek to use common infrastructure to support fixed telephony, wireless telephony, and various forms of Internet technology.

The philosopher Hegel, Karl Marx's teacher, propounded a concept he called the "Dialectic." He observed that societies developed technology and economic systems to support themselves; agrarian societies thought in terms of land ownership, while societies built on flocks and herds thought more in terms of temporary use of land that was otherwise not owned by anyone or considered a commons. When they needed to live close together, these systems would come into conflict, and a new system would emerge built on part of each of the older systems while also offering something new. He called the original systems the "thesis" and "antithesis," and the result the "synthesis."

I think this process is at work in global communications today. There is nothing wrong with the traditional telephone system, if you want to sit at your desk. But mobile telephony, Internet telephony, and Internet data exchange are very different, and they increasingly live together. We have seen the conflicts, and we are now seeing the synthesis of a new system of which, at this point, we can only guess the form. IP Mobility, along with other technologies, will have a place in that synthesis, but it remains to be seen exactly what or how.

I'll let Mahdavi and Stefan explain the part we have worked out to date and join them in working out the next steps.

Fred Baker
Cisco Fellow
Cisco Systems, Inc.
April 2005

Introduction

The Internet and mobile communications are defining how and when people access information, with mobile phones, PDAs, and laptops driving the need for "always-on" IP connectivity. One challenge to mobile data communication is moving data across different networks while maintaining communication. The solution to this problem is a standards-based protocol: Mobile IP. Mobile IP is an open standard defined by the IETF that allows users to keep the same IP address, stay connected, and maintain ongoing applications while roaming among IP networks.

Who Should Read This Book

This book is intended for anyone with a basic IP routing background who is interested in IP mobility. Having an understanding of how IP packets are routed through the Internet and the resulting security implications is useful. The book appeals to a wide spectrum of audiences, ranging from network and system engineers to graduate students.

Goals and Methods

This book introduces you to IP mobility and specifically Mobile IP. In the first part, you learn in detail the Mobile IP protocol and related security implications. The rest of the book walks you through increasingly more complex IOS configurations for real-world Mobile IP solutions. This book is well suited for both linear and random-access consumption. Readers who want to read from cover to cover will find little overlap between the chapters. Those intending a more random-access approach will find numerous cross references to help them navigate within the book. The chapters are laid out so that features are introduced in relation to the environment where they are to be used. Thus, you can find the information that you need based on the network environment that you are trying to achieve.

How This Book Is Organized

This book starts with a brief overview of mobility and wireless technology. It then presents a detailed introduction to the Mobile IP protocol, and it addresses the practical application of Mobile IP in real-world environments. It looks in depth at advanced Mobile IP features, including NAT traversal, integration with IPSec, and network mobility. Mobility solutions addressed in the book include enterprise campus wireless LAN and metropolitan mobility, for both individual devices and whole networks (network mobility). The book builds upon itself, with material presented in an earlier chapter being applicable to scenarios in later chapters.

The book delves into Cisco IOS Mobile IP configurations, demonstrating working implementations of the Cisco Mobile IP components. It includes troubleshooting methodologies for common failures and best practices. The book is supported by real-world examples throughout the text. Each example is designed to teach configuration, management, and troubleshooting—all of which are directly applicable to users' network mobility needs.

This book is divided into nine chapters and an appendix, and each chapter details an important facet of Mobile IP, as follows:

- Chapter 1, "Mobile and Wireless Technologies," introduces the concept of mobility and the requirements of mobility protocols. Wireless networking technologies are also introduced.

- Chapter 2, "Understanding Mobile IP," takes a detailed look at the Mobile IP protocol. The necessary components of a Mobile IP network are defined. Features, functions, and message flows are also covered.

- Chapter 3, "Mobile IP Security," examines security concepts related to Mobile IP, including protocol authentication and dynamic keying.

- Chapter 4, "IOS Mobile IP in the Lab," introduces Cisco IOS Mobile IP in an easy-to-learn lab format. A basic topology is built and evaluated, and then alternate scenarios are presented.

- Chapter 5, "Campus Mobility: Client-Based Mobile IP," looks at Mobile IP deployment in campus (intranet) networks. High-availability solutions and integration with AAA servers are covered.

- Chapter 6, "Metro Mobility: Client-Based Mobile IP," goes beyond the campus to look at metro mobility. Features covered include reverse tunneling, firewall and NAT traversal, and integration with VPN technologies.

- Chapter 7, "Metro Mobility: Cisco Mobile Networks," takes a close look at Cisco Mobile Networks, a Mobile IP client on a router. Basic configuration details are covered first, followed by integration topics including redundancy, QoS, and VPN.

- Chapter 8, "Deployment Scalability and Management," circles back to look at management and operation of the Mobile IP infrastructure. Home Address management, scalability considerations, and network management are explored.

- Chapter 9, "A Look Ahead," looks to the future of mobility, presenting current work and future ideas. Layer 2 integration challenges are addressed, and Mobile IPv6 is introduced. We finish with unstructured mobility and mobile ad hoc networking.

- Appendix A, "Answers to Review Questions," provides the answers to the "Review Questions" sections that appear at the end of each chapter.

- Appendix B, "IOS Mobile IP: Supported SNMP MIBs," contains a graphical representation of the Mobile IP Management Information Base (MIB) objects available in Cisco IOS.

CHAPTER 1

Mobile and Wireless Technologies

Today, the instantaneous communications capabilities of networks are quickly replacing the process of printing and delivering correspondence. The rise of the Internet has turned computers from data processing devices to real-time communications devices. E-mail, instant messaging, and web browsing are becoming the most popular applications. Mobile computing is driving the need to be connected even further. Users are rapidly adopting wireless LAN (WLAN) technologies because they expect real-time communications whenever and wherever they turn their computer on. Computers themselves are evolving into several new classes of devices, from smartphones and personal digital assistants (PDAs) to embedded navigation systems, all of which rely on real-time data communications.

Mobile data communications are not just about getting your e-mail and surfing the web. Many of the applications are more specific to individual industry. One of the best examples is a connected ambulance. Moving from an ambulance that has only voice radios to one that has real-time high-speed voice, video, and data significantly improves the level of care that can be offered to a patient. Now the on-scene paramedics can have access to medical records and hospital staff. The hospital can be ready when the patient arrives because all the data can be transmitted en route.

Mobility and wireless technology are not synonymous, but they do go hand in hand, especially for computing devices. Without wireless technology, mobile communications would be difficult. Carrying cables and plugging in at every location is inconvenient and does not allow connectivity while in motion. Wireless technology allows computing devices to stay connected while in motion, but only recently has this technology been able to meet the needs of the mass market. Cost has decreased, and speed and reliability have increased to the point where it is commonplace to see wireless technology integrated into computing devices rather than offered as a third-party add-on. Limitations to the technology still exist, though; for example, it is common for throughput to decrease as range and coverage area increase. This means that no single wireless technology is universally applicable. Just as in the wired world, LAN, Metro Area Network (MAN), and Wide Area Network (WAN) technologies are available, but unlike the wired world, each device connects directly to each network. Still, "mobile" devices are rapidly flooding the marketplace, but what makes a computing device mobile? A handle? Batteries? Wireless communications links?

Mobility

In general use, the term *mobile* is loosely defined. At a minimum, it implies that the noun with which it is paired is capable of moving easily. A mobile computer is a computer that is not confined to a desk by several large pieces of equipment and numerous wires. Current usage, however, is beginning to imply a greater degree of freedom. For example, a cordless phone is one that can only be used near its base station in the home, whereas a mobile phone can be used anywhere. These phones would not be considered mobile if they had to be plugged in wherever they were being used. On the same note, a mobile phone would not be considered truly mobile if the call was dropped every time it moved into a new cell site. When coupled with communications devices, mobility usually implies radio technology.

NOTE   It is important to note the difference between *mobility* and *nomadicity*. In this book, the latter refers to the ability to move from one location to another and start communications. Nomadicity can best be described by the laptop user who moves from one location to another, plugs in the laptop, obtains an Internet connection, and starts communicating. The user, however, will need to terminate and restart sessions and applications as a result of the move.

The common use of the term mobile computing implies nomadic computing. When a businessperson uses their laptop in the office, shuts it down, takes it home, and uses it at home — this is nomadic. If the user is responsible for establishing a new connection everywhere they go — this is nomadic. Our goal in the book is to facilitate a device that is *always* connected through the best available link.

Wireless Technology

The relationship between mobility and wireless is analogous for both telephony and data communications. Wireless telephony technology should be familiar to most readers and, as such, is used for description purposes in this chapter. Wireless telephony is already ubiquitous — cordless phones in the home and cell phones on the go — but how do they work and why are they different? The difference between cordless phones and mobile phones is the network infra-structure and wireless technology. Cordless phones are purchased as two parts: the handset and the base station. A handset can only talk to one base station without reprogramming. This is done to prevent our neighbors from making phone calls on our phone line. Cordless phones are often very-short-range devices; they are typically only usable within a few hundred feet of the base station. Increased range requires increased power. This is how early mobile phone systems operated: A single base station would serve an entire city. However, just as with radio and television, a limited number of channels are available to make calls. To make a business out of mobile phone service, operators needed a way to make tens of thousands of calls at a time, not just tens of calls.

Cellular telephone systems provide more efficient use of the radio spectrum. Cellular systems work by using many base stations with lower-power radios that each serve a small area. As shown in Figure 1-1, many base stations within a city can use the same channels for different calls. Building a network that allows users to maintain a call while roaming in and out of the coverage area of multiple base stations is much more complex than building a cordless phone. The need to change access links while maintaing a call is similar to the challenges of moving between LAN, MAN, and WAN data networks. Whether the topic is a cellular phone system or a mobile data network, the solution must address several challenges, which are discussed in the next section.

Figure 1-1   *Broadcast Radio Technology Allows Only One User per Channel in a City, Whereas Cellular Radio Technology Allows Channels To Be Reused*

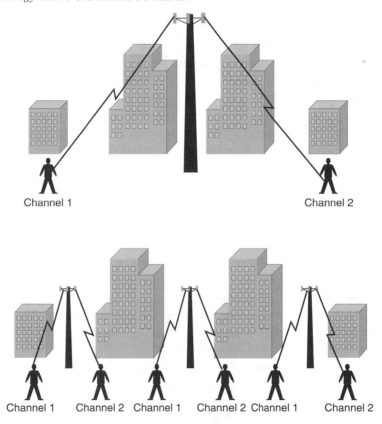

Challenges of Communications Mobility

Communications mobility is the ability for a device to communicate with another device from various locations over one or more access links (for example, Ethernet, 802.11, and so on). The ultimate goal—full mobility—adds the requirement of maintaining communications across access link changes. Just as you don't notice when your cell phone changes cell towers, the end user should never notice access link changes. In this context, mobility can mean changing from one subnet to another on an Ethernet network or making a telephone call in the car while passing from one cell site to another. Mobility can even mean moving from a high-speed Ethernet network at an office desk to a WLAN connection in a conference room. Regardless, all mobility solutions must be capable of locating a device and delivering traffic to that device. Specifically, a mobility solution must address the following four requirements:

- Location discovery
- Move detection
- Update signaling
- Path (re)establishment

Every communications mobility protocol can address these requirements in a different way. For example, some handle as much as possible in the core of the network, others at the edge of the network.

Location Discovery

For a network to deliver traffic to an end device, the network must know where to find the device. Networks use the following two approaches to find a device in a network:

- **Reactive approach**—Some protocols take a reactive approach by sending out a request only when traffic must be delivered.

  Airports often use this system, paging people to a courtesy telephone when a message is waiting for them. This is convenient because the airport does not need to keep track of where everyone is located at all times. It is also effective in airports because the frequency of the messages is low.

  If the frequency of messages increased, the system would fail because only so many messages can be delivered at one time. If an airport is divided into terminals, one for international traffic and one for domestic traffic, the paging system can be more efficient, because pages for domestic travelers only need to be broadcast in the domestic terminal.

  A similar type of hybrid scheme is used in cellular telephone networks. The network keeps track of which general area a phone is in, and when the network needs to deliver a call, it sends out a broadcast message in that area. This is efficient when little traffic needs to be delivered, because the network does not need to use a significant amount of resources tracking individual movements.

- **Proactive approach**—Some networks take a proactive approach and keep track of the exact location of each device at all times. While this might seem overwhelming, it can be implemented in a highly scalable fashion by bypassing the paging system. Today, fewer courtesy pages are broadcast in airports because so many people can communicate directly through mobile telephones without the need for a broadcast page.

Even though these are two completely different systems, the end result is the same—two parties in an airport can communicate with each other. As explored in Chapter 2, "Understanding Mobile IP," Mobile IP takes a similar approach.

Location discovery, whether it's reactive or proactive, is the method by which the network knows how to deliver traffic to the mobile device. The specific implementation of the location discovery is closely tied to the underlying technology and predicted traffic model.

Move Detection

While the term *move detection* has some clearly physical connotations, in this context, it is almost always logical. To put it simply, move detection is a change in available access links. Unlike fixed networking, where most devices have only one connection into the network, mobile devices often have several different paths available at a given time. The mobility protocol is then responsible for determining which of these paths is best and communicating this path as the device's current location. Cellular networks, for example, often have an overlap in the coverage area of their cell sites. The network then makes a determination, based on signal quality and other factors, of which cell site the device should associate with. In most cases, a logical move is the result of a physical move; however, if an access link fails, it is also treated as movement.

NOTE   For protocols that provide full mobility, sessions can be maintained when a device changes its access link. A location change that's based on move detection is called a *handover.*

Each time movement is detected, the system must determine whether this movement is equivalent to a change in location. Some protocols take a proactive approach, evaluating the optimal location with each movement. Others are reactive, looking for a new optimal link only when the existing link is no longer available. In some cases, the protocol is designed to allow the user to customize his handover algorithms.

Update Signaling

Both update signaling and path (re)establishment are concepts that already exist in IP routing protocols. *Update signaling* is equivalent to a routing update. Update signaling communicates the current location of the mobile device to the rest of the network. Update signaling communicates location changes and can inform the network that a device is still active in its current location. Signals can be sent on a per-device basis or they can be aggregated.

Path (Re)establishment

Path (re)establishment is similar to the concept of convergence in IP routing protocols. When a device signals that it has changed its location, the network must have some way to establish a path to the device, or if a path was already in use, to change that path so that traffic can be delivered to the device at its new location. This can be accomplished in different ways. Designs vary widely depending on whether the connection is circuit switched or packet switched. The important fact is that a communications mobility protocol must always be able to get traffic to and from the Mobile Node.

Full Mobility and the OSI Protocol Stack

Full mobility can be implemented several places in the Open System Interconnection (OSI) protocol stack. Figure 1-2 shows three common divisions of the OSI stack. At the bottom is the access technology, where many existing mobility protocols reside. The layers at the top are usually controlled by software applications, where no standard mobility protocol exists. In the middle, the network or IP layer is rapidly proving itself to be the ideal place for link- and application-independent services like mobility.

Figure 1-2   *Three Divisions of the OSI Stack*

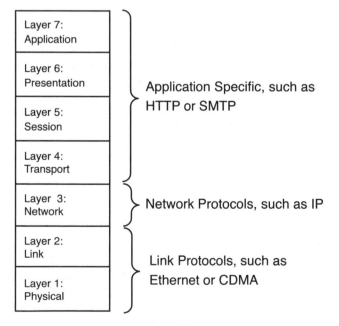

Mobility at Layer 2

Mobility integrated with the access technology has proven to be successful. The Layer 2 protocol is aware of all relevant changes in access links; thus, the information required for move detection and location discovery is readily available. User experience is generally positive, because handover can be quick and no impact on high-level applications exists. However, like many other aspects of Layer 2 protocols, scalability can be a problem.

Link layer mobility protocols alone are not capable of interaccess technology handover. Interaccess technology handover is especially important for data communications because of the wide range of speed and density of coverage provided by existing protocols. When a user is sitting at his desk, he wants to be able to take advantage of the high speed and low latency available through fixed Ethernet, but when he leaves his desk, he wants to maintain his connection through a WLAN. Mobility solutions at higher layers of the OSI stack are capable of providing roaming among diverse access technologies.

Mobility at Layers 4–7

Though there has been little effort to standardize a mobility protocol in Layers 4 through 7, many applications implement some level of mobility. Instant-messaging clients check regularly to ensure that the access link is still available and that the network address is the same. Many e-mail packages can handle IP address changes that occur between mail checks. When it comes to full mobility, most applications cannot maintain sessions when the access links change. If a user removes her fixed Ethernet cable while she is attempting to download a large e-mail attachment, the download fails. Few applications are even intelligent enough to resume or restart the transfer without error. Mobility at Layers 4 through 7 is not practical because applications must specifically be designed with mobility support. Each application must deal with mobility differently, common hooks are needed in the operating system to ensure that applications have all the information they need, and legacy applications must be retrofitted.

Mobility at Layer 3

Layer 3 (the network layer) and especially IP are ideal candidates for supporting full mobility protocols. IP is supported on a wide range of wired and wireless links, and is supported by many applications. IP mobility allows all IP-enabled applications, whether they use Transmission Control Protocol (TCP), User Datagram Protocol (UDP), or any other transport protocol, to seamlessly inherit full mobility across a diverse range of access link types. Users can roam from fixed Ethernet to wireless Ethernet to cellular, only noticing the degradation in speed and latency. The user does not need to restart applications, interrupt sessions, or reboot.

Combining Mobility Protocols

Both Layer 2 and 3 mobility solutions have their own unique advantages that dovetail nicely to create a full mobility solution. Many real-world mobility solutions rely on a combination of mobility solutions. Layer 2 mobility provides fast handover among access links in a small area and of the same technology. Layer 3 mobility is added on top of Layer 2 mobility to provide scalability and link-layer independence. Many of the current data offerings in mobile telephone systems use a combination of fast Layer 2 mobility and Mobile IP or a similar protocol for scalable Layer 3 mobility.

The Case for Mobile IP

Mobile telephone operators are not the only candidates for the Layer 3 mobility solution provided by Mobile IP. The following sidebar illustrates an example of the current plight of nomadic laptop users, and while Mobile IP isn't advantageous to dial-up users, it is useful to the average laptop user. Numerous public and private radio access technologies are well within the means of enterprise deployment, but none of these technologies can provide the ideal combination of ubiquitous coverage, high speed, and low cost. With Mobile IP, a device that has access to multiple radio networks can easily make use of the optimal link without user interaction.

Current Plight of Nomadic Laptop Users: Example

Most laptop users are familiar with the Nomadic laptop mobility protocol. It does not support full mobility, but it does allow limited mobile access, described as follows:

- **Location discovery**—Handled at Layer 8, the user layer. Users look for wired or wireless access each time they need to connect to the network, searching for Ethernet jacks and phone jacks, scanning for WLAN signals, and attaching cellular modems.

- **Move detection**—Handled at Layer 8, the user layer. When the cables are too short, the user must locate a new access link and manually reestablish a connection.

- **Update signaling**—Protocols like Dynamic Host Configuration Protocol (DHCP) and the IP Control Protocol (IPCP) part of Point-to-Point Protocol (PPP) provide a new IP address to users. Sometimes these assignments can trigger a dynamic Domain Name System (DNS) update, allowing inbound reachablity.

- **Path (re)establishment**—Applications must detect the connectivity changes and be restarted, or in some cases, the entire device must be rebooted.

While calling this a mobility protocol is a bit of an exaggeration, it clearly represents how mobility is accomplished in many cases. Throughout the rest of this book, we show that this is less than ideal and that real options exist to provide a better end-user experience in many cases.

Looking back at the ambulance example, it is easy to see that a solution that requires user interaction is not a viable option. Constant connectivity across a network enables new applications for a connected ambulance. Public safety applications like the connected ambulance are just the beginning. From fleet management in the transportation industry to sales force automation, the benefits of seamless mobility are endless.

Summary

For communications devices, users expect mobility to be more than just the ability to move. The goal of communications mobility is for a device to be fully operable while it is moving. Mobile telephony has set a standard that mobile computing devices need to live up to. These devices need to be fully functional whenever and wherever they are operated.

To achieve full mobility, a protocol must support location discovery, move detection, update signaling and path (re)establishment. These requirements can be met in different ways at any layer of the OSI model. Chapter 2 shows how these requirements are met at Layer 3 with the Mobile IP protocol. The chapter also discusses how Mobile IP interacts with different layers to achieve better mobility.

Review Questions

1 You would use a Mobile IP solution, rather than DHCP or a simple WLAN, when you are interested in which of the following?

   a Nomadic mobility

   b Intrasubnet mobility

   c Always-on IP mobility

   d Stationary IP communication

   e Link-layer mobility

2 What is the difference between nomadicity and mobility in the context of Mobile IP?

3 What are the four requirements that a mobility solution must address?

4 Link-layer mobility protocols by themselves are capable of handling interaccess technology handovers.

   a True

   b False

5 IP layer mobility allows all IP-enabled applications, whether they use TCP, UDP, or another transport protocol, to seamlessly inherit full mobility across a diverse range of access link types.

   a True

   b False

CHAPTER 2

Understanding Mobile IP

Mobile IP was originally approved as a draft standard of the Internet Engineering Task Force (IETF) in 1996. The original proposal was built on Request For Comments (RFCs) 2002–2006. Since then, a number of additional RFCs have added enhanced functionality and clarified the original standards. The core Mobile IP protocol, originally defined in RFC 2002, has been updated and is currently defined in RFC 3344. This chapter presents a combined view of the Mobile IP protocol in its current state, rather than examining each individual draft. Discussions of implementation issues not defined in the standard are also included.

Mobile IP: The Elevator Pitch

Mobile IP can be summed up in one, albeit long, sentence:

> Mobile IP is a dynamic routing protocol where end devices signal their own routing updates and dynamic tunnels eliminate the need for host route propagation.

In a nutshell, Mobile IP allows a user to roam across various IP subnets and access links, all the while maintaining continuous communication.

To understand the function of Mobile IP, a great analogy to use is the U.S. Postal Service. Postal mail is sent to you by placing a letter (the packet payload) in an envelope addressed to you (IP header). The letter arrives at your local post office and is routed to you at your Home Address, as shown in Figure 2-1. When you move, you tell the local post office (Home Agent) to forward packets to your new location (Care-of Address [CoA]). Now, when a letter addressed to your Home Address arrives at your local post office, it can now be readdressed (tunneled) to your new location (CoA). The letter then arrives at the post office that services your new location (Foreign Agent [FA]) and is delivered to you at your new location (CoA), as shown in Figure 2-2. This mail delivery is done with no effort (and usually even knowledge) by the original sender of the letter (Correspondent Node [CN]).

Figure 2-1 *Postal Service to Your Home*

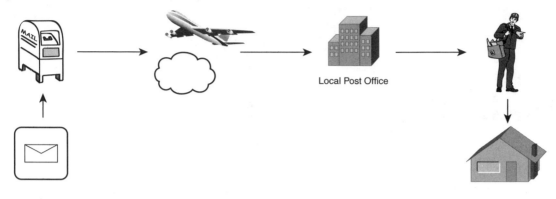

Local Post Office

Figure 2-2 *Postal Service When You Move*

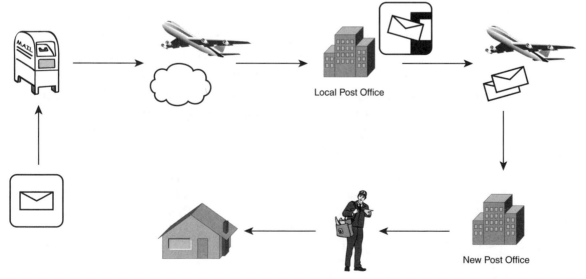

Inform Post Office of
your New Postal Address

Forwards your Mail
to NEW Postal Address

Local Post Office

New Post Office

Postal Delivery to your NEW Home

We now dive into what Mobile IP really is by dissecting this statement: Mobile IP is a dynamic routing protocol where end devices signal their own routing updates and dynamic tunnels eliminate the need for host route propagation.

Mobile IP Is a Dynamic Routing Protocol...

Although saying that Mobile IP is a dynamic routing protocol is a controversial statement, we stand by it. Some people call Mobile IP an address-management protocol, but Mobile IP still relies on existing address-management techniques, either static or dynamic. The core protocol does not attempt to control how IP addresses are managed or distributed. Extensions are available to distribute IP addresses to Mobile Nodes, but this is more an economy of signaling than a core feature. In the same way that the Point-to-Point Protocol (PPP) is not referred to as an address-management protocol simply because it is capable of distributing addresses, neither should Mobile IP.

Mobile IP has also been called an application. While some Mobile IP deployments resemble applications with a centralized "server" and clients on the edge, many other deployment scenarios resemble a classic routing infrastructure.

Finally, some say that Mobile IP is not a routing protocol because it is not capable of building a full topology on its own. While this is probably the most credible argument against it, we would argue that this is not a required feature of a routing protocol.

We maintain that Mobile IP is a dynamic routing protocol. To appreciate this statement, consider the characteristics of a dynamic routing protocol. The essence of a dynamic routing protocol is that it dynamically alters routing tables as routes (and reachability) change, and does not change how routing is done per se. It detects network topology changes and adapts by choosing best available paths and updating the routing table accordingly. The best available path is determined within the context of the dynamic routing protocol and varies from protocol to protocol because each is designed to meet specific needs. For example, some protocols are designed for scalability, while others are designed for fast convergence. These design decisions impact the choice of the best available path. Both Open Shortest Path First (OSPF) and Border Gateway Protocol (BGP) are dynamic routing protocols, but they each use different methods for selecting the best path.

In this light, Mobile IP is designed for mobility. It adapts to network topology changes. It selects best available path routes and inserts them into the routing table. Sounds like any other dynamic routing protocol!

...Where End Devices Signal Their Own Routing Updates...

Mobile IP is designed to provide highly scalable host routing for clients in a mobile (and usually wireless) environment. A Mobile Node can have one or more links attaching it to the network, and each link can have metrics associated with it. Using these metrics and link availability information, a Mobile Node informs the network through routing updates of the best path through which it should be reached, as shown in Figure 2-3. Because this path selection method is unlike any other, we propose calling it *edge intelligent*.

Figure 2-3   *Mobile IP Uses Routing Updates*

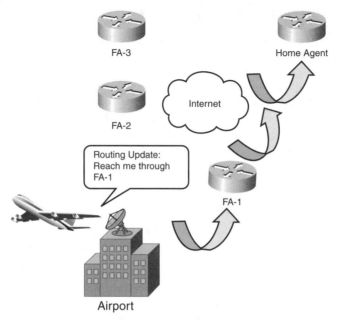

The idea of making all routing decisions at the edge might seem ill conceived, but it works well in a mobile environment for two reasons. First, on wireless networks, Mobile Nodes attach and detach rapidly, making it complex for the network to keep track of them. Imagine using a standard Interior Gateway Protocol (IGP) in an environment where hundreds of neighbors are on a single link and hundreds of topology changes occur every second. Moving much of the responsibility to the Mobile Node allows the network to scale more effectively. Second, because the speed and latency of wireless networks are often dramatically different from the fixed infrastructure, choosing a best path based solely on the access link is usually effective. Just as BGP's path vector approach provides a usable solution to inter-AS routing, Mobile IP's edge-intelligent design provides an effective solution to mobility routing.

...and Dynamic Tunnels Eliminate the Need for Host Route Propagation

Unlike other routing protocols, Mobile IP builds its own links; but don't expect a Home Agent to jump out of the rack and start laying fiber—they are all logical links. These logical links are known as *tunnels*. Tunneling usually connects two similar networks through a dissimilar network. For example, tunneling can carry a protocol like AppleTalk across a network that is not capable of routing AppleTalk.

However, as most other protocols are being replaced by IP, tunneling is finding more use linking similar routing domains across a dissimilar one. For example, an enterprise might use tunneling to link private networks in two remote sites across the Internet. This allows traffic with private addresses to be routed across a public network.

Mobile IP uses the same concept by tunneling across a routing domain that does not know how to route to the Mobile Node's current location, as shown in Figure 2-4. With Mobile IP, Mobile Nodes maintain a constant IP address as they move around the network. Supporting this with traditional routing protocols would require a host route for each Mobile Node. Every time a Mobile Node moves, the host route would have to be updated and the routing protocol would have to reconverge. This can work for a small number of Mobile Nodes with infrequent mobility, but when the frequency of routing updates increases, traditional routing protocols can fail.

Figure 2-4   *Mobile IP Uses Tunnels for Routing*

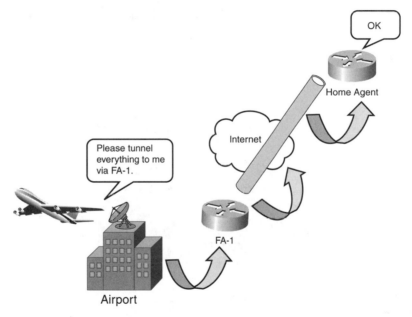

Instead, Mobile IP inserts host routes in at most two devices—the Home Agent and possibly a FA—and uses tunneling to deliver traffic across the network. This eliminates the need to propagate a host route across the network every time a Mobile Node moves, which would clearly not scale. In essence, Mobile IP uses tunnels to create an overlay routing domain, thus isolating frequent host route changes from the existing routing protocols.

Mobile IP: Components

As shown in Figure 2-5, a Mobile IP deployment can contain, at a minimum, a Home Agent and a Mobile Node, and can also contain a FA. A single router can serve as any or all of these three components. However, most common deployments use separate devices for each function or sometimes combine the Home Agent and FA into a single router. These functions can be enabled on existing access routers in the network, or they can be enabled on dedicated Mobility Agents. Other important concepts in Mobile IP include the Home Network, Home Address, and CoA.

Figure 2-5   *Components of a Simple Mobile IP Deployment*

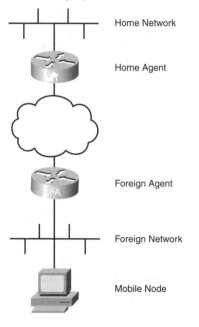

Home Network

Home Agent

Foreign Agent

Foreign Network

Mobile Node

Mobile Node

A *Mobility Node*, shown in Figure 2-6, can be any IP device running a Mobile IP client stack; Mobile Nodes can be anything from personal digital assistants (PDAs) and laptops to routers. The Mobile Node does its own move detection and thus must be able to detect logical movement and learn its current location. Logical movement is not simply the change in the access device, but a change in the subnet associated with the access link. If a Mobile Node remains still physically, it still can move logically if the access device it is associated with fails and it associates with a new one. When a Mobile Node decides to hand over, it must signal this change to the Home Agent, typically through a FA. (These terms are described in the sections "Home Agent" and "Foreign Agent," later in this chapter.) Note that the Mobile Node and Home Agent must share a security association for Mobile IP to be used.

Figure 2-6   *Overview of Mobile IP Components*

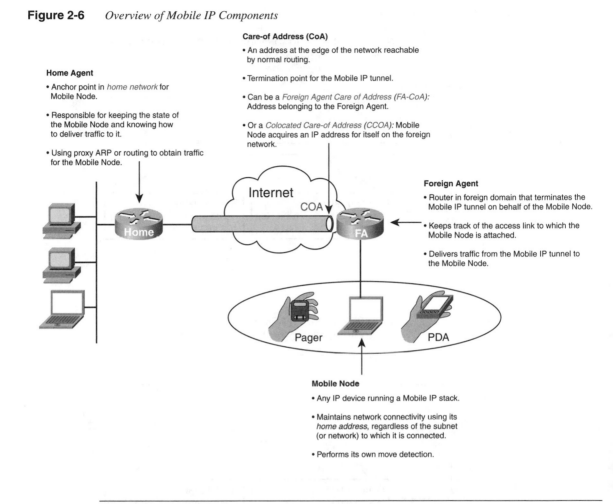

Care-of Address (CoA)
- An address at the edge of the network reachable by normal routing.
- Termination point for the Mobile IP tunnel.
- Can be a *Foreign Agent Care of Address (FA-CoA):* Address belonging to the Foreign Agent.
- Or a *Colocated Care-of Address (CCOA):* Mobile Node acquires an IP address for itself on the foreign network.

Home Agent
- Anchor point in *home network* for Mobile Node.
- Responsible for keeping the state of the Mobile Node and knowing how to deliver traffic to it.
- Using proxy ARP or routing to obtain traffic for the Mobile Node.

Foreign Agent
- Router in foreign domain that terminates the Mobile IP tunnel on behalf of the Mobile Node.
- Keeps track of the access link to which the Mobile Node is attached.
- Delivers traffic from the Mobile IP tunnel to the Mobile Node.

Mobile Node
- Any IP device running a Mobile IP stack.
- Maintains network connectivity using its *home address*, regardless of the subnet (or network) to which it is connected.
- Performs its own move detection.

NOTE   Even though Mobile IP is a Layer 3–based protocol, the line between Layer 2 and Layer 3 is often blurred. As we elaborate more on move detection and Mobile IP handover policy, you will see that Mobile IP cannot operate efficiently without Layer 2 interaction. The more information the Mobile Node has about Layer 2, the more intelligent its routing decisions can be.

Home Network and Home Address

Home is an important concept in Mobile IP, following the old cliché "home is where the route is," because Internet routing is based on the home IP address, as depicted in Figure 2-7.

Figure 2-7 *Home Is Where the Route Is*

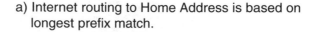

a) Internet routing to Home Address is based on longest prefix match.

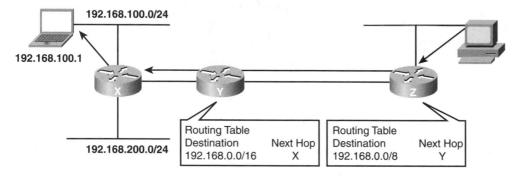

b) Internet routing doesn't work if address is not topologically correct (unless host routing).

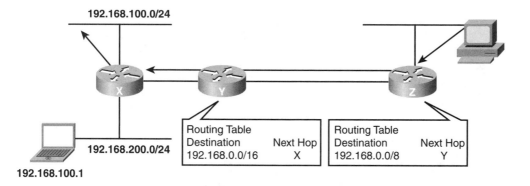

NOTE	IP routing scales effectively because large blocks of IP addresses can be aggregated based on their network prefix. IP networks are divided into subnetworks, or subnets. All hosts contained in a subnet share a common network prefix. The number of bits preceding the host portion of the address identifies the network prefix. All nodes on a subnet have the same network prefix. Traffic is delivered in the network by following the longest prefix routes.

A Mobile Node's IP address is referred to as its *Home Address*. The Home Address is allocated out of the Home Network, which is attached to the Home Agent. The Home Address is either statically assigned or dynamically allocated during the Mobile IP registration process. The concept of home in Mobile IP is simply an anchor point. The Home Network is the longest-prefix network advertised into traditional routing protocols. The goal of a Home Network is to avoid having to advertise host routes for each Mobile Node into the IGP routing protocol, a practice that would simply not scale.

When a Mobile Node is attached to its Home Network, Mobile IP is not needed, because traditional IP routing can deliver traffic to the Mobile Node as usual. When a Mobile Node has moved away from its Home Network and attaches to a new network, the new network/domain is referred to as the *foreign domain* or *visited domain*.

Home Agent

Traffic destined for the Mobile Node's Home Address continues to be delivered to the Home Network, even when the Mobile Node is no longer attached. This traffic must be redirected to the Mobile Node in its current location. This is the responsibility of the *Home Agent*. The Home Agent (refer to Figure 2-6) is a router capable of processing Mobile IP routing updates, called *registrations*, and forwarding traffic to the Mobile Node through dynamically created tunnels. If the Home Agent is in the forwarding path, it will forward traffic across the tunnel using a host route. If the Home Network is a physical network and the Home Agent is not in the forwarding path, the Home Agent will use proxy Address Resolution Protocol (ARP) to obtain all traffic destined for the Mobile Node and then forward it through the tunnel. Note that the Home Agent and Mobile Node must share a security association for Mobile IP to be used.

Care-of Address

The CoA is an IP address that is valid and routable at the Mobile Node's current point of attachment in the Foreign Network (refer to Figure 2-6). The Mobile Node informs the Home Agent of this CoA during the Mobile IP registration process. Encapsulated (tunneled) traffic from the Home Agent is then delivered to the *CoA*, which is the logical location of the Mobile Node in the foreign domain. The Mobile IP tunnel is between the Home Agent Address and the CoA. The CoA can be either of the following:

- Colocated CoA (CCoA)
- FA COA

Colocated Care-of Address

In CCoA mode, a Mobile Node acquires an IP address for itself on the Foreign Network, for example, through Dynamic Host Configuration Protocol (DHCP) or another address-management protocol. This address is known as the CCoA. In colocated mode, the Mobile Node has two addresses: the Home Address and the CCoA. The CCoA is valid and routable on the current link and receives tunneled traffic. Note that the Mobile Node must be capable of terminating the Mobile IP tunnel in the CCoA mode. The Home address is not routable on the current link but is used as the source and destination of all application traffic.

CCoA is considered an inefficient use of IP addresses because each Mobile Node requires a valid and routable address in each network it visits. Despite its inefficiency, CCoA mode is used often because it simplifies deployment. It is often coupled with private addressing to minimize the waste of IP addresses.

Foreign Agent Care-of Address

Another option is to use a FA–based CoA. In this case, many nodes share one CoA. A FA CoA is one or more of its interface IP addresses advertised by the FA, as described in the next section.

Foreign Agent

A *FA* is a router attached to the access link that is capable of terminating the tunnel on behalf of the Mobile Node (refer to Figure 2-6). The FA can advertise one or more of its IP addresses as a CoA. When a Mobile Node registers with its Home Agent, it registers through the FA. The FA keeps track of the access link to which the Mobile Node is attached. Traffic for the Mobile Node is tunneled from the Home Agent to the FA. After the FA removes the encapsulation header, it delivers the traffic to the Mobile Node. The FA must be connected to the Mobile Node's access link directly, because traffic can only be delivered through message authentication code (MAC) layer addressing. If the FA were to route the traffic, it would be sent back to the Home Agent and end up being caught in a routing loop.

Correspondent Node

Discussions of Mobile IP often include references to a CN. The CN is not a Mobile IP component but is a pedantic element that aids in the discussion of traffic flows. A CN is the peer of the Mobile Node in its IP communication, for example, another Mobile Node, a fixed node. If the Mobile Node is using a web browser, the CN would be the web server.

Mobile IP Protocol Concepts

Before we start putting together the pieces of the Mobile IP puzzle, we should take a closer look at the big picture. Given the components of the Mobile IP solution, how do they all work together? Earlier in the chapter, you learned that Mobile IP is a mobility protocol that allows a

Mobile Node to roam across various IP subnets and access links, all the while maintaining continuous communication. In Chapter 1, "Mobile and Wireless Technologies," we identified the four basic requirements for a mobility protocol: location discovery, move detection, update signaling, and path (re)establishment. We will briefly explain how Mobile IP addresses each of these requirements, and we then examine the details in the remainder of the chapter:

- **Location discovery**—In Mobile IP, two types of locations exist: the Home Network and the Foreign (Visited) Network. The type of network to which the Mobile Node is attached is central to the protocol, because each protocol results in a different type of Mobile IP handover and requires different Mobile IP signaling. The location is determined by examining Mobile IP agent advertisements, if one is received, or by examining the allocated Colocated CoA.

- **Move detection**—Mobile Nodes continually engage in the process of *move detection*, which is the act of monitoring changes in available paths into the network.

  Move detection rapidly becomes cloudy because the line between Layer 2 and Layer 3 is blurred. Features like proactive movement and simultaneous association with multiple Layer 2 access points complicate matters even further.

  Remember that Mobile IP is a Layer 3 protocol, and in this context, move detection is the process of keeping track of changes in Layer 3 paths that the Mobile Node can use to reach the network. Looking at this further in the light that Mobile IP is a routing protocol, this means that the Mobile Node must understand, as part of move detection, when candidate routes become available or disappear. To this end, whenever movement is detected, Mobile IP uses its Mobile IP handover policy algorithm to evaluate all candidate routes and determine whether a change in routing is necessary. A change in routing is known as a *Mobile IP handover*.

- **Update signaling**—After a Mobile IP handover has been initiated, the Mobile Node determines the type of Mobile IP signaling necessary based on its previous and new location type. This Mobile IP signaling takes the form of a *Registration Request (RRQ)* or a *Deregistration Request*. At this point, the FA, if one is being used, and the Home Agent evaluate the Registration or Deregistration Request and send either a success or failure Registration Reply (RRP) message to the Mobile Node. This signaling exchange is referred to as the *Mobile IP registration process*.

- **Path (re)establishment**—For successful Mobile IP registrations, a tunnel is established between the CoA and Home Agent. Conversely, for successful Mobile IP deregistrations, the tunnel is removed. In either case, the routing table of both the Home Agent and FA is updated to reflect the current routing path. At this point, the Mobile Node cycles back to the move detection state, and the process begins again.

Mobile IP Agent Discovery

Move detection and location discovery, two of the most important requirements of a mobility protocol, are addressed in Mobile IP through the use of agent advertisements. Mobile IP agent advertisements are built on top of the Internet Control Message Protocol (ICMP) Router Discovery Protocol (IRDP), which was first proposed in RFC 1256. IRDP consists of two messages that are enhanced to support Mobile IP, as follows:

- **Router advertisement**—A beacon that is sent at a defined interval by a router. The advertisement is a way for the router to say, "Hey, I'm out here, and here's what I can offer." When supporting Mobile IP, a router sends a router advertisement that contains an extension advertising the specific Mobile IP services that it supports, for example, reverse tunneling. The router is now saying, "Hey, I am a Mobility Agent, and here's what I can offer." These advertisements are known as Mobile IP agent advertisements, and they are sent either through IP multicast or IP broadcast.

- **Router solicitation**—A message that is sent by a node requesting that routers who hear this message send out their router advertisements. A Mobile IP agent solicitation is the same as a router solicitation, except that the TTL of the packet is set to 1. By sending a Mobile IP agent solicitation, the Mobile Node is asking, "Hey, are any Mobility Agents out there?" Solicitations by a Mobile Node allow location discovery to occur more quickly than if the Mobile Node had to wait for the periodic agent advertisement. A Mobile Node can send a solicitation through either multicast or broadcast.

Use of the Mobile IP agent advertisement and Mobile IP agent solicitation are depicted in Figure 2-8.

Figure 2-8   *Mobile IP Agent Discovery*

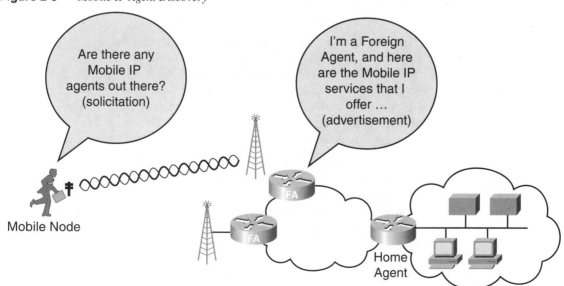

The use of these messages allows a Mobile Node to learn which Mobility Agents are out there and what Mobile IP services they are providing. The Mobile Node can also learn the specific subnets that are available on the link. Specifically, the Mobile Node pays attention to the following important fields and options bits in the Mobile IP advertisement extension:

- **Lifetime**—This is the maximum lifetime that the Mobility Agent can support a Mobile IP registration.

- **CoA(s)**—If the Mobility Agent is serving as a FA, this field specifies the Foreign Agent-Care-of Address (FA-CoA). Note that more than one advertised FA-CoA can exist.

- **R (Registration Required)**—This bit specifies that Mobile IP registration is required through this FA, regardless of whether the Mobile Node is using an FA-CoA or a CCoA.

- **B (Busy)**—This bit specifies that the FA is busy and cannot accept Mobile IP registrations from additional Mobile Nodes.

- **H (Home Agent)**—This bit specifies that the Mobility Agent offers service as a Home Agent.

- **F (FA)**—This bit specifies that the Mobility Agent offers service as a FA.

- **M (Minimal Encapsulation)**—This agent supports receiving tunneled datagrams that use minimal encapsulation.

- **G (GRE Protocol)**—This agent supports receiving tunneled datagrams that use the generic routing encapsulation (GRE) protocol.

- **T (Reverse Tunneling)**—This bit specifies that the FA supports reverse tunneling. Reverse tunneling is described in Chapter 6, "Metro Mobility: Client-Based Mobile IP."

Example 2-1 shows the agent advertisement message in detail. In this example, the Mobility Agent is a FA with CoA 192.168.100.6, supporting GRE and reverse tunneling. The FA is advertising mobility support for 10 hours.

Example 2-1 is a packet capture and decode of an actual agent advertisement taken with Ethereal, a network protocol analyzer. Protocol analyzers are widely used for troubleshooting and provide a field-by-field view of the packet.

Example 2-1 *Mobile IP Agent Advertisement Protocol Detail*

```
Internet Protocol, Src Addr: 192.168.100.6, Dst Addr: 255.255.255.255
    Version: 4
    Header length: 20 bytes
    Differentiated Services Field: 0x00 (DSCP 0x00: Default; ECN: 0x00)
    Total Length: 54
    Identification: 0xd838
    Flags: 0x00
    Fragment offset: 0
    Time to live: 1
    Protocol: ICMP (0x01)
    Header checksum: 0xbce0 (correct)
    Source: 192.168.100.6 (192.168.100.6)
```

continues

Example 2-1 *Mobile IP Agent Advertisement Protocol Detail (Continued)*

```
        Destination: 255.255.255.255 (255.255.255.255)

Internet Control Message Protocol
    Type: 9 (Router advertisement)
    Code: 0
    Checksum: 0x6ba4 (correct)
    Number of addresses: 1
    Address entry size: 2
    Lifetime: 30 seconds
    Router address: 192.168.100.6
    Preference level: 0

    Ext: Mobility Agent Advertisement Extension
        Extension Type: Mobility Agent Advertisement Extension (16)
        Length: 10
        Sequence Number: 3
        Registration Lifetime: 36000
        Flags: 0x15
            0... .... = Registration Required: False
            .0.. .... = Busy: False
            ..0. .... = Home Agent: False
            ...1 .... = Foreign Agent: True
            .... 0... = Minimal Encapsulation: False
            .... .1.. = GRE: True
            .... ..0. = Reserved: False
            .... ...1 = Reverse Tunnel: True
        Reserved: 0x00
        Care-Of-Address: 192.168.100.6 (192.168.100.6)

    Ext: Challenge Extension
        Extension Type: Challenge Extension (24)
        Length: 4
        Challenge: B858BED2
```

Here are the descriptions of the fields in the IP Header:

- **Destination Address**—Advertisements must be sent to either the limited broadcast address (255.255.255.255) or the all-systems multicast address (224.0.0.1). Responses to solicitations can be either unicast to the Mobile Node or can be sent as a broadcast/multicast.

- **TTL**—Must always be set to 1, because the FA must be on the same link as the Mobile Node and the advertisement must not be forwarded to another link.

Here are the descriptions of the fields in the ICMP Header:

- **Type**—Type 9 is used for agent advertisements, and Type 10 is used for agent solicitations.

- **Code**—The code can either be 0 if the advertising agent is a fully capable router or 16 if it is only to be used as a Mobile IP agent.

- **Lifetime**—This is the maximum amount of time a Mobile Node should consider this agent as being reachable without hearing a new advertisement. The agent should send at least three advertisements during this window.

- **Router Address**—The router should list all the IP addresses that are configured on the interface from which the advertisement is being sent. These can be used as CoAs.

Here are the descriptions of the fields in the Mobility Advertisement Extension:

- **Type**—Type 16 is used for the Mobility Advertisement Extension.

- **Sequence Number**—This is a number that increases with each advertisement, starting at 0x0 after a reboot. When the maximum (0xFFFF) is reached, the agent begins with 0x00FF to distinguish a rollover from a reboot.

- **Registration Lifetime**—This is the maximum lifetime that the agent can accept in a registration.

- **Registration Required Flag**—The Mobile Node must register with a FA on this link, even if it wants to use a Colocated CoA.

- **Busy Flag**—When set, this FA is not currently accepting new registrations.

- **Home Agent Flag**—This agent offers Home Agent services.

- **FA Flag**—This agent offers FA services.

- **Minimal Encapsulation Flag**—This agent is capable of processing minimally encapsulated packets, as defined in RFC 2004.

- **GRE Flag**—This agent is capable of processing packets encapsulated with the GRE protocol, as defined in RFC 1701.

- **Reserved**—This originally specified Van Jacobson header compression support. This was removed in the second revision of the RFC because it was deemed unusable.

- **Reverse Tunnel**—This FA is capable of reverse tunneling.

- **CoA**—This is one or more IP addresses that the Mobile Node can use as its CoA if it registers through this FA.

Here are the descriptions of the fields in the Prefix Length Extension:

- **Type**—Type 19 is used for the prefix length extension.

- **Prefix Length**—Network prefix lengths are specified in order for each respective router address listed in the IRDP extension.

Here are the descriptions of the fields in the Challenge Extension:

- **Type**—Type 24 is used for the FA Challenge Extension.

- **Challenge**—This is a pseudorandom challenge that provides replay protection at the FA.

Location Discovery

Recall that a Mobile Node can find itself in two types of locations: the Home Network and the visited network. To identify which one of these network locations it is currently in, the Mobile Node must look at two parts of the agent advertisement. To determine whether it attached to its Home Network, the Mobile Node compares its Home Address and prefix to the router address(es) in the IRDP portion of the message, which identify each subnet that is routed to the link. If any of the router addresses is on the Mobile Node's Home Network, the Mobile Node knows it is at home. If the Mobile Node is not at home, it looks at the CoA(es) listed in the message. The *Care-of Address Extension* carries one or more IP addresses from the FA. These address(es) can be the same as the interface address(es) advertised in the router address portion of the advertisement, or they can be address(es) from other interfaces. When we look at Mobile IP deployment scenarios starting in Chapter 4, "IOS Mobile IP in the Lab," you see that the recommended CoA for a FA is a single loopback address, not a physical interface address.

If the Mobile Node does not receive an agent advertisement on a link, it can attempt to use a dynamic addressing mechanism such as DHCP to determine its current location. The address it obtains through the dynamic addressing mechanism can be used as a CCoA during the Mobile IP registration process.

NOTE   As you see in the next section, some aspects of location discovery and move detection are intentionally vague or left out of the standard because they do not impact interoperability. This allows tremendous flexibility in the implementation of Mobile Node clients, but makes it difficult for us to tell you how the Mobile Node will behave. What we present here is either directly addressed in the standard or introduced as a common, but not standard, feature.

One of these undefined portions of the standard surrounds how a Mobile Node can determine whether it should use a FA–based CoA or a CCoA. Common logic would suggest that a Mobile Node wait for a Mobile IP agent advertisement, possibly following a solicitation, and then attempt to use a CCoA, if necessary. In the interest of speed, some Mobile Nodes attempt to solicit for a Mobile IP advertisement and begin the DHCP process of obtaining a Colocated CoA at the same time, assuming that the DHCP address can be released if a FA is found. Some Mobile Nodes avoid the uncertainty by forcing the user to define which type of CoA is to be used on a per-interface basis.

Move Detection and Mobile IP Handover Policy

Move detection is the process that the Mobile Node uses to determine changes in the usability of its access links. This information is coupled with the Mobile IP handover policy to determine when the Mobile Node needs to initiate a Mobile IP Handover, as defined in the section "Mobile IP Handover," later in this chapter. The two are so tightly coupled in Mobile IP that move detection often implies Mobile IP handover policy, although some important distinctions exist.

NOTE   Before we go any further, we take a closer look at access links. Every Mobile Node has at least one interface that it can use to connect back into the network. With only one access link available, the Mobile IP handover policy is relatively easy to determine. More-complex algorithms become necessary when a Mobile Node has more than one access interface. Adding to the challenge, some link types associate with only one "base station" at a time, similar to the way Ethernet works—the cable has two ends, one at the client and the other at the base station. However, more advanced link types allow the client to communicate with more than one base station at a time. The latter is ideal for Mobile IP because the Mobile Node can maintain its association with one base station while registering through another.

A Mobile IP handover policy governs the Mobile Node's behavior upon move detection and can be classified as either *reactive* or *proactive*. The RFC specifies two reactive Mobile IP handover policy algorithms, described in the following two sections, but the option to use other algorithms is left up to Mobile Node implementers. With these reactive algorithms, it is hard to distinguish between move detection and Mobile IP handover policy, because move detection is based strictly on Mobile IP messages. On the other hand, proactive algorithms show the importance of separating the two concepts. The proactive algorithms track movement, but they only trigger a Mobile IP handover when a better communication link is available, as described in the section "Link-State Triggers," later in this chapter. Mobile Nodes are not restricted to using a single Mobile IP handover policy. The Mobile IP handover policy algorithms described in the next sections do not have standardized names, but names are used here to show the key characteristics of the algorithm.

Steady-State Algorithm

The first Mobile IP handover policy defined in the RFC can be classified as the *steady-state algorithm*.

In this algorithm, the Mobile Node holds on to its current FA as long as it can. After the Mobile Node establishes a valid registration with a FA, it continues to listen for advertisements from other FAs. However, the Mobile Node does not register with a new FA until the current FA's advertisement lifetime has expired. The steady-state algorithm is depicted in Figure 2-9. This means that even if the Mobile Node hears an agent advertisement from another FA on the same interface, it does not register through the new FA until the current FA's advertisement expires.

The steady-state algorithm minimizes the number of Mobile IP registrations, because a Mobile Node does not attempt to register through a new FA as long as it thinks it still has connectivity through its current FA. In a sense, it aims to maintain a constant link for communication between the Mobile Node and FA. However, the problem is that the Mobile Node could go the entire *hold time* (the amount of time that the Mobile Node considers the Mobility Agent still reachable without having received an agent advertisement) without connectivity.

Figure 2-9 *Steady-State Algorithm*

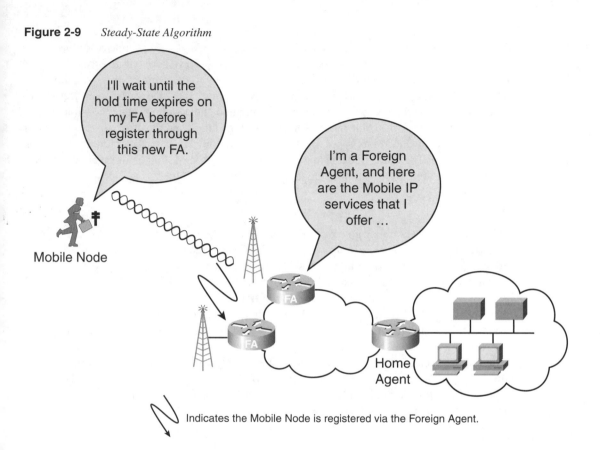

Indicates the Mobile Node is registered via the Foreign Agent.

New Network Algorithm

The new network algorithm requires the use of the *prefix length extension*, which specifies the network prefix lengths in order for each respective router address that is listed in the agent advertisement. Using the Mobile IP agent advertisement and the prefix length extension, the Mobile Node knows exactly which subnets are available on the current link, whether it is on the Home Network or a Foreign Network. When a Mobile Node hears an advertisement on that link advertising a different subnet, it can assume that it has changed its point of attachment to the network. Specifically, the Mobile Node compares the network prefix(es) of its current Mobility Agent's advertisement against any newly received agent advertisements. If they differ, the Mobile Node can assume that it has roamed and needs to initiate a Mobile IP handover. Use of the new network algorithm is depicted in Figure 2-10.

Figure 2-10 *New Network Algorithm*

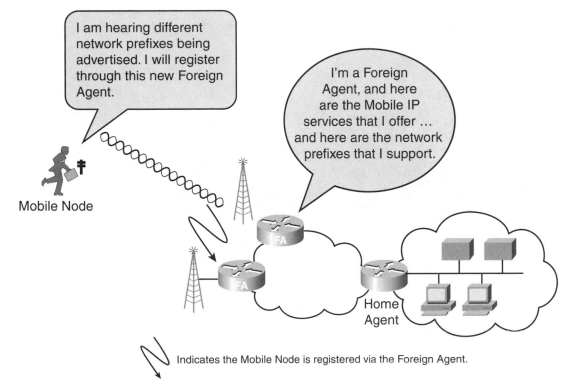

Indicates the Mobile Node is registered via the Foreign Agent.

The new network algorithm is more efficient than the steady-state algorithm, because the Mobile Node does not wait until the hold time expires before it considers a new Mobility Agent. Rather, with this method, a Mobile Node can hand over in less than the new network's advertisement interval. However, if the new network advertisement interval is longer than the previous network's hold time, this method is less efficient than the steady-state method.

Link-State Triggers

The ideal Mobile IP handover policy is to use link-state triggers and can be considered either reactive or proactive, depending on the action taken. This method is not specified in the core Mobile IP RFC because it cannot be implemented at Layer 3, but rather relies on information from Layer 2. Moreover, the quality and quantity of link-state triggers are device and access-link specific. However, in real-world implementations, many Mobile Nodes are in fact capable of detecting link state effectively, for example, when physical cables are unplugged and when wireless links hand over. Using this Layer 2 information along with Mobile IP agent solicitations, the Mobile Node can determine even more quickly whether it has moved. For example, as illustrated in Figure 2-11, if the Mobile Node receives a Layer 2 trigger that its wireless Local Area Network (LAN) connection is handing over, the Mobile Node can solicit for Mobile IP agent advertisements on the new wireless link. Upon hearing a new agent advertisement in response to the solicitation, the Mobile Node can immediately register with its Home Agent.

Figure 2-11 *Using Link-State Triggers*

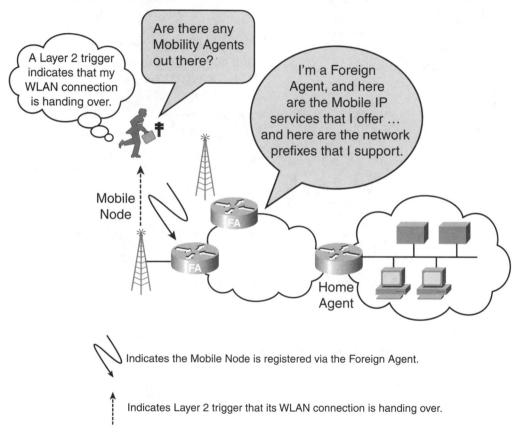

When using link-state triggers, move detection latency is reduced to the sum of the link-state detection and notification delay, and the Mobile IP solicitation and agent response delay.

When using link-state triggers proactively, the Mobile Node makes an active choice to initiate a handover, even if its existing link is still functional. In this context, a proactive handover can be at Layer 2 or Layer 3, and might be from one interface to another, or it might be to force an interface to reassociate with a new base station. When a Mobile Node forces an interface to move, it behaves just like a link-state change. However, now, rather than the interface telling the Mobile Node it has moved, the Mobile Node tells the interface to move. This can be useful in wireless environments, where the Mobile Node can determine information, such as signal strength and quality, about other base stations. A proactive handover due to link-state triggers is most often implemented between two interfaces, which is one of the most powerful features of Mobile IP. Although not defined in RFC 3344, nearly all Mobile IP clients include some from of proactive handover.

NOTE   Proactive handover is similar to route selection in traditional routing protocols. Valid agent advertisements are combined with a series of metrics to determine which advertisement is the best to use. Typical metrics include link bandwidth and link cost, although other metrics, like signal strength and latency, could also be applied. Metrics do not need to be standardized because they are assigned and used only by the Mobile Node. The network infrastructure does not perform route selection. Depending on the implementation, metric precedence is either predefined or user controllable. Typically, metrics are evaluated independently. For example, cost is evaluated first, and if cost is equal, bandwidth is evaluated. For example, if a Mobile Node has a 10-Mbps wireless LAN link, a 56-kbps cellular link, and a 128-kbps satellite link, the Mobile Node can adjust the metric so that cellular is preferred over satellite because of the associated cost of the satellite link.

Mobile IP Handover

In the previous sections, we looked at how move detection and Mobile IP handover policy initiate a Mobile IP handover. Before we look at the messaging that performs a Mobile IP handover, we look at the possible types of handover. Using the information in agent advertisements, the Mobile Node can determine one of the following, as illustrated in Figure 2-12:

- **Did I leave my Home Network?**—This implies a Mobile IP handover from the Home Network to a Foreign Network. When a Mobile Node leaves its Home Network, it initiates a new Mobile IP registration to its Home Agent.

- **Did I roam to a different Foreign Network than the one I was already visiting?**—This implies a Mobile IP handover from one FA to another. In this case, the Mobile Node determines from its CoA whether a Mobile IP reregistration is necessary. If the CoA has changed, the Mobile Node initiates a Mobile IP reregistration. (If two access networks are connected to the same FA, the Mobile Node can hear the same CoA and not need to reregister.)

- **Did I come back to my Home Network?**—This implies a Mobile IP handover from a Foreign Network to the Home Network. When the Mobile Node returns to its Home Network, it performs a Mobile IP *deregistration* to ensure that the Home Agent no longer attempts to tunnel its traffic. Remember that when a Mobile Node is attached to its Home Network, Mobile IP is not used for forwarding, because the standard IGP routing already delivers traffic to the Home Network.

Figure 2-12 *Types of Mobile IP Handovers*

Did I leave my home network? — Home Network to Foreign Network handover.
Did I move to another Foreign Agent? — Foreign Agent to Foreign Agent handover.
Did I return back to my home network? — Foreign Network to Home Network handover.

Mobile IP Registration

When the Mobile Node determines that is has moved, whether roaming across different FAs or returning home, it initiates a Mobile IP handover by entering into the Mobile IP registration phase. During this phase, the Mobile Node signals this location update to its Home Agent. This signaling is accomplished through a Mobile IP RRQs, one of the most important messages in Mobile IP. RRQ messages are the equivalent of a routing update, because they inform the network how to deliver traffic to the Mobile Node (through the CoA). A RRP is a positive or negative acknowledgment of the RRQ, and can be originated by either the Home Agent or FA. A depiction of the registration message exchange when the Mobile Node is in a Foreign Network is shown in Figure 2-13.

For a Mobile IP handover other than returning home, upon successful exchange of a Mobile IP RRQ and Mobile IP RRP, the Mobile Node is said to be *registered* with the Home Agent (and FA if one is used) for the lifetime specified by the Home Agent in the RRP. Thus, in addition to sending RRQs as location updates, the Mobile Node must also send a RRQ to continue its registration if the lifetime is about to expire.

Figure 2-13   *Registration Message Exchange in Foreign Network*

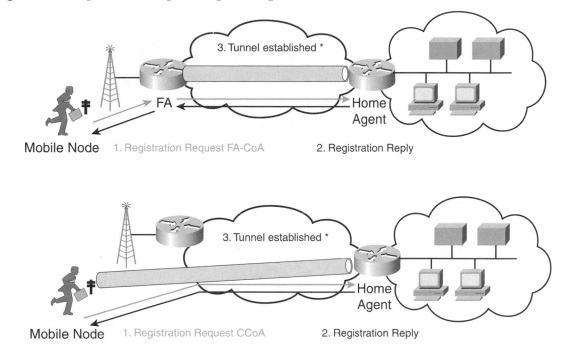

* if registration process is successful.

For a Mobile IP handover when returning home, the Mobile Node is said to be *deregistering* during the RRQ and RRP message exchange.

The RRQ and RRP messages are center to the Mobile IP registration phase. They are sent through User Datagram Protocol (UDP) signaling with destination port number 434.

NOTE   The UDP transport layer protocol is chosen over Transmission Control Protocol (TCP) because it is lighter-weight than TCP. The overhead and retransmission mechanism in TCP is unwarranted, because the RRQ messages can be retransmitted by the Mobile Node if an RRP is not received.

The message exchange must be unambiguous and secure because it alters routing to the Mobile Node. To this end, the messages are comprised of major components as follows.

RRQs are comprised of the following three major components:

- **Identification**—Unique identification of the RRQ and unique identification of the Mobile Node
- **Service Requests**—Negotiation of Mobile IP services
- **Authentication Parameters**—Security parameters for message authentication

Registration Replies are also comprised of the following three major components:

- **Identification**—Unique identification to match the RRP to the RRQ, and unique identification of the Mobile Node
- **Reply Codes**—Status of the Mobile Node's registration
- **Authentication Parameters**—Security parameters for message authentication

In the next sections, we look into the details of each message and describe how they impact behavior on the different Mobile IP entities. After you gain an understanding of what the messages look like and what they convey, we look into message delivery and how the messages accomplish the Mobile IP handovers outlined in the section "Mobile IP Handover," in this chapter.

Identification

A crucial aspect of the Mobile IP registration message exchange is that the messages must be unique and specific in their identity. Two types of identification appear in each RRQ and RRP message: one to identify the Mobile Node and one to identify the registration or reply message itself. A unique Mobile Node identifier is required to determine who the request is coming from, what services are available for this Mobile Node, and which authentication tokens should be used for this Mobile Node. Mobile Node identification is either through a statically allocated Home Address (Home Address field) or a Network Access Identifier (NAI) extension, defined in RFC 3846, which can be used with dynamic Home Address allocation, as described in Chapter 8, "Deployment Scalability and Management."

NOTE   The NAI concept was first introduced as a way to support PPP roaming. Users are identified by either a username or a username and a realm, represented in the form user@realm. While an NAI looks similar to an e-mail address, the realm portion does not need to be a fully qualified domain name. The use of a realm allows users to be classified into groups; the groups can signify different administrative domains, different service classes, or both. The username portion uniquely identifies the individual within that group.

The second identifier in the Mobile IP messages uniquely identifies the registration or reply message. This field is referred to as the *identification field* in the RRQ and RRP, and is chosen by the Mobile Node to uniquely distinguish each registration attempt. The identification field allows the Mobile Node to correlate each RRQ with its corresponding received RRP. Several pending RRQs can exist for a Mobile Node at a given time, and hence, the Mobile Node can match each outstanding RRQ with its RRP. The identification field prevents replay attacks of the RRQ specifically, because it is unique in each RRQ and thus thwarts a bad-intentioned node from keeping a copy of an RRQ and replaying it at a later time. Use of the identification field is covered in depth in Chapter 3, "Mobile IP Security."

Services

A key outcome of the Mobile IP registration phase is for the Mobile Node and Home Agent to agree on the Mobile IP services that are to be provided during the lifetime of the registration. You might have already pieced together how this "negotiation" occurs, but we risk stating the obvious. A Mobility Agent advertises the Mobile IP services that it is willing to provide in its agent advertisements. The Mobile Node then requests particular services in its RRQ. The FA and Home Agent either accept or reject these requests in the RRP.

Most of the services that a Mobile Node can request center around the Mobile IP tunnel and associated delivery options. For example, a Mobile Node can request that a specific CoA be used as the tunnel endpoint, and a particular encapsulation be used for the tunnel. Services can be requested either by setting specified option bits in the RRQ or by appending appropriate Mobile IP extensions. The use of extensions allows new services to be added to the Mobile IP protocol at any time. (Mobile IP includes provisions for 256 types of extensions, but extension subtypes can add an unlimited number of extensions.) All Mobility Agents must understand extensions of type 0–127 (considered critical extensions), or the entire RRQ that contains the extension must be silently discarded. This is because Mobile IP connectivity can depend on the nonoptional parameters conveyed in these extensions, and if an agent does not understand what is being requested, simply ignoring the extension and processing the rest of the request are likely to result in problems. On the other hand, options that do not critically affect connectivity, namely, extensions of type 128–255, might be ignored if they are not understood, with the rest of the RRQ, including all extensions, processed as normal.

Service Fields and Bits

The standard services offered in Mobile IP are best described by the different option bits and relevant fields in the RRQ, which are as follows:

- **CoA field**—The Mobile Node requests that the Mobile IP tunnel terminate at this address. This address can be an FA-CoA or a CCoA.

- **Lifetime field**—The Mobile Node requests Mobile IP services for this time period. If this field is set to 0, the Mobile Node is requesting a deregistration, either because it has roamed back to the Home Network or it is powering down.

The options bits are S, B, D, M, G, and T; when set to 1, the bits mean the following:

- **S**—A Mobile Node is requesting the use of simultaneous bindings. This requires the Home Agent to duplicate all packets and forward them to multiple CoAes.

- **B**—A Mobile Node is requesting that broadcast datagrams from its Home Network be delivered to it.

- **D**—The Mobile Node is specifying that it can perform the Mobile IP tunnel decapsulation, that is, the Mobile Node is using a CCoA and, thus, is the tunnel endpoint.

- **M**—The Mobile Node is requesting that the Home Agent use minimal encapsulation, as defined in RFC 2004, instead of IP-in-IP encapsulation for the Mobile IP tunnel.

- **G**—The Mobile Node is requesting that the Home Agent use GRE, as defined in RFC 1701, instead of
  IP-in-IP encapsulation for the Mobile IP tunnel.

- **T**—The Mobile Node is requesting reverse tunneling for packets originated by the Mobile Node. (Reverse tunneling is described in Chapter 6.)

To perform a Mobile IP handover other than returning home, the Mobile Node sends a RRQ, requesting relevant Mobile IP services and requesting that the Home Agent tunnel its packets to the CoA specified for the lifetime requested. If the RRQ and requested services are accepted by the FA and Home Agent, a RRP indicating success is received by the Mobile Node, with the registration lifetime specified in the lifetime field. The actual lifetime of the registration is determined by the Home Agent in the RRP and can differ from the lifetime requested by the Mobile Node in the RRQ.

On the other hand, if the RRQ is rejected, a RRP with a failure code (as outlined in the section "Registration Reply Codes," later in this chapter) is received by the Mobile Node. Many Mobile IP services are negotiated in this manner, that is, the Mobility Agent rejecting the RRQ sends a RRP with an appropriate error code, indicating to the Mobile Node how to amend its request.

If a Mobile Node commences a Mobile IP handover to return home or if it decides to power down, it sends a RRQ with the lifetime field set to 0 and the CoA field set to its Home Address. This type of RRQ is known as a *deregistration*.

Broadcast Support

If the Mobile Node requests that broadcast datagrams (by setting the B bit) be forwarded from its Home Network, care must be taken to ensure that the broadcasts do not appear on the visited network, but are delivered directly to the Mobile Node. The action that the Home Agent takes to ensure this depends on where the Mobile IP tunnel is terminating in the Foreign Network.

In the case that the tunnel terminates on the FA, the Home Agent encapsulates the broadcast datagram in a unicast IP packet destined for the Mobile Node's Home Address. This encapsulated packet is then sent through the Mobile IP tunnel as any other datagram, resulting in double encapsulation. The outer encapsulation allows the packet to be sent down the Mobile IP tunnel, and the inner encapsulation allows the FA to know which Mobile Node to forward the inner broadcast datagram. It is the responsibility of the Mobile Node to remove this inner encapsulation header to receive the broadcast datagram. This implies that the Mobile Node must be able to decapsulate packets to request broadcast support.

When the Mobile Node is using a CCoA and registering directly with the Home Agent, the Home Agent simply tunnels the broadcast datagram as any other packet destined for the Mobile Node. The extra inner encapsulation is not necessary because datagrams are tunneled directly to the Mobile Node.

Simultaneous Bindings

When the Mobile Node requests simultaneous bindings (by setting the S bit), it is requesting that the Home Agent maintain this mobility binding in addition to mobility binding(s) that the Home Agent might already have for it. If the Home Agent accepts the request, it duplicates each data packet and sends a copy to the CoA in each of the mobility bindings simultaneously, as shown in Figure 2-14.

Simultaneous binding support is often interpreted as a feature necessary to have a Mobile IP handover occur without packet loss. Mobile IP is often perceived as a "break before make" protocol, that is, the current Mobile IP connection is lost before a new Mobile IP registration is made. Using simultaneous bindings is perceived as making Mobile IP a make before break protocol because the bindings seem to provide a good communication path before the old path goes away. In practice, these characterizations are, for the most part, link-layer phenomena, and while simultaneous bindings can achieve a Mobile IP handover without packet loss, to leverage it with a single roaming interface, the underlying link layer must be designed for proper support. However, even then, a significant advantage over a standard Mobile IP handover would be unlikely.

Figure 2-14   *Simultaneous Bindings*

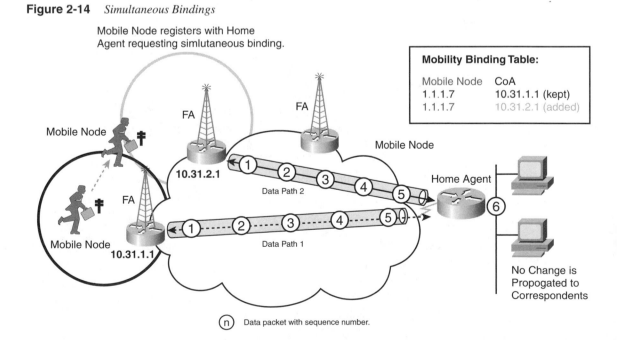

Regardless of whether simultaneous bindings are used, Mobile IP generally switches over instantly without packets being discarded by the Home Agent. This can be clearly seen when two different link types are being used and a Mobile Node is handing over from one active link to another active link. Packets to the Mobile Node are tunneled through the initial link until a reregistration is accepted by the Home Agent. At this point, the Home Agent immediately starts forwarding packets to the new CoA. As long as both links are active, no packets are lost, providing a Mobile IP handover without packet loss and without simultaneous bindings, as illustrated in Figure 2-15.

NOTE   Here is the worst case: If the initial link is slower than the new link, some packets can arrive out of sequence. However, this problem is not solved with simultaneous binding support, because it is an effect of the link speed, not the Mobile IP routing. However, if the link-layer capabilities of the Mobile Node were such that it could associate with two lossy links at the same time, simultaneous bindings can improve the probability that the Mobile Node can correctly receive its packets, because they are tunneled to both locations.

Figure 2-15 *Mobile IP Handover Without Simultaneous Bindings*

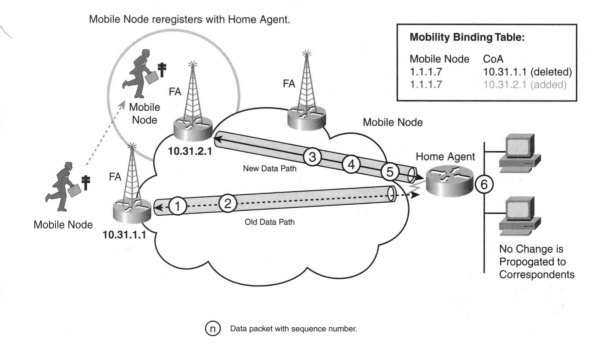

Authentication

Mobile IP authentication is covered in depth in Chapter 3, but you should understand the authentication concepts at this stage to understand the full capability of the Mobile IP registration messages and any appended Mobile IP extensions. To this end, we provide an overview of the concepts and refer you to Chapter 3 for more details.

Like other routing protocols, Mobile IP uses digital signature–style authentication to protect routing updates (that is, the RRQ and RRP) and is accomplished using authentication extensions (AEs). Different types of authentication extensions exist, each used to establish a bidirectional trust relationship between two specific Mobile IP entities. The critical purpose of the authentication extensions is to verify the sender of the message or portion of the message and to ensure that the message (or portion) was not altered while in transit.

Unlike other routing protocols, authentication between the Mobile Node and its Home Agent is mandatory for all routing updates. Because the registration messages alter routing to the Mobile Node, the information exchanged during the registration phase must be protected. To accomplish this, the Mobile Node–to–Home Agent Authentication Extension (MHAE) provides a bidirectional trust relationship between the Mobile Node and its Home Agent. It is the only authentication extension that is required in every RRQ and RRP. Other authentication extensions facilitate a bidirectional trust relationship between the Mobile Node and the FA (MFAE), the FA and the Home Agent (FHAE), and the Mobile Node and an authentication, authorization, and accounting (AAA) server (Mobile Node-AAA), as seen in Chapter 3.

The security of any appended Mobile IP service extensions depends on their placement relative to the authentication extensions present in the Mobile IP messages. For example, the FA can append a service extension after the mandatory MHAE and then secure it with an FHAE. Thus, controlling the placement of service extensions in this way allows extensions to be added and removed by individual Mobile IP entities in the path without impacting the integrity of the data protected by other authentication extensions. For example, Figure 2-16 shows how the MHAE authenticates only the information between the UDP header and the MHAE, while the FHAE protects the information between the UDP header and the FHAE, that is, including the FA-appended extensions.

Figure 2-16   *Use of Mobile IP Authentication Extensions*

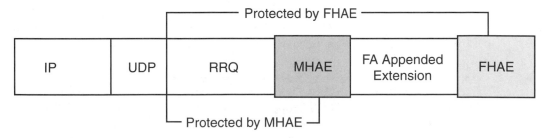

Relevant Address Fields

The different IP address fields within the Mobile IP RRQ message and the IP tunnel header depend on the registration situation and Mobile IP handover. Although it might seem confusing at first, it is quite straightforward. The possible Mobile IP handovers lead to the following four main registration scenarios:

- A Mobile Node registering with an FA-CoA through a FA
- A Mobile Node registering with a CCoA directly with its Home Agent
- A Mobile Node registering with a CCoA through a FA
- A Mobile Node deregistering with its Home Agent

In scenarios 1–3, the Mobile Node can operate either with a statically allocated Home Address or it can request a dynamically allocated Home Address. If the Mobile Node is requesting a dynamically allocated address, the Home Address field of the RRQ is 0.0.0.0. Table 2-1 outlines the different scenarios and IP address values.

Table 2-1   *Registration Request Address Field and IP Header Values Set by the Mobile Node*

	1 FA-CoA through FA	2 CCoA to Home Agent	3 CCoA through FA	4 Deregistration
IP Source Address	Mobile Node's Home Address or 0.0.0.0	$CCoA^2$	$CCoA^2$	Mobile Node's Home Address[3]
IP Dest. Address	An interface address on the FA	Home Agent's IP address	An interface address on the FA	Home Agent's IP address
Home Agent Address	Home Agent's IP address	Home Agent's IP address	Home Agent's IP address	Home Agent's IP address
CoA	$FA\text{-}CoA^1$	$CCoA^2$	$CCoA^2$	Mobile Node's Home Address[3]
Home Address	Mobile Node's static Home Address or 0.0.0.0 for dynamic allocation			Mobile Node's Home Address[3]

[1]This is the FA-CoA learned from the FA advertisement.

[2]This is an address in the foreign domain that is obtained through DHCP, manual configuration, or other means.

[3]This is either the Mobile Node's static Home Address or the dynamically allocated Home Address.

Example 2-2 shows the RRQ message in detail. In this example, the Mobile Node has an NAI (user@example.com) and is requesting that a Home Address be dynamically allocated. The Mobile Node is registering through a FA (192.168.100.28) with its Home Agent (192.168.101.1). It is requesting a registration lifetime of 2 hours and is appending an mobile foreign challenge extension (MFCE) and Mobile Node-AAA extension on top of the mandatory MHAE. (The MFCE and Mobile Node-AAA extensions are described in Chapter 3.)

Example 2-2 is a packet capture and decode of a RRQ taken with Ethereal, a network protocol analyzer. Protocol analyzers are widely used for troubleshooting and provide a field-by-field view of the packet.

Example 2-2   *Mobile IP Registration Request Protocol Detail*

```
Internet Protocol, Src Addr: 0.0.0.0 (0.0.0.0), Dst Addr: 192.168.100.28
  (192.168.100.28)
    Version: 4
    Header length: 20 bytes
    Differentiated Services Field: 0x00 (DSCP 0x00: Default; ECN: 0x00)
        0000 00.. = Differentiated Services Codepoint: Default (0x00)
        .... ..0. = ECN-Capable Transport (ECT): 0
        .... ...0 = ECN-CE: 0
    Total Length: 118
    Identification: 0x6c41
    Flags: 0x00
        .0.. = Don't fragment: Not set
        ..0. = More fragments: Not set
    Fragment offset: 0
    Time to live: 255
    Protocol: UDP (0x11)
    Header checksum: 0x2a71 (correct)
    Source: 0.0.0.0 (0.0.0.0)
    Destination: 192.168.100.28 (192.168.100.28)

User Datagram Protocol, Src Port: mobileip-agent (434),
    Dst Port: mobileip-agent (434)
    Source port: mobileip-agent (434)
    Destination port: mobileip-agent (434)
    Length: 98
    Checksum: 0xe7f7 (correct)

Mobile IP
    Message Type: Registration Request (1)
    Flags: 0x00
        0... .... = Simultaneous Bindings: False
        .0.. .... = Broadcast Datagrams: False
        ..0. .... = Co-lcated Care-of Address: False
        ...0 .... = Minimal Encapsulation: False
        .... 0... = GRE: False
        .... .0.. = Van Jacobson: False
        .... ..0. = Reverse Tunneling: False
    Lifetime: 7200
    Home Address: 0.0.0.0 (0.0.0.0)
    Home Agent: 192.168.101.1 (192.168.101.1)
    Care of Address: 192.168.100.28 (192.168.100.28)
    Identification: Jan 13, 2003 12:52:34.389797056
    Extensions
        Extension: Mobile Node NAI Extension
```

continues

Example 2-2   *Mobile IP Registration Request Protocol Detail (Continued)*

```
            Extension Type: Mobile Node NAI Extension (131)
            Extension Length: 12
            NAI: user@example
      Extension: Mobile-Home Authentication Extension
            Extension Type: Mobile-Home Authentication Extension (32)
            Extension Length: 20
            SPI: 0x00000100
            Authenticator: CF62301B0031DB59959A12B3E0AC939C
      Extension: Mobile Node-FA Challenge Extension
            Extension Type: MN-FA Challenge Extension (132)
            Extension Length: 4
            Extension: 179823C4
      Extension: Generalized Mobile-IP Authentication Extension
            Extension Type: Generalized Mobile-IP Authentication Extension (36)
            Gen Auth Ext SubType: MN AAA Extension (1)
            Extension Length: 20
            SPI: 0x00000002
            Authenticator: DF0461262E7DDB651E2C68B9180EC3AC
```

Here are the descriptions of the fields in the IP Header:

- **Source Address**—This is the CoA if the request has been forwarded by the FA or if the Mobile Node is using a Colocated CoA. Otherwise, the source is the Mobile Node's Home Address. If the Mobile Node does not have a Home Address, it is 0.0.0.0.

- **Destination Address**—This is either the Home Agent's IP address or the source address from the agent advertisement, but not necessarily the CoA.

- **Destination Port**—The destination port in the UDP Header is always 434.

Here are the descriptions of the fields in the Mobile IP Registration:

- **Type**—This is 1 for a RRQ and 2 for a RRP.

- **Simultaneous Bindings Flag**—The Mobile Node would like the Home Agent to duplicate packets and send them to multiple CoAes.

- **Broadcast Datagrams Flag**—The Mobile Node would like broadcast packets from the Home Network to be tunneled to its current location.

- **Colocated Colocated Care-of Address (CCoA) Flag**—The Mobile Node is using a Colocated CoA and not a FA.

- **Minimal Encapsulation Flag**—The Mobile Node would prefer to use minimal encapsulation for the tunnel instead of IP-in-IP encapsulation.

- **GRE Flag**—The Mobile Node would prefer to use GRE for the tunnel instead of IP-in-IP encapsulation.

- **Van Jacobson Flag**—This flag has been deprecated because it was deemed unimplementable.

- **Reverse Tunneling Flag**—The Mobile Node would like traffic to be reverse tunneled.

- **Lifetime**—This is the length of time in seconds that the Mobility Agent can retain an active binding. The lifetime value can range from 0 to 65,535 seconds. If the lifetime is 0, the Mobile Node is deregistering. A lifetime value of 65,535 is infinite.

- **Home Address**—This is the Mobile Node's Home Address. If the Home Address is set to 0.0.0.0, the Mobile Node would like a Home Address to be dynamically allocated.

- **Home Agent**—This is the IP address of the Mobile Node's Home Agent. This can be 0.0.0.0 if dynamic Home Agent assignment is being used.

- **CoA**—This is the address that the Mobile Node would like all traffic tunneled to.

- **Identification**—The identification field prevents replay attacks. It is usually represented as an NTP-style timestamp.

- **Extensions**—These begin with a type and length and then are followed by extension-specific data.

Registration Reply Codes

A RRP is sent either by a FA or a Home Agent in response to a RRQ. In the case of an FA-CoA, if the FA accepts the RRQ from the Mobile Node, it forwards the request to the Home Agent. However, if the FA rejects the RRQ or cannot forward the request to the Home Agent, it immediately sends a RRP with an appropriate error code, and does not propagate the reply to the Home Agent. Similarly, if the FA receives a RRP from the Home Agent and deems the reply to be invalid, it generates a new RRP with the appropriate error code. The possible FA reply codes are as follows:

```
64 reason unspecified
65 administratively prohibited
66 insufficient resources
67 mobile node failed authentication
68 home agent failed authentication
69 requested Lifetime too long
70 poorly formed Request
71 poorly formed Reply
72 requested encapsulation unavailable
73 reserved and unavailable
77 invalid care-of address
78 registration timeout
80 home network unreachable (ICMP error received)
81 home agent host unreachable (ICMP error received)
82 home agent port unreachable (ICMP error received)
88 home agent unreachable (other ICMP error received)
```

The FA attempts to use a specific reply code so that the Mobile Node knows why the registration was rejected. For example, the FA can send back error code 72 to indicate that the requested encapsulation [is] unavailable so that the Mobile Node can request a different encapsulation type in its next registration attempt.

When the Home Agent receives the RRQ, it generates a RRP. The Home Agent either responds with a successful reply code or an appropriate error code. The possible Home Agent reply codes are as follows:

```
Registration successful:

    0 registration accepted
    1 registration accepted, but simultaneous mobility
      bindings unsupported

Registration rejected by the home agent:

    128 reason unspecified
    129 administratively prohibited
    130 insufficient resources
    131 mobile node failed authentication
    132 foreign agent failed authentication
    133 registration Identification mismatch
    134 poorly formed Request
    135 too many simultaneous mobility bindings
    136 unknown home agent address
```

Registration Delivery

By this time—although this might fall into the same category as saying that a stop sign says "STOP"—a Mobile IP RRQ is initiated by a Mobile Node to commence a Mobile IP handover. The delivery details of the RRQ and RRP messages during the Mobile IP handover depend on whether a FA is being used. A Mobile Node can either forward a RRQ directly to the Home Agent if it is operating in CCoA mode without a FA or it is deregistering from its Home Network; otherwise, it forwards the request to the FA. The behavior of the Mobility Agents depends on the success of the messages and the type of Mobile IP handover being performed.

Regardless of the Mobile IP handover, when a FA receives a RRQ, it first verifies any necessary security associations. It then verifies that it is capable and allows the Mobile IP services requested by the Mobile Node. If the FA cannot or does not provide the requested services, it generates a RRP with an appropriate failure code, as described in the previous section.

If the FA can provide all the requested services, it creates an entry in its pending *registration table*. The pending registration table tracks RRQs that have not yet received a reply from the Home Agent. A pending registration is held by the FA for a maximum of 7 seconds before assuming that the Home Agent is unavailable. If an RRP is not received from the Home Agent, the FA generates a RRP with a registration timeout error code.

When the Home Agent receives the RRQ, either from the FA or directly from the Mobile Node, it begins by verifying the relevant security associations, as covered in Chapter 3. After the authenticity of the RRQ has been verified, the Home Agent begins to process the request, and if at any time the Home Agent cannot successfully support the request of the Mobile Node, it sends a RRP with an appropriate error code, as described in the previous section.

After this point, the behavior of the Mobility Agents depends on the type of Mobile IP handover being initiated in the RRQ.

Mobile IP Handover Other Than Returning Home

For a RRQ initiating a Mobile IP handover other than returning home, as the first step in processing the RRQ, the Home Agent determines whether a Home Address must be allocated for the Mobile Node by examining the home address field of the RRQ. (If the Mobile Node is requesting that a Home Address be dynamically assigned, it sets the Home Address field of the RRQ to 0.0.0.0, as described in the section "Relevant Address Fields," earlier in this chapter.) If a dynamic Home Address is needed, the Home Agent allocates an address to the Mobile Node that can be retained for as long as the Mobile Node is registered with the Home Agent. Details of dynamic Home Address allocation can be found in Chapter 8.

The Home Agent then updates the Mobile Node's mobility binding, if it already exists, or creates a new mobility binding for the Mobile Node. The mobility binding is a structure that keeps track of the attributes of an active Mobile Node. The Home Agent uses the binding to monitor which Mobile IP services are in use by the Mobile Node, the current CoA, and the lifetime of the registration. The Home Agent maintains the mobility binding in a *binding table*, which is a database of all the active Mobile Nodes and is a similar concept to the database in OSPF. Mobility bindings are uniquely indexed within the binding table by the Mobile Node's Home Address and are removed if the lifetime of the binding expires.

The Home Agent uses the information in the mobility binding to create a Mobile IP tunnel between itself and the CoA. It updates its routing table so that traffic for the Mobile Node is sent on the tunnel. The Home Agent then sends a gratuitous ARP on the Home Network to attract all traffic for the Mobile Node. This ensures that the Mobile Node's traffic is delivered to the Home Agent and, thus, can be sent down the Mobile IP tunnel to the Mobile Node. The result of the registration message exchange can be seen in Figure 2-17.

Finally, the Home Agent sends a RRP to the Mobile Node, either through a FA, if one is used, or directly. If the Home Agent allocated a dynamic Home Address for the Mobile Node, it includes the assigned address in the home address field of the RRP.

When the FA receives the RRP and deems the reply valid, it considers the Mobile Node to be visiting on its network. It moves the pending registration entry for the Mobile Node into its visitor table. The *visitor table* keeps track of all the Mobile Nodes with active sessions and is analogous to the binding table in the Home Agent. The visitor entry is not removed until the lifetime expires or until a Deregistration Reply, as described in the next section, is received.

Figure 2-17 *Result of a Successful Mobile IP Registration*

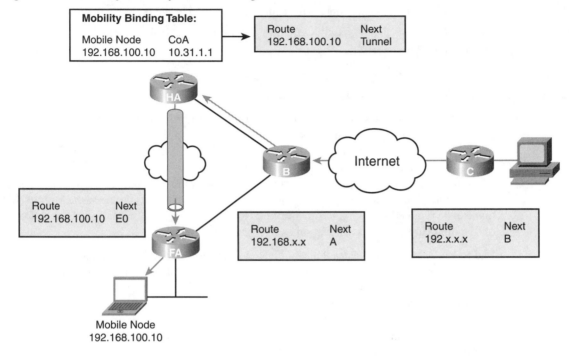

Mobile IP Handover Returning Home

Upon successful receipt of a Deregistration Request by a Mobile Node initiating a Mobile IP handover to return home or powering down, the Home Agent tears down the Mobile IP tunnels and dismantles (removes) the mobility binding. At this point, Mobile IP is no longer used for routing to the Mobile Node. The Home Agent sends a RRP, in this case known as a *Deregistration Reply*, to the Mobile Node.

If the FA receives the Deregistration Reply, it removes the corresponding Deregistration Request from its pending registration table and removes the Mobile Node's visitor table entry. The FA can only receive a Deregistration Reply for a Deregistration Request that it forwards. The FA forwards the Deregistration Reply to the Mobile Node.

Upon deregistration, the Mobile Node sends out a gratuitous ARP on the Home Network to ensure that its traffic is delivered to it and is no longer delivered to the Home Agent. Typically, the Mobile Node surrenders a dynamically allocated Home Address at this point.

Mobile IP Example

We now look at a Mobile IP example to get a good feel for the protocol. Consider a Mobile Node with a single interface whose Home Address is 192.168.10.30 and Home Agent is 192.168.10.1. In this example, the Mobile Node roams away from home to FA 192.168.100.6, and then to another FA, 192.168.200.6. It then finds itself still roaming, but not within the domain of a FA. At this point, it obtains a Colocated CoA and continues to roam. After some time, it returns home. The example is as follows:

1 The Mobile Node powers on and hears a Mobility Agent advertisement with the H bit set and router address as 192.168.10.1. Using this information and other relevant information from the advertisement, the Mobile Node recognizes that it is at home and does nothing.

2 At some later time, the Mobile Node hears another Mobility Agent advertisement with the F bit set, router address as 192.168.100.6 with a prefix length extension of /24, and CoA as 192.168.100.6. The Mobile Node detects that it has moved into a foreign domain and can request services by this FA. Using the new network algorithm, the Mobile Node determines that it needs to initiate a Mobile IP handover.

3 The Mobile Node sends a RRQ to its Home Agent through the FA. It conveys its new CoA (192.168.100.6) and its Home Address (192.168.10.30). As required, the Mobile Node appends an MHAE with the correct security credentials. The IP source of the RRQ is the Mobile Node's Home Address (192.168.10.30), and the IP destination is the FA (192.168.100.6).

4 The FA receives the RRQ, validates the requested services, creates an entry in its pending registration table, and forwards it on to the Home Agent. The IP source of the RRQ is now the FA 192.168.100.6, and the IP destination is the Home Agent 192.168.10.1.

5 The Home Agent authenticates and then validates the RRQ. The Home Agent establishes the mobility binding and Mobile IP tunnel to the CoA, sends a gratuitous ARP on the Home Network, and sends a positive RRP to the Mobile Node through the FA (the IP source is the Home Agent 192.168.10.1, and the IP destination is the FA 192.168.100.6). As required, the Home Agent appends an MHAE with the correct security credentials.

6 The FA receives the RRP, verifies that it is a successful reply, and changes the pending registration entry into a visitor entry for the Mobile Node. The FA then forwards the RRP to the Mobile Node using link-layer addressing.

7 The Mobile Node receives the RRP and enjoys the established Mobile IP services for the lifetime granted, or until it moves again and must reregister.

8 At some time later, the Mobile Node hears a Mobility Agent advertisement with the F bit set, router address 192.168.200.6 with a prefix length extension of /24, and CoA of 192.168.200.6. This time, the Mobile Node uses the steady-state algorithm and, thus, does not do anything until its current FA's advertisement expires, even though it hears this new FA advertisement.

9   Upon expiry of its current FA's advertisement, the Mobile Node initiates a Mobile IP
    handover and sends an updated RRQ to its Home Agent with the new CoA of
    192.168.200.6. The RRQ and RRP follow the same logic as previously described, and the
    Mobile Node successfully registers with the new FA.

10 The Mobile Node realizes that it has not heard an advertisement from its FA in some time
    and that the hold time is about to expire. It sends out an agent solicitation in hopes of
    finding a FA.

11 The Mobile Node receives no Mobility Agent advertisements and realizes that it is still
    roaming away from home, but is not under the domain of a FA. It then sends a DCHP
    request to obtain a CCoA (192.168.250.7) in the Foreign Network. It sends a RRQ directly
    to its Home Agent with the D bit set, the CCoA as 192.168.250.7, and the Home Address
    as 192.168.10.30. The IP source is the CCoA 192.168.250.7, and the IP destination is the
    Home Agent 192.168.10.1. The Home Agent sends a positive RRP directly to the Mobile
    Node 192.168.250.7.

12 At some time later, the Mobile Node hears a Mobility Agent advertisement with the H bit
    set and router address 192.168.10.1 with prefix length extension /24, and realizes that it is
    back home. It initiates a Mobile IP handover and sends a RRQ with the IP source as its
    Home Address (192.168.10.30) and IP destination as the Home Agent (192.168.10.1). It
    sets the CoA as its Home Address (192.168.10.30) and lifetime as 0 to indicate that it is
    deregistering its mobility binding. The Mobile Node sends out a gratuitous ARP on its
    Home Network to ensure that its traffic is delivered to it and is no longer tunneled by the
    Home Agent.

Tunneling

Rather than distribute routing information to the entire network, Mobile IP builds single-hop
logical links, or tunnels, to the edge of the Foreign Network, where the Mobile Node is
attached. A tunnel, just like any other link, can carry any IP packet between its endpoints. In
Mobile IP, the tunnel endpoint in the Foreign Network is either a FA–based CoA or a CCoA.
When a Home Agent has several Mobile Nodes registered through the same FA, traffic to all
nodes is delivered through a single-tunnel FA-CoA. A Home Agent can have several tunnels to
the same CoA, but the encapsulation protocol must be different for each tunnel.

Encapsulation

The default tunneling protocol in Mobile IP is IP-in-IP encapsulation, as defined in RFC 2003. Encapsulated packets are delivered as the payload of a new IP packet. The header of this new packet is referred to as the *outer header*. The destination of the outer header is the tunnel endpoint, and the source is the encapsulating device. For the forward Mobile IP tunnel, the destination is the CoA and the source is the Home Agent.

IP-in-IP is a simple protocol that requires little effort on the part of the Home and FAs. All field values in the outer header are chosen and set by the Home Agent with the exception of the type of service and don't fragment fields. Type of service values are copied from the inner packet to help preserve end-to-end quality of service of the packet. The "don't fragment bit" is set in the outer header if it is set in the header of the encapsulated packet, or if the Home Agent chooses to set it. This can enable tunnel path MTU discovery, as described in Chapter 6.

The Mobile Node can request an alternate encapsulation method for the tunnel. Both minimal encapsulation and GRE are available as options in the Mobile IP RRQ.

Minimal encapsulation, defined in RFC 2004, is an attempt to reduce the size of the inner header by eliminating the duplicate information found in IP-in-IP encapsulation. That is, the original packet header is compressed by removing the redundant information that is in the outer IP header. Minimal encapsulation is useful if the tunnel must traverse a low-bandwidth link, where every bit counts. In practice, the low-bandwidth link is usually the last link. Thus, in the case of registration through a FA, the increased processing overhead required by the tunnel endpoints does not justify the bandwidth savings.

GRE is an existing tunneling protocol that transports different network layer protocols across IP networks. GRE is defined in RFC 1701 and includes an extra 4-byte header between the outer and inner IP headers. GRE is used in some cases because of existing support for accelerated encapsulation on the Home Agent.

Triangle Routing

Mobile IP uses an asymmetric routing path referred to as *triangle routing*. Basically, traffic for the Mobile Node goes from the CN to the Home Agent to the Mobile Node, and return traffic goes directly from the Mobile Node to the CN, thus forming a triangular path, as shown in Figure 2-18. The main reason that the Mobile Node does not simply inform the CN of its new location and establish symmetrical routing can be summed up in one word: security.

Figure 2-18 *Triangle Routing*

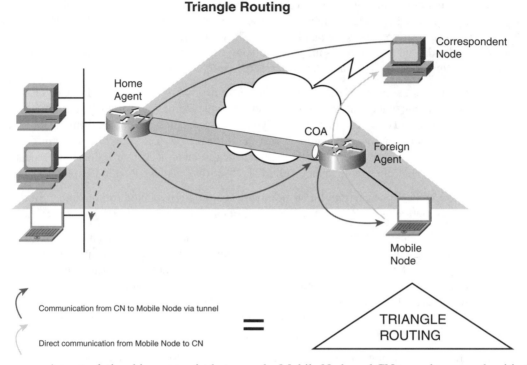

A trust relationship must exist between the Mobile Node and CN to exchange such critical information during the Mobile IP registration process; otherwise, the communication between the nodes is subject to simple DoS attacks. For example, a rogue node can just send a bogus registration message to the CN conveying a false CoA and simply hijack the Mobile Node's traffic. Because a trust relationship between a Mobile Node and every possible CN is highly unlikely, Mobile IP falls back to secure and reliable communication through triangle routing and the trusted Home Agent.

IP routing, as it is defined, does not use the source address of a packet in the delivery process. Mobile IP takes advantage of this fact in an attempt to optimize traffic delivery. That is, packets from the Mobile Node are sent using the Mobile Node's Home Address as the source address, even while on the Foreign Network, and are delivered directly to their destination using a default gateway, the FA. The Mobile Node must forward traffic through one of the router addresses listed in the FA advertisement and must not send ARP requests when it is in a Foreign Network.

Return routing to the Mobile Node follows standard IP routing to the Mobile Node's Home Network prefix. When traffic arrives at the Home Network, the Home Agent intercepts that traffic using either routing, gratuitous ARP, or a similar technique. The Home Agent then forwards the Mobile Node's traffic through the tunnel to the CoA.

In Chapter 6, we discuss a feature called *reverse tunneling*, which allows data packets originated by the Mobile Node on the Foreign Network to be forwarded back to the Home Agent through a reverse tunnel. These packets then follow standard routing from the Home Agent to their destination. Reverse tunneling removes the notion of triangle routing and ensures that the packets from the Mobile Node are topologically correct. This is necessary to overcome security measures being deployed in the Internet today. A detailed discussion of reverse tunneling is given in Chapter 6.

Summary

In this chapter, we discussed how Mobile IP is a dynamic routing protocol where end devices signal their own routing updates and dynamic tunnels eliminate the need for host route propagation, thereby providing a scalable solution. We looked at how the Mobile IP protocol solves the mobility challenges of location discovery and move detection using agent advertisements and agent solicitations, and we discussed the concept of a Mobile IP handover. You saw how Mobile IP handovers are accomplished during the Mobile IP registration phase using routing updates, namely, the RRQ and RRP messages. We examined the behavior of the Mobile Node, FA, and Home Agent during these phases, and you saw how routing is accomplished while the Mobile Node is in the Foreign Network, and while it is at home.

In the coming chapters, we examine the security aspects of Mobile IP and highlight the major concepts of IOS Mobile IP configuration in a simple lab topology. We then apply all this knowledge to real-world use of Mobile IP, in both a private intranet environment and the global Internet. Along the way, we introduce enhanced Mobile IP features, along with the specific IOS commands necessary to invoke these features.

Review Questions

1 List the major entities in a Mobile IP deployment.

2 Mobile IP provides which of the following features? (Select two.)

   a A dynamic security association between the Mobile Node and Home Agent that changes as the Mobile Node roams across different subnets

   b Seamless roaming across IP subnets

   c Redirection routing to the Mobile Node based on the distance to the Mobile Node's new location

   d Mobility transparent to CNs

   e Host-specific routing to the Mobile Node

3 In Mobile IP, when a Mobile Node moves to another domain, how do the CNs now communicate with the Mobile Node?

   a The Mobile Node informs the CN of its movement, and thus a dynamic tunnel is created between the CN and the Mobile Node's CoA. The CN sends packets for the Mobile Node through the tunnel.

   b The CNs communicate as normal with the Mobile Node, sending packets to the Mobile Node's home IP address. The Home Agent intercepts the packets and forwards them to the Mobile Node through a dynamic tunnel established between the Home Agent and CoA.

   c The CN sends packets to the home network and requests the Home Agent to tunnel the packets to the Mobile Node through the Mobile Node's CoA.

   d The CN suspends communication with the Mobile Node until the Mobile Node returns home.

4 Which two features of a mobility protocol are facilitated by agent advertisements in Mobile IP?

   a Location discovery

   b Move detection

   c Update signaling

   d Path (re)establishment

5 Which of the following is not used for move detection?

   a The router address and prefix length extension portion of the agent advertisement

   b The CoA portion of the agent advertisement

   c Link-state information

   d RRQ message

6 Mobile IP handover occurs at Layer 2.

   a True

   b False

7 Name three different types of Mobile IP handover policy algorithms. Briefly describe each one.

8 How does a Mobile Node know whether it is on its Home Network or a Foreign Network?

   a By comparing the lifetime granted in its current Mobile IP registration against that advertised in Mobile IP agent advertisements

   b By comparing the FA address configured on the Mobile Node against that advertised in the Mobile IP agent advertisements

    c By comparing its CoA against the Home Agent address advertised in Mobile IP agent advertisements

    d By comparing its Home Address and network prefix against those advertised in Mobile IP agent advertisements

9 A Mobile Node finds itself away from home on a network with a FA. Describe the Mobile IP registration process, starting with how the Mobile Node learns that it is not home.

10 What types of CoAes can a Mobile Node use on a Foreign Network?

11 Which of the following are advantages of a Mobile Node using a FA CoA? (Select two.)

    a Many Mobile Nodes can roam off of the same CoA, which saves address space in IPv4.

    b The Mobile Node can retain the same FA CoA as it moves across different foreign domains.

    c The Mobile Node can be preconfigured with the FA CoA.

    d The same tunnel between the Home Agent and FA can support numerous Mobile Nodes.

    e The Mobile Node does not need to reregister with its Home Agent when it moves to a different foreign domain.

12 Which of the following indicate situations when the Mobile Node would use a Colocated CoA? (Select two.)

    a If the Mobile Node is statically configured with a Colocated CoA

    b If the Mobile Node doesn't hear an agent advertisement from a FA on the foreign domain

    c If the Mobile Node doesn't hear an agent advertisement from its Home Agent on the foreign domain

    d If the Mobile Node cannot detunnel its own packets

    e If the FA is not providing services that the Mobile Node would like

13 How does a Mobile Node signify to the Home Agent that it would like a dynamic Home Address to be assigned?

14 Describe the steps that a FA follows during the registration process.

15 Describe the steps that the Home Agent follows upon receiving a RRQ from a Mobile Node.

16 What is triangle routing?

17 What does a Mobile Node do upon returning home?

CHAPTER 3

Mobile IP Security

The previous chapters characterized Mobile IP as a routing protocol, and when it comes to security, Mobile IP is no different. Just like other routing protocols, the security features in Mobile IP are designed to authenticate routing peers and ensure the integrity of routing update messages. As such, all the security methods in Mobile IP are designed to protect only the control plane traffic, namely, the Registration Request (RRQ) and Registration Reply (RRP).

In this chapter, we explore the two mechanisms that are used in Mobile IP to provide secure communication among the different Mobile IP entities: authentication extensions and replay protection. This chapter delves into the various components of the authentication extension and illustrates precisely how messages are secured. You see why some authentication extensions between certain Mobile IP entities (the Home Agent and Mobile Node) are mandatory while some are not. You also see why replay protection is needed in Mobile IP and how it is achieved with timestamps or nonces.

The most challenging trust relationship in Mobile IP is between the Mobile Node and Foreign Agent (FA), simply because the Mobile Node cannot have a security relationship with every FA to which it can roam. In this chapter, we look into clever mechanisms that afford security between a FA and its visiting Mobile Nodes without requiring preconfiguration of the Mobile IP entities.

The first part of the chapter assumes a static security relationship that is used in the authentication extensions. Later in the chapter, we investigate different approaches to dynamically administering a security association between Mobile IP entities. Specifically, we look into ways to change the security association dynamically, or even to set up a security association between Mobile IP entities when one does not already exist.

NOTE   Mobile IP secures control traffic and does not interact with data traffic per se. However, Mobile IP can easily be combined with existing protocols designed to secure data traffic, for example, IP Security (IPSec). More detailed discussions of the integration of Mobile IP with IPSec are covered in Chapter 7, "Metro Mobility: Cisco Mobile Networks," and Chapter 8, "Deployment Scalability and Management."

Protocol Authentication Extensions

In a routing protocol, it is important for peers to trust one another and to ensure that the messages they exchange have not been altered in transit. False routing updates from untrusted peers or altered updates from trusted peers can wreak havoc on a network, for example, causing traffic for multiple prefixes to be routed incorrectly or even blackholed.

Even though Mobile IP limits the impact of rogue updates because each routing update is for an individual host and only affects that host, it is just as important to secure the routing control messages. In fact, because Mobile IP is an overlay routing protocol often used across multiple autonomous systems, it is more vulnerable to attack. Because the Mobile IP control messages traverse multiple routers, or those claiming to be routers, it is necessary to ensure that a control message is *from who it says it is from* and *says what it was intended to say*. If the RRQ and RRP messages are not properly secured, a roaming Mobile Node's traffic can easily be hijacked. You have probably realized that a Mobile Node at home is not subject to the same vulnerabilities as a roaming Mobile Node.

The Mobile IP protocol uses security authentication extensions to provide peer authentication and message integrity. As the name suggests, the authentication extension is an extension containing relevant security information that is appended to the end of the message. The authentication extensions are designed to allow extensive flexibility through their extension type and placement within the message. That is, different types of authentication extensions secure messages between different Mobile IP entities. Moreover, the authentication extensions secure a specific part of the Mobile IP messages, depending on where the part is placed within the message.

The critical purpose of the authentication extension is to verify the sender of the message and to ensure that the message was not altered while in transit.

The extension types are allocated to allow authentication between various pairs of peers. The following four Mobile IP extension types, allocated for authentication, currently exist:

- Mobile Node–Home Agent Authentication Extension (abbreviated as MN-HA or MHAE)
- Mobile Node–FA Authentication Extension (abbreviated as MN-FA or MFAE)
- FA–Home Agent Authentication Extension (abbreviated as HA-FA or FHAE)
- Generalized Authentication Extension (abbreviated as GNAE)

The GNAE is a catchall for new types of Mobile IP authentication extensions. It allows more authentication extensions to be created without consuming more Mobile IP extension types, which are limited. The only current use of the GNAE is to define the Mobile Node–authentication, authorization, and accounting (AAA) Server Authentication Extension (MN-AAA).

Authentication extensions allow flexibility in authenticating various parts of the registration message with various peers. Thus, as information is added to the registration control messages, it can be protected without altering the protection to pre-existing portions of the control message. For example, a Mobile Node can secure its RRQ with an MHAE and forward the request to its FA. The MHAE protects the information preceding it, namely, the base RRQ. In turn, the FA might want to append an extension to the RRQ and secure the extension with an FHAE. The two extensions secure different subsets of the message and are between different Mobile IP entity pairs. That is, the base RRQ is secured between the Mobile Node and Home Agent, and the entire message, including the appended extension, is secured between the FA and Home Agent. Figure 3-1 shows a Mobile IP RRQ and mandatory MHAE that is appended by an extension by the FA and then secured with the FHAE.

Figure 3-1   *Authentication Extension Placement and Protection*

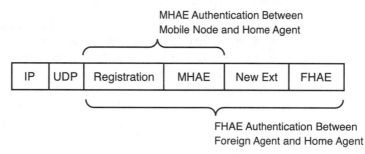

Security Associations

The next natural question then is "What relevant security information do authentication extensions contain, and how do these extensions secure messages?"

For Mobile IP entities to use an authentication extension between them, they must first share a security relationship. This relationship is in the form of a set of predefined parameters configured into each node, which are collectively known as a *security context*. A security context is comprised of the following components:

- Algorithm and mode to be used in crypto computations
- Shared key between the peers
- Replay protection method

(We look at each of these components in more detail in subsequent sections.)

Theoretically, each node can have more than 4 billion individual security contexts per peer. A group of one or more security contexts that are shared with an individual peer is referred to as a *security association*. It is also common for the term *security association* to be used interchangeably with the term *security context*. This is likely because security associations are often made up of only one security context.

NOTE   The ability to support multiple security contexts gives Mobile IP operators enormous flexibility and control over security association management. Multiple contexts can be used between each node to minimize the impact of brute-force attacks by rotating through the keys with each registration. You can also change keys without requiring both nodes to be updated at the same time. For example, an administrator could add the new security context to the Home Agent. Then, when the Mobile Node is available for update, the new context can be added and the old one removed. Finally, the old context can be removed from the Home Agent.

After the shared association is in place, the entities can now send messages securely.

The sender computes a cryptographic keyed hash of the message using an algorithm and shared key, places this value in the authentication field of the authentication extension, and sends the message. The algorithm and keys that protect a message are implied by the sender within the authentication extension, which is part of the protected portion of the message. To verify the integrity of a message, the recipient computes its own cryptographic keyed hash of the same portion of the message (the message *not* including the authenticator value) using the same algorithm and shared key. It then compares the computed hash to the authenticator value in the appropriate authentication extension, as shown in Figure 3-2. If the two match, the message is considered to be authenticated.

Figure 3-2   *Authentication in Mobile IP Using Extensions*

Sender: message to be protected + algorithm + secret keys = HASH 'A'

Receiver: message received UP TO and WITHOUT the HASH received
+ algorithm implied to be used + secret keys = HASH 'B'

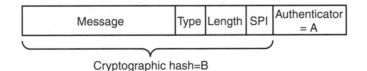

If A=B, message authenticated

If HASH 'B' is identical to HASH 'A,' the receiver has some assurance the message was received as it was sent by a node which knows how to identify the algorithm, and that algorithm's shared secret.

SPI

A specific security context is identified in the authentication extension by the *security parameter index (SPI) value*. The SPI is a 4-byte value that is configured as either a hexadecimal or decimal value. (Unfortunately, this can often lead to confusion because the peer devices can require the SPI value to be specified in different formats.) If a security violation is received on a RRQ, the SPI value is the first item that should be verified, because it identifies the security context to use in authenticating the message.

Of the over four billion values, the values 0 through 255 are reserved for specific contexts defined in IETF standards. The only reserved SPI values currently allocated are the Challenge Handshake Authentication Protocol (CHAP) and CHAP Hash-based Message Authentication Code (HMAC), 2 and 3 respectively, which are used in the MN-AAA Authentication Extension. This is discussed in the section "MN-AAA Authentication," later in this chapter.

NOTE   It is common to use SPI value 100 hex or 256 decimal when configuring the first security context because it is the first nonreserved value.

Algorithm and Mode

The authenticator value in the authentication extension is a message authentication code (MAC), which can be thought of as a fingerprint. For each registration message, a hash algorithm calculates the unique fingerprint value, which is of smaller total length than the original message. Thus, given that more possible values exist for the original message than do unique fingerprint results, the algorithms are designed so that the result is as unique as possible. The ideal algorithm results in 50 percent of the bits in the hash changing by changing just 1 bit in the message.

It is difficult to derive a message that would produce the same result. For example, if the message is the classic sentence "The quick brown fox jumped over the lazy dog," an algorithm whose result identified the message as "containing 36 letters, 3 of which are *es*" would be less than ideal. Many sentences would produce the same result, and it is easy to create one. It would be more secure to say that it "contains 36 letters and at least 1 of each letter in the alphabet." Coming up with a sentence to match this identification would be much more difficult!

The Mobile IP standard originally defined MD5, as described in Request For Comment (RFC) 1321, as the required algorithm for the Mobile Node-Home Agent and FA-Home Agent authentication extensions. However, this was later determined to be vulnerable to attack. MD5, as defined in RFC 1321, is often described as *prefix-suffix mode*. The standard was later amended to define HMAC, as described in RFC 2104, as the required algorithm and mode instead of prefix-suffix MD5. HMAC is a method of computing a hash of the message and is cryptographically stronger.

The MN-AAA Authentication Extension uses CHAP and CHAP-HMAC for computing the authenticator, as described in the section "MN-AAA Authentication," later in this chapter. The standard also allows implementers to use other methods such as Secure Hash Algorithm (SHA) or RIPEMD-160 in their implementations, but this is not common.

Key

The authenticator is computed using a key that is shared between the two peers. The node that initiates the message uses the key to compute the value in the authentication extension. The node that receives the message uses the same key value and computes the authenticator over the registration message and compares the result to the value in the authentication extension. If the two values match, the authentication is accepted. The default key is 128 bits long and is usually represented by 32 hex characters. RFC 3344, "IP Mobility Support for IPv4," states the following:

The default algorithm is HMAC-MD5 [23], with a key size of 128 bits. The FA MUST also support authentication using HMAC-MD5 and key sizes of 128 bits or greater, with manual key distribution. Keys with arbitrary binary values MUST be supported.

...More authentication algorithms, algorithm modes, key distribution methods, and key sizes MAY also be supported for all of these extensions.

This leaves the implementation open for software developers and has lead to many different keying options. Specifically, key length varies widely, some vendors support keys of only 128 bits, and others support longer or shorter keys. This problem becomes even worse when vendors attempt to use plain-text keys and convert them. Some vendors take text of any length and convert it straight to hex; others add 0s to the key to ensure that it is 128 bits long. This results in some interoperability problems among different vendors' components. Fortunately, almost every vendor supports a 128-bit key configured in hex so that interoperability is still possible.

Selection of the key is important. Keys should be unique to each user and should be random. Good random keys can usually be used because a user does not need to remember them. These keys are typically typed in once and stored.

Replay Protection Methods

Authentication in the Mobile IP control messages can be strong if proper keys are selected, but because no data is guaranteed to be unique in each registration message, these messages are vulnerable to replay attacks. That is, a malicious third party could capture the registration message used in a given location and then resend that message after the Mobile Node has left, disrupting the data flow and redirecting traffic to the attacker. To avoid this kind of attack, Mobile IP offers the following two replay protection methods:

- **Timestamp**—Timestamp support is required in all Mobility Agent and nodes
- **Nonces**—Optional

By using timestamps or nonces, a unique value is placed in a field of the registration message. The receiver can then verify that it is a unique message and ignore the message if it is not unique, suspecting it to be a replay. Whichever method is used, the unique identifier that makes every message different is contained in the 64-bit identification field of the registration message.

Timestamp Replay Protection

Timestamp replay protection relies on the availability of a real-time timestamp placed in each registration message and the algorithm, as shown in Figure 3-3. The timestamp is sent in the identification field and is encoded in the manner specified by the Network Time Protocol (NTP).

Figure 3-3   *Mobile IP Timestamp Replay Protection Algorithm*

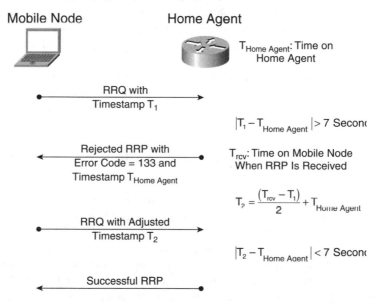

$$|T_1 - T_{Home\ Agent}| > 7\ \text{Secon}$$

$$T_{rcv}\text{: Time on Mobile Node When RRP Is Received}$$

$$T_2 = \frac{(T_{rcv} - T_1)}{2} + T_{Home\ Agent}$$

$$|T_2 - T_{Home\ Agent}| < 7\ \text{Secon}$$

The NTP timestamp format is a 64-bit unsigned fixed-point number. The first (higher) 32 bits, known as the *integer portion*, represent the number of seconds since 12:00 a.m. on January 1, 1900. The remaining (lower) 32 bits, or fractional portion, represent the fraction seconds. Unlike NTP, when insufficient clock granularity is available, the data should be padded with quality random data rather than 0s. When generating random data, the timestamp must be greater than any previously used timestamp, or the message will be discarded as being out of sequence.

When a message is received, the timestamp is verified to ensure that the time in the identification field is within a configured interval of its current time. This interval is typically 7 seconds and should not be less than 3 seconds. If the Home Agent finds that the difference between the timestamp and the current time is greater than the allowed interval, it rejects the registration with an error code of 133, registration id mismatch. The Home Agent also updates the higher 32 bits with the current timestamp in the RRP. Upon receipt of the RRP, the Mobile Node matches the sent RRQ message to the received reply by comparing the lower 32 bits and then updating its time by computing an offset. The offset is the difference between the Mobile Node's time and the Home Agent's time, plus the estimated latency of the link. The latency is estimated by halving the time difference from when the RRQ was sent and when the reply was received. The Mobile Node then attempts to reregister with this updated timestamp.

Nonces Replay Protection

Nonces are a concept where the identification field is split into two 32-bit values; the low-order values are allocated by the Mobile Node and the high-order values are allocated by the Home Agent. For every RRQ, the Mobile Node generates a new lower-order value. The Home Agent copies that value into the lower-order portion of the identification field in the reply and generates a new random value for the high-order portion. The values generated by the Home Agent are then saved and used as the high-order portion of the identification field in the next RRQ sent by the Mobile Node. Because the Home Agent always knows what the next high-order portion of the identification field is supposed to be and the Mobile Node changes the lower-order portion, it can easily determine whether a message is being replayed.

Mobile Node and Foreign Agent Authentication and Challenge Mechanism

The Mobile Node-FA Authentication Extension is intended to provide authenticated communication between the Mobile Node and FA. However, it suffers from several deployment problems that have kept it from widespread adoption. Use of the original Mobile Node-FA Authentication Extension would require every Mobile Node to have a key for every FA it visited, and every FA to have a key for every potential Mobile Node. Clearly, key management and distribution on such a scale is simply not practical. Moreover, the MFAE also does not provide replay protection because the timestamp and nonces methods are between the Home Agent and Mobile Node only. (Refer to the section "Replay Protection Methods," earlier in this chapter.)

In most deployment cases, this was not an issue because Mobile Node-FA authentication was not needed. However, when Mobile IP was adopted as part of the CDMA 2000 standard, authentication at the FA was deemed necessary precisely for replay concerns, but it could not be easily achieved using the Mobile Node-FA Authentication Extension. Again, one of the major problems was key distribution. Not only was it not part of the standard, but with intercarrier roaming, it was also not desirable to send actual key values to roaming partners.

A more practical and easily achievable security mechanism was needed. It was cleverly realized that the solution might already be in the air, so to speak! AAA servers based on the Remote Authentication Dial-In User Service (RADIUS) protocol (which is described in Chapter 5, "Campus Mobility: Client-Based Mobile IP") were already widely deployed and had a proven method for authenticating roaming users in a dial-up environment. This existing capability, along with the existing replay protection used in dial-up, was then leveraged to provide secure authentication at the FA, namely, authentication through a AAA server and the CHAP for replay protection. The Mobile IP Working Group formalized the technique in RFC 3012 and introduced the following new extensions to Mobile IP to support the technique:

- FA Challenge Extension for agent advertisements
- Generalized Authentication Extension with MN-AAA authentication subtype
- Mobile Node-FA Challenge Extension for RRQs

NOTE   The Generalized Authentication Extension with subtype 1 (MN-AAA authentication) is simply referred to as the *MN-AAA Authentication Extension*.

FA Challenge

Point-to-Point Protocol (PPP)-based dial-up uses an authentication mechanism referred to as the CHAP. CHAP integrates authentication and replay protection into a single protocol. The authenticating device, in this case the FA, issues a *challenge,* which is a random number that is valid for a specified amount of time, and then expires.

The FA often offers multiple challenge values that are valid for a specified amount of time, known as the *challenge window,* as shown in Figure 3-4. By issuing a challenge, the FA is basically saying, "For a RRQ to be valid, you must include a challenge value from within my challenge window. And by the way, you can only use a particular challenge value once." The challenge is sent in an extension to the agent advertisement called the Mobile IP Agent Advertisement Challenge Extension and, when copied into the RRQ, allows the FA to ensure that the request is not a replay.

A challenge can also be sent in a RRP so that the Mobile Node does not have to wait to learn of new challenges in agent advertisements. For example, if a RRQ is denied by the FA because of a bad challenge, the FA can inform the Mobile Node of a new challenge in the RRP. Because agent advertisements and registration replies are confined to the link on which they are sent, only Mobile Nodes on that link would learn the challenge values.

Figure 3-4 *Challenge Window*

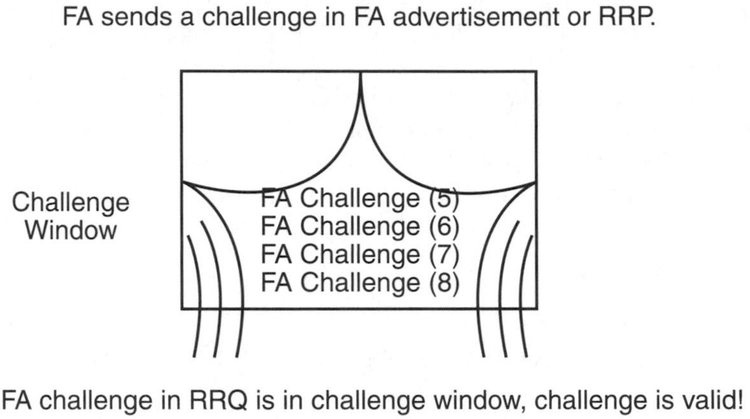

FA sends a challenge in FA advertisement or RRP.

Challenge
Window

FA Challenge (5)
FA Challenge (6)
FA Challenge (7)
FA Challenge (8)

If FA challenge in RRQ is in challenge window, challenge is valid!

A Mobile Node copies a valid challenge value into an extension—the Mobile Node-FA Challenge Extension—and appends the extension to the RRQ it sends to the FA. This extension must be secured by either an MFAE, if one exists, or the Mobile Node-AAA extension described in the next section. Ah, the raised eyebrows! Yes, the notion that the MFAE exists seems to contradict the need for this mechanism, but keep in mind that while the MFAE provides authentication, it doesn't provide replay protection.

Upon receiving the challenge in the RRQ, the FA first checks whether the challenge is indeed valid before authenticating the message. This is simply because validating the challenge is an easier and faster process than authenticating the Mobile Node. This is a process similar to the nonces' process described in the section "Nonces Replay Protection," earlier in this chapter. If the FA determines that the challenge is not valid, it rejects the RRQ and sends a RRP with one of the following newly defined error codes:

- **104 Challenge**—Value is unknown.
- **105 Challenge**—Value is missing in the RRQ.
- **106 Challenge**—Value has expired or has already been used.

At this point, the Mobile Node must reregister with a valid challenge value. Note that RFC 3012 does not mandate that a FA must reject the RRQ if a challenge is invalid. However, accepting invalid challenge values is as good as not having the mechanism to begin with. Figure 3-5 illustrates the FA Challenge (FA Challenge) mechanism.

Figure 3-5   *Mobile IP FA Challenge Flow*

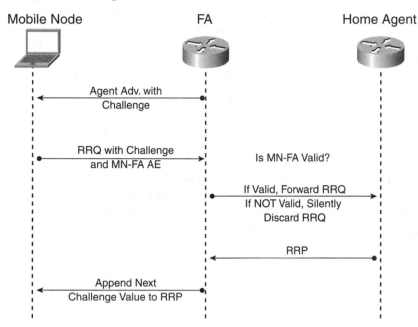

MN-AAA Authentication

The MN-AAA Authentication Extension is similar to other authentication extensions, but is intended to be processed by a AAA server, which is discussed in more depth in Chapter 5. Recall that the MN-AAA Authentication Extension is the Generalized Authentication Extension with Subtype 1, as defined in RFC 3012.

NOTE   When using the AAA model for authentication, a AAA server typically exists for the home domain, and a AAA server for the foreign domain. Sometimes, they can in fact be the same physical server; however, the functionality is distinct.

The MN-AAA extension can only be generated by the Mobile Node, because the Mobile Node and its home AAA server are the only entities with the proper credentials. The Mobile Node appends the MN-AAA Authentication Extension to a RRQ. Although this might be stating the obvious, the MN-AAA Authentication Extension can authenticate RRQs, but it cannot be used in the RRP because the reply is generated by a FA or Home Agent.

The most common use of the MN-AAA Authentication Extension is with a specialized SPI called the CHAP_SPI, an SPI value of 2, which is designed to mimic a PPP CHAP authentication request to a RADIUS server. This allows off-the-shelf RADIUS servers to be used rather than requiring a custom AAA infrastructure. RFC 3012, "Mobile IPv4 Challenge/Response Extensions," has also been amended to support CHAP-HMAC to eliminate the same MD5 vulnerability, as discussed in the section "Algorithm and Mode," earlier in this chapter.

With the MN-AAA Authentication Extension and the FA Challenge, FAs can now authenticate RRQs without needing the pre-existing security key. When the FA receives a RRQ with the MN-AAA extension, it computes a hash on the message and sends a portion of this hash, along with the authenticator value sent in the MN-AAA, to its AAA server, which likely consults the Mobile Node's home network AAA server. A trust relationship is assumed to exist between the two AAA servers. The appropriate AAA server completes the hash computation using the stored password for the Mobile Node and compares the hash that it computed with the authenticator value that was sent. If they match, an authentication accept message is returned to the FA. In this way, the FA can authenticate the Mobile Node. Figure 3-6 shows the same call flow for an FA Challenge as in Figure 3-5, but with the Mobile Node using the MN-AAA Authentication Extension.

Figure 3-6 *Mobile IP FA Challenge Flow Using the MN-AAA Authentication Extension*

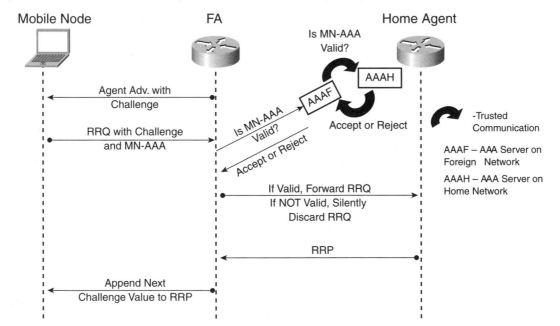

Unlike the other authentication extensions, the MN-AAA is designed to accommodate a textual password. This password is typically used for dial-up authentication as well. The use of a single authentication infrastructure allows a simplified deployment and management. Note that the MN-AAA is not a replacement for the Mobile Node-Home Agent Authentication Extension.

Dynamic Keying

The complexity of managing static preshared keys can be a daunting task, especially for larger enterprises. Deploying a client-based Mobile IP solution would be cost prohibitive if each Mobile Node needed to be manually configured with one or more keys. Couple this with the fact that any static security key is usually reissued (rekeyed) periodically to prevent rogue nodes from capturing a key and using it indefinitely. Even if you consider a network with 100 Mobile Nodes, each having 2 keys, that would result in 200 keys that an administrator would need to manually configure. By the time she finished configuring all the keys, it might be time to reissue each of those keys!

Instead, wouldn't it be nice if the mandatory Mobile Node-Home Agent key could be generated dynamically? Or, even if a preshared key existed, wouldn't it be nice if session keys could be dynamically generated so that the Mobile Node and Home Agent wouldn't need to be rekeyed periodically. That is, a security key (session key) could be generated dynamically for each Mobile IP session from a static key. Because the session key would be valid only for that session, in a sense it is being rekeyed for each session.

Dynamic keying reduces the need to provision new keys on the Mobile Node and Home Agent also protects against rogue nodes that are trying to crack the key. Remember, when it comes to cryptography, it is not a matter of *if* the encryption can be broken but *when*. The goal is to make the cracking so difficult that the data is irrelevant by the time the encryption can be broken. For example, if someone can capture your encrypted sales figures, but it takes him 1000 years to read them, is that data relevant? To make the capturing of the encrypted data even more difficult, imagine that the sales report is split into five pieces—each encrypted using a different key. Then it would take five times as long to read it! It is more difficult to break the code if you have less data and you have an effective cryptography system. The same premise is used for dynamic keying systems in Mobile IP.

Standards-Based Dynamic Keying

An IETF draft, "AAA Registration Keys for Mobile IPv4," authored by Perkins and Calhoun, is nearing standardization to provide a replacement for the static preshared keys used in Mobile IP authentication. This draft, while attempting to be AAA-server agnostic, does not appear to be usable with a RADIUS server and is definitely not usable with existing AAA servers. The draft is designed to use the advanced features of a Diameter server. (Diameter is designed to be a replacement for RADIUS.) Diameter has not been widely adopted, and as such, this draft did not seem like the ideal way to simplify enterprise deployment. In fact, without a larger Diameter deployment base, this draft, though perhaps useful, will be limited in the places it can be used.

Cisco Dynamic Security Association and Key Distribution

The Cisco Dynamic security association and Key Distribution feature was designed to derive dynamic session keys on the Mobile Node and Home Agent. It integrates with common enterprise infrastructure as part of the Zero Configuration Client, or ZeCC, solution. ZeCC, covered more in Chapter 5, in turn is designed to integrate with existing services, including Dynamic Host Configuration Protocol (DHCP), RADIUS, and Windows domain controllers.

Cisco Dynamic security association and Key Distribution uses vendor-specific extensions to the RRQ and reply messages to derive session keys on both peers. The basic message flow is shown in Figure 3-7. RFC 2759, "Microsoft PPP CHome AgentP extensions version 2 (MS CHAPv2)," is used with Windows login credentials obtained at the Mobile Node to authenticate the initial RRQ. A hash of the hashed user password along with data from the initial RRQ generate a permanent key from which transient session keys are generated. Either the permanent key or transient session keys can then perform Mobile Node–Home Agent authentication. To accomplish this key establishment, five vendor-specific extensions can be used, and four other extensions are defined to carry configuration information.

Figure 3-7   *Cisco Dynamic Security Association and Key Distribution Call Flow*

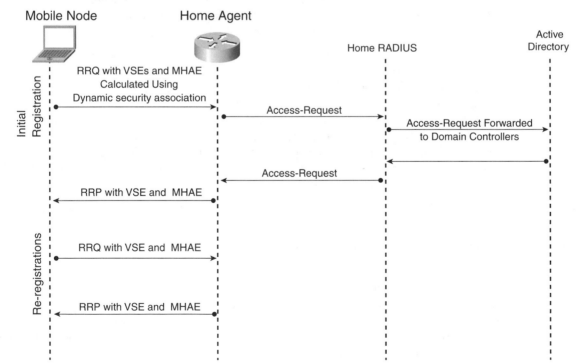

Session Index Extension

The session index differentiates between multiple devices being operated by the same user. For example, if a user has a laptop and a personal digital assistant (PDA) both running Mobile IP and using the same Windows login credentials, separate keying sessions must be maintained for each device.

The session index is a textual name, usually the host name or network ID of the Mobile Node. The session index is combined with the network access identifier (NAI) to form a session identifier. The session identifier is similar to the IP Address/SPI pair that identifies the Mobile Node's security association. A typical session identifier would be user.pda or user.laptop. The use of a session index extension is optional.

Security Association Setup Extension

MHAE requires more than just a key to be completed. A security context, identified by an SPI value, must also contain the authentication algorithm and the replay protection method. The security association setup extension allows the Mobile Node to inform the Home Agent how to build a complete security association. The Mobile Node selects a random unused value between 256 and 65,535 for use as an SPI, and the node identifies the authentication algorithm, replay protection method, and key it will use. The Mobile Node can send one security association setup extension for the permanent key and can send another for the transient key. If, after the first registration, the Mobile Node or Home Agent desires a new transient session key, it computes the new key and includes an security association setup extension with the new SPI, algorithm, and replay protection. Either the Home Agent or Mobile Node can rekey at any time.

Domain Extension

Microsoft Windows authentication allows users to be associated with a domain. The domain is similar to the realm portion of the NAI. If multiple domains are in use within an enterprise, the domain extension must carry the domain name of the user. This allows the AAA server to route the query to the proper domain controller for authentication. This extension is optional.

Challenge Extension

MS CHAPv2 requires the use of a challenge value similar to that in FA CHAP, as described in the section "FA Challenge," earlier in this chapter. This value can be a random number chosen by the Mobile Node. The recommended CHAP value is a 16-byte concatenation of the Home Agent address, the Care-of Address (CoA), and the identification field. Having the Mobile Node generate its own challenge defeats the purpose, but because the replay protection defined in the Mobile Node-Home Agent security association already protects against replay attacks, the challenge is not necessary. The challenge essentially maintains compatibility with the existing protocol so that infrastructure does not need to be updated. The challenge extension is mandatory.

Authentication Response Extension

The authentication response extension carries the authenticator value computed over the RRQ using MS CHAPv2 and a hash of the user password. This provides the bootstrap authentication that authenticates the initial RRQ from which the dynamic Mobile Node-Home Agent keys can be derived. This extension is mandatory but is only used in the initial RRQ. After the session keys have been derived, they are used in the MHAE to authenticate registration update messages.

Configuration Extensions

While not related to the derivation or distribution of security associations, four more extensions are defined as part of Cisco Dynamic security association and Key Distribution to facilitate the zero-configuration client solution. These extensions are as follows:

- The Home network prefix extension allows the Home Agent to inform the Mobile Node of the prefix or netmask that should be used with the assigned home address.

- The Domain Name System (DNS) server extensions provide the Mobile Node with DNS servers it should use during the session.

- The DHCP server extension and the DHCP client identifier extension are optional parameters that allow the Mobile Node to acquire configuration options from and maintain a lease with the DHCP.

Location Privacy

Beyond the basic concepts of authentication and authorization, *location privacy* often comes up in Mobile IPSec discussions. The concern is that the Mobile IP registration process divulges too much information about the location, both physically and logically, of a Mobile Node, its home network, and as such, the person to whom the Mobile Node belongs. For example, if a delivery company has Mobile Nodes in each vehicle, it could easily determine whether a driver had left his route and gone home for lunch by evaluating the physical location of the CoA used by the Mobile Node. The Mobile Node might also not want the foreign network to know where the node is from.

However, the privacy implications in Mobile IP v4 are debatable. Because no support exists for route optimization, only the operator of the Home Agent has direct access to the CoA information. It is clearly possible to use a location-discovery mechanism like traceroute to discover the location of a Mobile Node, but this can be blocked. While location privacy should be considered when evaluating the security impacts of a Mobile IP solution, these impacts are rarely formidable enough to preclude deployment.

Summary

As a routing protocol, Mobile IP provides an extensive set of features to ensure the integrity of each routing update as a registration message traverses its peers. Just as with other routing protocols, Mobile IP does not provide provisions for securing user data, nor does it preclude the use of existing security protocols like IPSec. In the next chapter, security associations appear as a required part of the configuration in our lab example. In Chapter 5, examples of a ZeCC-configuration Mobile IP client are demonstrated. Chapter 6 introduces the integration IPSec with Mobile IP to provide data security.

Review Questions

1 What are the two key features that secure the Mobile IP registration messages?

2 What prevents a rogue node from setting up the mobility binding for the Mobile Node on the Home Agent?

    a All Mobile IP control packets traverse the home AAA server, where the packet is authenticated.

    b The Home Agent discards any Mobile IP control packet if the IP source address does not equal that of the Mobile Node's home address.

    c The Mobile Node and Home Agent share a security association, and all Mobile IP control packets must be authenticated between the Mobile Node and Home Agent.

    d The FA performs egress filtering and drops any Mobile IP control packets that do not emanate from the Mobile Node's CoA.

3 List the different types of Mobile IP authentication extensions, and describe their purpose.

4 Describe how the MHAE and FHAE can secure the same RRQ.

5 What elements comprise a security context? How is a security context identified?

6 What is the standard hash algorithm that must be supported in a Mobile IPv4 deployment?

7 To verify the integrity of a message that has an authentication extension appended, the recipient does which of the following?

    a The recipient compares the authenticator value in the appended extension to that stored in the security association for the sender.

    b The recipient computes a cryptographic hash on the authenticator value and compares it to the value stored in the security context.

    c The recipient indexes the security association with the SPI and finds the authenticator value to compare to the value in the extension.

    d The recipient computes a cryptographic hash of the message and compares it to the authenticator value in the appended extension.

8 Replay protection in registration messages is needed for which of the following reasons?

   a To thwart off reflection and replay attacks, where the message is retransmitted at a later time

   b To ensure that data flow is not disrupted and traffic is not redirected by the attacker

   c To guarantee that a unique field exists in the registration messages

   d A and B only

   e A and C only

   f A, B, and C

9 Briefly describe the timestamp replay protection method.

10 Briefly describe the nonces replay protection method.

11 How does the Mobile Node secure registration messages using the FA Challenge mechanism?

   a The Mobile Node appends a valid challenge value to a registration message that it learns from the FA's advertisements.

   b The Mobile Node appends a valid challenge value that it learns from its Home Agent in a reply message secured with the MHAE.

   c The Mobile Node appends a valid challenge value from a pool of challenge values with which it is preconfigured.

   d The Mobile Node appends a valid challenge value that it learns from the FA through link-layer signaling.

12 What is the challenge window?

13 The MN-AAA Authentication Extension can secure RRQs and registration replies.

   a True

   b False

14 Why is the session index extension used in Cisco dynamic security association and key distribution?

CHAPTER 4.

IOS Mobile IP in the Lab

This chapter highlights the major concepts of IOS Mobile IP configuration in a simple lab topology. It presents in detail the most important concepts in IOS Mobile IP configuration. We start out by using six routers to examine each component individually. Several alternatives requiring fewer routers are presented at the end of the chapter. The idea here is to introduce Mobile IP configuration in its simplest form. All of the solutions presented in upcoming chapters are built on the information presented here. The topology presented here was not created just for this example, but is used by the authors as a baseline for most of their Mobile IP lab work.

Building the Baseline Topology

Figure 4-1 shows the basic topology, which is designed to demonstrate all the basic functionality in clearly separated components. It consists of Mobile IP entities—a single Home Agent, two Foreign Agents (FAs), and a Mobile Node—and non-Mobile IP entities—a Correspondent Node (CN) and an intermediate system (IS). Each of these devices is a router capable of running IOS software, as shown in Table 4-1. Feature navigator on Cisco.com can ensure that all features are available on the selected platform.

Figure 4-1 *Basic Lab Topology*

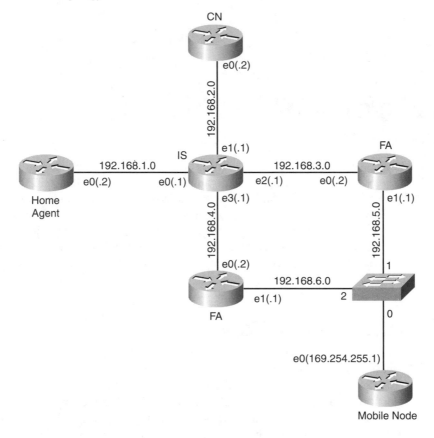

Table 4-1 *Required IOS Software Versions*

Device	Software Version*
Home Agent	IOS Release 12.0(1)T or higher
FAs	IOS Release 12.0(1)T or higher
Mobile Node	IOS Release 12.2(4)T or higher
CN	Any IOS version
IS	Any IOS version with OSPF

*If possible, IOS Release 12.3 or higher should be used in the Mobility Agents—Home Agents and FAs—so that all the features covered in this book are available.

Note that the Mobile Node in this topology is a "mobile router" (see Chapter 7, "Metro Mobility: Cisco Mobile Networks"). Although the mobile router is covered later in this book, it is used in this example to provide a complete solution that is independent of a specific Mobile Node client. The mobile router has essentially the same basic configuration attributes as a simple Mobile Node and thus provides not only a Mobile Node example but also a mobile router example for later reference.

Intermediate System Configuration

The IS shows the interaction between Mobile IP and traditional routing protocols and, as such, has no Mobile IP–specific configuration. However, inclusion of the ISs more accurately models real-world scenarios and allows better understanding of a Mobile IP deployment. In Example 4-1, each interface is assigned an IP address, and the Open Shortest Path First (OSPF) routing protocol is configured for all interfaces.

Example 4-1   *Intermediate System Final Configuration*

```
hostname IS
!
interface Ethernet0/0
 ip address 192.168.1.1 255.255.255.0
!
interface Ethernet1/0
 ip address 192.168.2.1 255.255.255.0
!
interface Ethernet2/0
 ip address 192.168.3.1 255.255.255.0
!
interface Ethernet3/0
 ip address 192.168.4.1 255.255.255.0
!
router ospf 1
 log-adjacency-changes
 network 192.168.0.0 0.0.255.255 area 1
!
end
```

Correspondent Node Configuration

The CN is used as a peer for traffic from the Mobile Node. Many Mobile IP labs are built without a CN and IS; while this allows basic functionality testing, it does not demonstrate real-world behavior. The use of a CN demonstrates the routing infrastructure as well as the Mobile IP infrastructure, and the interaction of the two. The CN needs only to be configured with an IP address on the interface. Although the CN is a router in Example 4-2, it could easily be replaced with a computer.

Example 4-2 *CN Final Configuration*

```
hostname CN
!
interface Ethernet0/0
 ip address 192.168.2.2 255.255.255.0
!
end
```

Home Agent Configuration

Home Agent configurations entail the following three basic tasks:

- Enabling the Home Agent
- Configuring the home networks
- Configuring the Mobile Nodes that are supported by the Home Agent

We will step through the three tasks and introduce the IOS configuration commands that are needed on the router. The configuration shown in this section demonstrates the base configuration of the Home Agent. Later chapters introduce more features, but keep in mind that you should always keep the configurations as short as possible and enable only the necessary features.

The foremost task is to simply enable the Mobile IP functionality. Note that regardless of which Mobile IP entity the router is functioning as, the Mobile IP routing process needs to be configured as follows:

```
router mobile
```

When the Mobile IP process is running, one or more Mobility Agents can be enabled. To configure this router as a Home Agent, use the following command:

```
ip mobile home-agent
```

The next step is to configure the home networks and Mobile Nodes that are to be supported by the Home Agent. IOS Mobile IP supports two types of home networks, physical home networks and virtual home networks. Each Mobile Node that is supported by a Home Agent must reside on one of these types of home networks.

Physical Home Network Configuration

When a Home Agent supports physical home networks, it allows Mobile Nodes to attach directly to their home network. The physical home networks are defined on a Home Agent's physical interface. When a Mobile Node is attached to its home network, all Mobile IP functionality is inactive for that Mobile Node, and normal IP routing delivers traffic. When the Mobile Node is not attached to the home network, the Home Agent uses proxy Address Resolution Protocol (ARP) to divert traffic to the Mobile Node in its current location. Route propagation for a physical home network is handled directly by interior routing protocols, just as it would be for an interface with no Mobile Nodes. To use a physical home network, simply assign the interface an IP address and ensure that it is not shut down.

NOTE When using physical home networks, if the interface is down, Mobile Nodes cannot register with the Home Agent.

Virtual Home Network Configuration

A Home Agent also supports Mobile Nodes that reside on a virtual home network. Virtual home networks are similar to loopback interfaces, but they are Mobile IP specific. Similar to a loopback interface, a virtual network is always up and not susceptible to physical failures, thereby ensuring higher availability. Virtual networks only support nodes that never physically come home. Virtual networks are expressed as a network number and mask. To define a new virtual network on the Home Agent, use the following configuration command with *address* as the network number and *mask* as the network mask:

```
ip mobile virtual-network address mask
```

Unlike physical interfaces, however, routing information about virtual networks can only be originated by the Home Agent when mobile routes are redistributed into the interior gateway protocol. Redistribution of Mobile IP routes only redistributes the virtual networks; it does not redistribute the individual host routes that reach the Mobile Nodes. The section "Examining the Routing Table," later in this chapter, shows how Mobile IP routes appear in the routing table and how redistribution works.

NOTE Redistribution allows routes from one routing domain to be translated and injected into another routing domain. Use care when redistributing routes to maintain a functional routing topology.

Specific configuration of redistribution varies from protocol to protocol, but generally, it should be configured on the Home Agent as follows:

```
redistribute mobile
```

The next step is to configure Mobile Nodes to reside on a particular home network.

Mobile Host Configuration

The essence of a Home Agent configuration centers around configuring the Mobile Nodes that it supports and appears on one or more lines beginning with the **ip mobile host** command. This command defines which Mobile Nodes are allowed to register, which services they are allowed to use, and how to authenticate them. (The security association itself is configured separately, as described in the next section of this chapter.) The **ip mobile host** command requires a Mobile Node or group of Mobile Nodes to be defined and associated with a home network.

In the following example command, we consider a simple case—defining a range of Mobile Nodes identified by their home address (192.168.100.10 through 192.168.100.20) and associating them with a virtual network (192.168.100.0 with mask 255.255.255.0):

```
ip mobile host 192.168.100.10 192.168.100.20 virtual-network 192.168.100.0
   255.255.255.0
```

The Home Agent also needs to be configured with the Mobile-Home security association for each Mobile Node. The security association can be configured either in a AAA server or on the command line, as described in the examples of the next section.

Security Association Configuration

The security association between the Home Agent and a Mobile Node is mandatory; it is also the only one used in this chapter. A security context is configured on the Home Agent one per line, and each line is usually associated with one Mobile Node. (Remember a security association is made up of one or more security contexts.) In some cases, several Mobile Nodes can share the same security key, but this is generally not recommended. At a minimum, one Mobile Node-Home Agent (MN-HA) security context is configured for each mobile host entry, but the standard allows for far more. If multiple security contexts, which are differentiated by using different security parameter index (SPI) values, are configured for a single mobile host, the IOS mobile router implementation will round-robin through all keys. In this case, each Registration Request (RRQ) uses a different security context going from the lowest to the highest SPI value and then starting over again. The Home Agent always uses the same security context that was used in the RRQ by the Mobile Node when the Mobile Node sends a Registration Reply (RRP).

NOTE   Configuration of security associations for IOS Mobile IP is always done from the perspective of the agent that is to use that security association. For example, the **ip mobile secure foreign-agent…** command configures an Home Agent-FA security association on the Home Agent. If the same command were configured on the Mobile Node, it would imply an MN-FA security association.

In the case of a router serving as both a Home Agent and FA, the configuration of keys for Mobile Nodes is slightly different. Specifically, you must be able to differentiate the Mobile Node-Foreign Agent (MN-FA) and MN-HA keys in this hybrid case. Because IOS uses the **host** command to refer to the Mobile Node in Home Agent configurations and the **visitor** command to refer to the Mobile Node in FA configurations, the same is done for security associations. Thus, the **ip mobile secure host** command configures the Home Agent-Mobile Node (HA-MN) security association, while the **ip mobile secure visitor** command configures the FA-MN security association.

As with all security context, the HA-MN security context must be indexed with an SPI. The SPI in IOS is specified as a hexadecimal value. Finally, the key, algorithm, and mode must be specified. You can specify keys as an ASCII value or a hexadecimal value. To avoid errors, hexadecimal keys are recommended because the use of ASCII keys is not standardized. A complete HA-MN security association is as follows:

```
ip mobile secure host 192.168.100.10 spi 100 key hex
    1234567890abcdef1234567890abcdef algorithm hmac-md5
```

Home Agent Final Configuration

Example 4-3 shows the final configuration of a router serving as a Home Agent. The Home Agent supports Mobile Nodes (192.168.100.10 through 192.168.100.20) residing on virtual network 192.168.100.0. The only Mobile Node configured with a security association is 192.168.100.10, and thus, it is the only Mobile Node allowed to register and roam.

Example 4-3   *Home Agent Final Configuration*

```
hostname HA
!
interface Ethernet0/0
 ip address 192.168.1.2 255.255.255.0
!
router mobile
!
router ospf 1
 redistribute mobile subnets
 network 192.168.0.0 0.0.255.255 area 1
!
ip mobile home-agent
ip mobile virtual-network 192.168.100.0 255.255.255.0
ip mobile host 192.168.100.10 192.168.100.20 virtual-network 192.168.100.0
   255.255.255.0
ip mobile secure host 192.168.100.10 spi 100 key hex
   1234567890abcdef1234567890abcdef algorithm hmac-md5
!
end
```

Foreign Agent Configuration

The FA configuration used in this lab is simple and represents the most common implementation. Complex FA configurations are typically only used in mobile Internet service provider deployments of Mobile IP. A basic FA configuration requires the definition of the Care-of Address (CoA) and activation of roaming interfaces.

Recall that for any Mobile IP entity, the IOS Mobile IP process must be started before any Mobile IP commands can be accepted on the router. Again, this is accomplished with the **router mobile** command.

FA functionality is enabled with a single global statement that also specifies the interface to be used as the CoA. In the following example command, Ethernet interface 1/0 is configured with FA functionality:

```
ip mobile foreign-agent care-of Ethernet1/0
```

When the FA service has been enabled on the router, each interface that can accept Mobile Nodes needs to be configured. The interface-level command is as follows:

```
ip mobile foreign-service
```

Finally, because Mobile IP agent advertisements are part of Internet Control Message Protocol (ICMP) Router Discovery Protocol (IRDP) advertisements, IRDP must be configured. The default timers for IRDP are long and do not facilitate timely handovers unless solicitation is used. In Example 4-4, the timers have been lowered because no link state triggers exist. Three relevant values exist for IRDP configuration: **maxadvertinterval**, **minadvertinterval**, and **holdtime**. If the *min* and *max* values are used together, a random value in between the two is generated for each advertisement. The holdtime should typically be three times the maximum to ensure that the agent is truly gone and not just experiencing a brief packet loss. Configuration values for IRDP timers are in seconds. Note that the advertisement timers can also be adjusted on the Home Agent with similar IRDP commands. Unless specified through configuration commands, the default IRDP values are a maximum interval of 5 minutes and a holdtime of 15 minutes.

Examples 4-4 and 4-5 show the configuration of routers serving as FAs. In Example 4-4, the FA allows Mobile Nodes to roam on interface E1/0 with FA–Care-of Agent (FA-CoA) 192.168.5.1. In Example 4-5, the FA allows Mobile Nodes to roam on interface E1/0 with FA-CoA 192.168.6.1. In both examples, the IRDP agent advertisement timers are adjusted.

Example 4-4   *FA1 Final Configuration*

```
hostname FA1
!
interface Ethernet0/0
 ip address 192.168.3.2 255.255.255.0
!
interface Ethernet1/0
 ip address 192.168.5.1 255.255.255.0
 ip irdp
 ip irdp maxadvertinterval 4
 ip irdp minadvertinterval 3
 ip irdp holdtime 9
 ip mobile foreign-service
!
router mobile
!
router ospf 1
 log-adjacency-changes
 network 192.168.0.0 0.0.255.255 area 1
!
ip mobile foreign-agent care-of Ethernet1/0
!
end
```

Example 4-5   *FA2 Final Configuration*

```
hostname FA2
!
interface Ethernet0/0
 ip address 192.168.4.2 255.255.255.0
!
interface Ethernet1/0
 ip address 192.168.6.1 255.255.255.0
 ip irdp
 ip irdp maxadvertinterval 4
 ip irdp minadvertinterval 3
 ip irdp holdtime 9
 ip mobile foreign-service
router mobile
!
router ospf 1
 log-adjacency-changes
 network 192.168.0.0 0.0.255.255 area 1
ip mobile foreign-agent care-of Ethernet1/0
!
end
```

Mobile Node Configuration

In this chapter, the Mobile Node is an IOS router running the IOS Mobile Networks feature. For this example, only a small subset of the IOS Mobile Networks features is used; full coverage is available in Chapter 7. The Mobile IP client used in IOS Mobile Networks is built on the same standard as a Mobile IP client for a PC or personal digital assistant (PDA) and, thus, requires all the same basic configura-tion attributes. In general, each Mobile Node must be configured with its identification, Home Agent's IP address, and a security association shared with the Home Agent.

IOS Mobile Networks uses a static home address for identification that needs to be configured on an interface before it can be used by the Mobile IP client. You should configure the home address on a loopback interface so that the home address is always up. The home address is a host address and, as such, needs to be configured with a /32 mask. (If the loopback does not have a host mask, traffic for other nodes on the Mobile Node's home network cannot follow the default route, but is routed to the loopback and get dropped.)

The real mask of the home network is configured with the **ip mobile router address** command. One or more physical interfaces need to be specifically configured as roaming interfaces. These interfaces also must be configured with an IP address to enable IP traffic on that interface. Note that the IP address does not need to be valid and routable. Addresses are commonly used from the autoconf space, but you can pick any IP address.

As with all Mobile IP entities, the **router mobile** command is required to enable the Mobile IP process on the mobile router. After enabling Mobile IP, the Mobile IP client configuration is invoked with the **ip mobile router** command, setting the router in mobile router configuration mode. In this mode, the home address and home network subnet mask are configured with the

address subcommand, and the Home Agent address is configured with the **home-agent** sub-command, as shown in the following example:

```
router mobile
 ip mobile router
  address 192.168.100.10 255.255.255.0
  home-agent 192.168.1.2
```

Finally, the mandatory security association with the Home Agent needs to be configured. This security association needs to *exactly match the one configured on the Home Agent, as follows:*

```
ip mobile secure home-agent 192.168.1.2 spi 100 key hex
   1234567890abcdef1234567890abcdef algorithm hmac-md5
```

Recall that the security association is configured from the perspective of the Mobile IP entity on which the command is invoked, that is, this line is configuring the MN-HA security association.

Example 4-6 shows a mobile router configuration with a home address of 192.168.100.10 and a Home Agent address of 192.168.1.2. Note that the home address is configured on the loopback interface, and interface E0/0 is configured as the roaming interface.

Example 4-6   *Mobile Node Final Configuration*

```
hostname MN
!
interface Loopback0
 ip address 192.168.100.10 255.255.255.255
!
interface Ethernet0/0
 ip address 169.254.255.1 255.255.255.0
 ip mobile router-service roam
!
router mobile
!
ip mobile secure home-agent 192.168.1.2 spi 100 key hex
   1234567890abcdef1234567890abcdef algorithm hmac-md5
!
ip mobile router
 address 192.168.100.10 255.255.255.0
 home-agent 192.168.1.2
!
end
```

Operation and Evaluation/Troubleshooting

In the lab environment, roaming is simulated by toggling the FA to which the mobile router's roaming interface is connected. This is typically done by assigning different virtual LAN (VLAN) numbers to each FA and changing the VLAN assignment for the roaming interface on the mobile router. After the mobile router's roaming interface is connected to a FA at Layer 2, the mobile router should automatically register with the Home Agent through the FA.

The different mobility entities can be probed to assess proper functioning of the Mobile IP process.

Home Agent

Even though Mobile IP is an edge-intelligent routing protocol (that is, all routing decisions are made by the Mobile Node), a network administrator often does not have access to the Mobile Node for troubleshooting. Because the Home Agent is the anchor point in the network, it is a logical starting point for evaluation. The first checklist task at the Home Agent is to verify that the Mobile Node indeed has a mobility binding using the **show ip mobile binding** command. If no binding exists for the Mobile Node, the **show ip mobile host** command can provide information about any previous failed registration attempts.

Example 4-7 shows the output if the security association on the Mobile Node (192.168.100.10) did not match the one configured on the Home Agent. The output of the **show ip mobile host** command displays the failure as "Last code," which in this example is a failed authentication. The output also shows when the Home Agent last accepted a registration from the Mobile Node, and when the registration was last denied. In this example, the Mobile Node had four failed registration attempts, and had never successfully registered with the Home Agent.

Example 4-7   **show ip mobile host** *Command*

```
HA#show ip mobile binding 192.168.100.10
Mobility Binding List:
HA#show ip mobile host 192.168.100.10
Mobile Host List:

192.168.100.10:
    Allowed lifetime 10:00:00 (36000/default)
    Roam status -Unregistered-, Home link on virtual network 192.168.100.0 /24
    Accepted 0, Last time -never-
    Overall service time 00:00:21
    Denied 4, Last time 07/24/03 13:43:29
    Last code 'MN failed authentication (131)'
    Total violations 4
    Tunnel to MN - pkts 0, bytes 0
    Reverse tunnel from MN - pkts 0, bytes 0
HA#
```

Using the information learned through troubleshooting, the Mobile Node configuration can be corrected to send a proper RRQ message to the Home Agent. Upon successful authentication and validation of the RRQ, a mobility binding is established on the Home Agent, as shown in Example 4-8. A valid binding, however, might not indicate that everything is functioning correctly. Thus, you should also verify that the last accepted registration is more recent than the last denied registration using the **show ip mobile host** command.

Example 4-8   *Valid Mobility Binding*

```
HA#show ip mobile binding 192.168.100.10
Mobility Binding List:
192.168.100.10:
    Care-of Addr 192.168.6.1, Src Addr 192.168.4.2
    Lifetime granted 10:00:00 (36000), remaining 09:59:52
    Flags sbdmg-t-, Identification C2CA6BA8.4489393C
    Tunnel0 src 192.168.1.2 dest 192.168.6.1 reverse-allowed
    Routing Options -
HA#
```

Mobile Node

After looking at the Home Agent, the next best place to troubleshoot is at the Mobile Node. (The FA is often reserved for last, because the only deterministic way to identify the active FA is to look at the CoA that the Mobile Node is using.) Each Mobile IP client offers a different set of tools for troubleshooting, but the basic premise is the same as those available in IOS. Follow these troubleshooting steps:

1 Ensure that the Mobile Node has received agent advertisements from one or more FAs.

2 Determine which FA the Mobile Node has selected and whether the registrations are indeed accepted by the foreign and Home Agents. Also, the registration might be accepted, but the reply is dropped by the network.

3 Determine whether and how data traffic is flowing.

Example 4-9 shows the output of the **show ip mobile router agent** command, which lists all currently valid agent advertisements. Because this mobile router is only seeing one FA, you can easily determine which FA is being used. Note that most clients have some method of indicating which FA is being used. This is useful when proceeding to the FA for further troubleshooting. If no FAs have been heard, it is likely a physical layer problem or a FA configuration problem.

Example 4-9   *Current Agent Advertisements*

```
MN#show ip mobile router agent

Mobile Router Agents:

Foreign agent 192.168.5.1:
    Care-of address 192.168.5.1
    Interface Ethernet0/0, MAC aabb.cc00.6801
    Agent advertisement seq 30828, Flags rbhFmG-t, Lifetime 36000
    IRDP advertisement lifetime 9, Remaining 6
    Last received 07/20/03 19:49:07
    First heard 07/19/03 18:11:37
```

When you have determined that the Mobile Node has a valid FA, the next step is to look at the registration status. Example 4-10 shows the output of the **show ip mobile router** command. In the Monitor section of the output, the status of the registration is displayed, along with the current FA and CoA.

Example 4-10 *Registration Status*

```
MN>show ip mobile router

Mobile Router
    Enabled 07/20/03 15:00:42
    Last redundancy state transition NEVER

Configuration:
    Home Address 192.168.100.10 Mask 255.255.255.0
    Home Agent 192.168.1.2 Priority 100 (best) (current)
    Registration lifetime 65534 sec
    Retransmit Init 1000, Max 5000 msec, Limit 3
    Extend Expire 120, Retry 3, Interval 10

Monitor:
    Status -Registered-
    Active foreign agent 192.168.6.1, Care-of 192.168.6.1
    On interface Ethernet0/0
    Tunnel0
```

Finally, if the registration looks good and matches what the Home Agent has for the registration, you likely have a data plane problem. Check the interface counters and verify that traffic is coming into an out of the Mobile Node. You often find outbound traffic, but no inbound traffic. In this case, you likely have a problem with the tunneling. A number of common tunneling problems and solutions are covered in Chapter 6, "Metro Mobility: Client-Based Mobile IP," and Chapter 8, "Deployment Scalability and Management."

FA

The FA stores the state of active Mobile Nodes in the visitor table. The output of the **show ip mobile visitor** command, shown in Example 4-11, is similar to the output of the **show ip mobile binding** command on the Home Agent. However, visitor entries in the FA can be misleading for troubleshooting. Entries are not flushed from the visitor table until the lifetime expires, so a Mobile Node could have briefly visited the FA, but the visitor entry can remain for many hours if the lifetime is long. Note that using the Registration Revocation mechanism, described in Chapter 6, alleviates this problem.

Example 4-11 *FA Visitor Table Entry*

```
FA1#show ip mobile visitor
Mobile Visitor List:
Total 1
192.168.100.10:
    Interface Ethernet1/0, MAC addr aabb.cc00.6a00
    IP src 192.168.100.10, dest 192.168.5.1, UDP src port 434
    HA addr 192.168.1.2, Identification C2EDFF2A.72710D54
    Lifetime 10:00:00 (36000) Remaining 08:16:14
    Tunnel0 src 192.168.5.1, dest 192.168.1.2, reverse-allowed
    Routing Options -
```

Mobile Nodes that have not successfully completed registration are kept in the pending visitor table, which is visible with the show ip mobile visitor pending command. If communication problems exist between the FA and Home Agent, several entries are often in the pending table. However, in most cases, entries do not stay in the pending table long enough to be visible.

Examining the Routing Table

You should also understand what the routing table will look like. All routes controlled by Mobile IP are marked with an *M* in the routing table. The Home Agent has two kinds of Mobile IP routes in its routing table, home networks and Mobile Nodes. If a home network is configured as a virtual network, it appears in the routing table as an M route; otherwise, it appears as a connected route. For each Mobile Node that has an active binding, you also find a host route in the routing table. As shown in Example 4-12, the Mobile Node route shows the tunnel that is being used as the next hop.

Example 4-12 *Routing Table on the Home Agent*

```
HA#show ip route
Codes: C - connected, S - static, R - RIP, M - mobile, B – BGP
       D - EIGRP, EX - EIGRP external, O - OSPF, IA - OSPF inter area
       N1 - OSPF NSSA external type 1, N2 - OSPF NSSA external type 2
       E1 - OSPF external type 1, E2 - OSPF external type 2
       i - IS-IS, su - IS-IS summary, L1 - IS-IS level-1, L2 - IS-IS level-2
       ia - IS-IS inter area, * - candidate default, U - per-user static route
       o - ODR, P - periodic downloaded static route

Gateway of last resort is not set

O    192.168.4.0/24 [110/20] via 192.168.1.1, 01:52:00, Ethernet0/0
O    192.168.5.0/24 [110/30] via 192.168.1.1, 01:52:00, Ethernet0/0
O    192.168.6.0/24 [110/30] via 192.168.1.1, 01:52:00, Ethernet0/0
C    192.168.1.0/24 is directly connected, Ethernet0/0
O    192.168.2.0/24 [110/20] via 192.168.1.1, 01:52:00, Ethernet0/0
     192.168.100.0/24 is variably subnetted, 2 subnets, 2 masks
M       192.168.100.10/32 [3/1] via 192.168.6.1, 01:51:55, Tunnel0
M       192.168.100.0/24 is directly connected
O    192.168.3.0/24 [110/20] via 192.168.1.1, 01:52:00, Ethernet0/0
```

Example 4-13 looks at the routing table of the IS. The point of including the IS in the topology explored in this chapter is to show that only the home network route is redistributed. In Example 4-13, the virtual network appears as a Type 2 external OSPF route.

NOTE   The individual host routes for the Mobile Nodes are not redistributed. Isolation of the network from the host routes is a key feature of Mobile IP.

Example 4-13   *Routing Table on the IS*

```
IS>show ip route
Codes: C - connected, S - static, R - RIP, M - mobile, B - BGP
       D - EIGRP, EX - EIGRP external, O - OSPF, IA - OSPF inter area
       N1 - OSPF NSSA external type 1, N2 - OSPF NSSA external type 2
       E1 - OSPF external type 1, E2 - OSPF external type 2
       i - IS-IS, su - IS-IS summary, L1 - IS-IS level-1, L2 - IS-IS level-2
       ia - IS-IS inter area, * - candidate default, U - per-user static route
       o - ODR, P - periodic downloaded static route

Gateway of last resort is not set

C       192.168.4.0/24 is directly connected, Ethernet3/0
O       192.168.5.0/24 [110/20] via 192.168.3.2, 01:58:45, Ethernet2/0
O       192.168.6.0/24 [110/20] via 192.168.4.2, 01:58:45, Ethernet3/0
C       192.168.1.0/24 is directly connected, Ethernet0/0
C       192.168.2.0/24 is directly connected, Ethernet1/0
O E2 192.168.100.0/24 [110/20] via 192.168.1.2, 01:58:45, Ethernet0/0
C       192.168.3.0/24 is directly connected, Ethernet2/0
```

Alternative Topologies

While the topology presented in the previous sections is ideal for learning Mobile IP in the lab, it requires a significant number of routers and is beyond the facilities of many small labs. The following topologies present several methods for integrating different Mobile IP components.

Single-Router Topology

At the opposite end of the spectrum from the topology shown in Figure 4-1, Figure 4-2 demonstrates a lab scenario using only a single-router topology. Coupled with a pair of computers—one acting as a Mobile Node and the other acting as a CN—this solution has most of the capabilities but is more complex to understand because all the functions are integrated. One key behavior about this configuration is that IOS Mobile IP does not use tunneling when the Home Agent and FA are on the same router. Instead, the forwarding entries are updated based on the interface to which the Mobile Node is attached.

Figure 4-2 *Single-Router Test Topology*

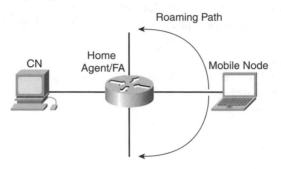

Other Options for Single-Router Topology

In between these two topologies are a number of other options. Eliminating the IS and replacing the CN with a computer are good options that can have minimal impact on the testing. Without the IS, it will not be clear how the redistribution works, but Mobile IP still functions the same. You can also combine the two FAs into one FA with two interfaces, but it will not be clear when the Mobile Node changes links, because the CoA does not change using the configuration in Example 4-4. To ensure that a CoA change is seen, each interface where the Mobile Node attaches needs to be configured as a CoA and the **interface-only** option should be used. Normally with two CoAes configured, the FA would advertise both addresses out both interfaces. However, with the **interface-only** command, only the address of the physical interface is advertised.

Summary

This chapter presented a pedantic Mobile IP example as a learning tool and highlighted the major concepts of IOS Mobile IP configuration in a simple lab topology. We introduced IOS configuration commands and looked at basic configuration of the Home Agent, FA, and Mobile Node. We considered common troubleshooting areas on the different Mobile IP entities, and we showed how to evaluate the proper functioning of the Mobile IP process.

The remaining chapters build on the basic understanding of the protocol from Chapters 2 and 3—and the hands-on configuration in this chapter—to help build real-world solutions. Applying Mobile IP to real-world deployments enables a good understanding of the benefits and implications of Mobile IP. The solutions are broken down by the size of the roaming area and the client options.

Review Questions

1   Draw a basic Mobile IP topology.

2   Which command enables the Mobile IP process on a router?

3   What are virtual networks and why are they used?

4   Give an example of a basic Home Agent configuration with the following features: Home Agent address 192.168.1.2, virtual network 192.168.100.0/24, and Mobile Node 192.168.100.10 residing on the virtual network. Don't forget to include the Mobile-Home security association.

5   Give an example of a FA configuration with the following features: FA address 192.168.3.2 and CoA 192.168.5.1 on Ethernet 1/0.

6   Give an example of an IOS Mobile Networks configuration with Home Agent 192.168.1.2 and Home Address 169.254.255.1.

7   A router can serve as a Home Agent and FA at the same time.

   a   True

   b   False

8   Configuration of security associations for IOS Mobile IP is always done from the perspective of the agent that is to use that security association.

   a   True

   b   False

9   List two commands that are useful for troubleshooting on the Home Agent.

10   Name a command that is useful for troubleshooting on the FA.

CHAPTER 5

Campus Mobility: Client-Based Mobile IP

This chapter builds on fundamentals explored in the lab environment in the previous chapter to build a reliable campus mobility solution. Adding mobility to a campus network can provide significant productivity benefits. One of the biggest benefits is improved user experience, especially for multimedia applications like desktop video conferencing and screen sharing. Users can go from the fast fixed Ethernet on their desktop to wireless LAN (WLAN) in the conference room without interrupting their work. Not only does this improve the user experience, but it also improves WLAN performance by keeping traffic on the fixed network when it is available. Mobile IP also enables a range of hand-held applications, such as personal digital assistant (PDA)-based voice and on-campus delivery tracking and security.

The chapter begins by characterizing the campus mobility model and then delves into features designed to simplify and enhance Mobile IP deployments in such environments. Specifically, the chapter looks closely at various options for security key management, Home Agent redundancy for high availability, and quality of service (QoS) integration. Keep in mind that the book introduces features in a progressive manner, and thus, the features addressed in this chapter can be used in Mobile IP environments discussed in later chapters.

Campus Mobility Model

Campus mobility refers to mobility within a single administrative domain, whether it is an entire university campus, a hospital, or a couple of conference rooms in a hotel. The main assumption in this model is that communication is within the campus (intranet), and no roaming exists across global Internet connectivity.

A good example of a campus intranet is a corporate campus. Consider a corporate facility of many units/departments, as shown in Figure 5-1. Assume that every unit/department has its own Local Area Network (LAN) segment (either Ethernet or 802.11, or both) and that the various segments are connected through a gateway router to a high-speed backbone, allowing the different departments to communicate with one another, albeit with proper security credentials. Note that this allows communication as long as the different hosts stay within their LAN, which can be limiting, especially in this mobile age.

Figure 5-1 *Typical Corporate Campus*

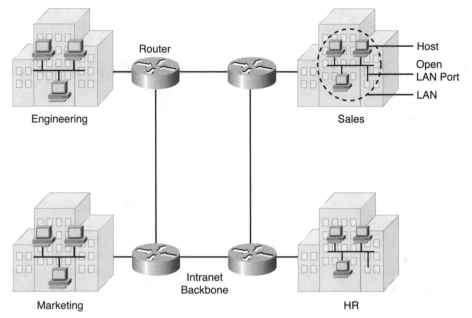

Deploying Mobile IP in this environment allows the network to become "campus mobile" capable, because Mobile IP client hosts can now roam around the campus and still maintain connectivity. This can be accomplished by various configurations, including simply installing Mobility Agent functionality on the gateway routers and installing Mobile IP client software on the portable hosts, for example, laptops, as shown in Figure 5-2.

The first step toward simplifying Mobile IP deployments in the campus mobility environment is efficiently managing the security keys. This is accomplished by storing the security associations in an authentication, authorization, and accounting (AAA) server.

Storing Security Associations in AAA

A AAA server is a separate centralized database that can store and maintain security associations. It is especially helpful to incorporate a AAA server into the network architecture for scalability reasons. For example, if a Home Agent is supporting hundreds or thousands of Mobile Nodes, the Mobile Node-Home Agent (Mobile Node-Home Agent) security associations can be stored on the AAA server instead of the Home Agent, freeing memory on the Home Agent. This allows the Home Agent to service more Mobile Nodes as the number of users on the network grows. When using a AAA server, the Home Agent queries the AAA server for the credentials necessary to authenticate a Mobile Node, as shown in Figure 5-3.

Figure 5-2   *Mobile Corporate Campus with Users Roaming Inside the Network Only*

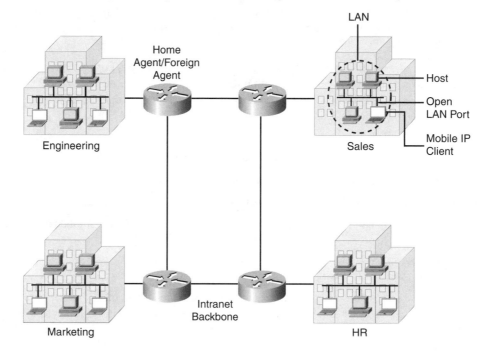

Figure 5-3   *Integration of a AAA Server into a Mobile IP Network*

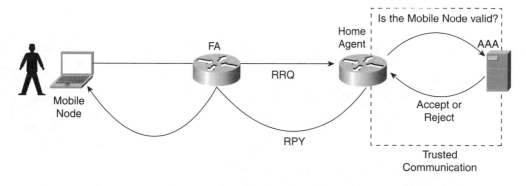

Another advantage of using a AAA server is that it allows maintenance and administrative functions to be streamlined, facilitating ease of support. With a AAA server, Home Agent configurations do not need to be altered every time a Mobile Node is added or removed. This model of having a fixed configuration on the Home Agent and dynamic user information on a AAA server has already proven effective and scalable.

When a AAA server is introduced into the network, it must be configured to share a trust relationship with the Mobility Agents that it supports. The trust relationship between mobility entities and AAA servers is not part of Mobile IP, but rather is configured according to the AAA implementation.

When a AAA server is introduced into the Mobile IP architecture, both entities (the Mobility Agent and AAA server) need to be configured for proper integration. Throughout this section, we introduce the IOS configuration commands that are needed on the Mobility Agent to leverage the AAA architecture.

The first step is to configure the Mobility Agent to retrieve the security association from the AAA server using a specific AAA protocol, such as one of the following:

- Remote Authentication Dial-In User Service (RADIUS)
- Terminal Access Controller Access Control System Plus (TACACS+)

This is accomplished using the following global IOS configuration commands on the Mobility Agent:

```
aaa new-model
aaa authorization ipmobile
```

The next task is to configure the entities to share a trust relationship. This configuration is related to the AAA protocol and not a specific Mobile IP configuration. In any case, once a protocol-specific trust relationship is established through the AAA protocol, the AAA server and Mobility Agents can now exchange sensitive security information. Cisco IOS only supports storing the Mobile Node-Home Agent security association in a AAA server; other types of security associations are rarely used and, as such, must be configured on the command-line interface (CLI).

Because the AAA server stores Mobile Node-Home Agent security associations, it needs a way to identify the specific security association needed by the Home Agent. As advanced as Cisco products are, they cannot read minds—at least not yet! Thus, the Mobile IP user must be uniquely identified on the AAA server. To this end, the Mobile Node is identified on the AAA server, either by a statically assigned home IP address or other username (for example, Mobile Node Network Access Identifier [NAI] without the realm portion). The realm portion of the NAI can route the AAA request to the appropriate server. Configuration of this routing is specific to the AAA infrastructure and, as such, is beyond the scope of this book.

In general, AAA servers are designed to provide *yes* or *no* responses to authentication requests so that passwords do not have to be distributed. However, for Mobile IP purposes, it is not enough for the Home Agent to simply know whether the Mobile Node is authenticated. Rather, the Home Agent must retrieve the Mobile Node-Home Agent secret key because it needs that key to compute the authenticator value to be included in the Registration Reply (RRP). To this end, Cisco IOS typically bypasses authentication on the AAA server to receive the Mobile Node-Home Agent key as a textual authorization attribute. The AAA server then provides the Home Agent with the Mobile Node's Mobile Node-Home Agent security association through a

Cisco vendor-specific authorization attribute. At this point, the Home Agent can authenticate the Mobile Node as usual.

NOTE

It is important to understand the difference between Mobile IP authentication and AAA authentication. Processing of the Mobile Node-Home Agent Authentication Extension always occurs on the Home Agent and requires the key to be on the Home Agent. Because RADIUS authentication can only return a pass/fail answer to the network access server (NAS), the Mobile Node-Home Agent security association must be stored on the AAA server as an authorization attribute. However, RADIUS requires a positive authentication before it can return authorization attributes to the NAS. In a sense, AAA authentication must be passed before Mobile IP credentials can be retrieved. Most RADIUS servers can be configured so that if no AAA password is configured for the user, the server assumes positive AAA authentication. Alternatively, each Mobile IP authentication request is sent with *cisco* as the user password. If the RADIUS server does not support default authentication, a password of *cisco* can be used for each Mobile Node account.

In many cases, a AAA server already exists in the network and is configured with secure passwords for each user. In these scenarios, Mobile Node-authentication, authorization, and accounting (MN-AAA) authentication can perform AAA authentication with a secure password. MN-AAA requires the use of a Foreign Agent (FA) and requires the FA to be configured to forward the MN-AAA extension to the Home Agent rather than strip it off.

The Cisco Zero Configuration Client (ZeCC), described in the section "Cisco ZeCC," later in this chapter, is an ideal option for integrating with an existing authentication infrastructure. With the Cisco ZeCC, Mobile Node-Home Agent keys do not need to be configured for each Mobile Node.

It should now be clear that the AAA server does not *authenticate* an entity per se, but rather it provides the requesting Mobility Agent with the security association through a AAA protocol, for example, RADIUS or TACACS+.

As one would expect, some latency might be involved in processing a Mobile Node's Registration Request (RRQ) because now the Home Agent must first consult the AAA server for the Mobile Node's security association. While this is true, some Cisco IOS features can mitigate this latency. security association *caching* is a mechanism that allows the security association to be locally stored on the Home Agent when it has been retrieved from the AAA server. Then, the next time the Home Agent must authenticate the Mobile Node, the Home Agent only needs to consult its local cache. You might be thinking, "But if you are retrieving the security associations just to store them on the Home Agent, what is the benefit of caching?" Good question. The idea behind caching is that only the security associations for the Mobile Nodes that are currently active (roaming) are kept in the Home Agent's cache, while the security associations of nonroaming Mobile Nodes are kept on the AAA server. Thus, caching still allows the benefits of using a AAA server, while reducing the latency incurred with having to consult the AAA server. Depending on the configuration, the security association can either be deleted from the cache automatically after a binding terminates or it can be kept permanently on the Home Agent. The security associations can also be manually cleared.

The following options are available as part of the **ip mobile host** global configuration command to allow use of a AAA server and the associated caching of the security association:

- **aaa**—This option specifies that the security association is stored on a AAA server (TACACS+ or RADIUS).

- **load-sa**—This option specifies that security associations are cached (or loaded) into RAM after retrieval. If the Mobile Node is an NAI host, the security association is cleared from the cache after the binding is deleted. For non-NAI hosts, the security association is kept permanently in the cache. Caching provides significant benefits in most deployments.

- **permanent**—This option specifies that the security association for NAI hosts is kept permanently in the cache after retrieval from the AAA server. Exercise care when using this option, because as the user population changes, the Home Agent memory could fill with unnecessary security associations.

Looking at the security association caching, you might wonder what happens if the security association is changed on the AAA server and corresponding entity—for example, Mobile Node—after it has been downloaded to local cache. No worries. One option allows the Home Agent to requery the AAA server if the authentication fails based on the security association in the local cache. The **resync-sa** feature has some intelligence built in to thwart denial of service (DoS) attacks on the AAA server by allowing only one AAA query per Mobile Node in a specified interval. Use the following command to achieve the requery behavior when authentication fails, with the *seconds* argument specifying the interval that the Home Agent must wait before requerying the AAA server:

```
ip mobile home-agent resync-sa seconds
```

The next question is "What happens if the Mobile Node is no longer authorized to use my network?" In this case, you should remove the security association from the AAA server and the local cache in the router. This can be accomplished in two ways. The first is by using the **clear ip mobile secure** command on the command line. While effective, the CLI is not ideal for automated provisioning and management systems. For these advanced systems, you can also flush a cached security association using the Simple Network Management Protocol (SNMP) set queries on objects defined in the Cisco Mobile IP Management Information Base (MIB), as discussed in Chapter 8, "Deployment Scalability and Management."

RADIUS

RADIUS is a AAA protocol that provides authentication and accounting services in a client/server model. RADIUS-specific messages and attributes are used for communication between the client—called a NAS—and server. In the context of a Mobile IP deployment, the NAS is the Mobility Agent, for example, Home Agent, and the server is the AAA server.

RADIUS uses User Datagram Protocol (UDP) as the transport mechanism and only encrypts the password portion of packets, with the remainder of the packet sent in the clear text. Thus, RADIUS is considered lighter-weight than TACACS+, which uses Transmission Control Protocol (TCP) (and is recommended for use in Mobile IP deployments over TACACS+.) (TACACS+ is described in the next section of this chapter.) However, because the packet is not encrypted, the security association transits the network in the clear. If enhanced security is necessary, IP Security (IPSec) can protect the RADIUS traffic.

After configuring the use of AAA on the Mobility Agent, the AAA protocol–specific configurations must be added. Use the following configuration commands on the Home Agent to specify which RADIUS server should be used, and the security between the Mobility Agent and RADIUS server:

- **radius-server host host**—Specifies a RADIUS server host.
- **radius-server key key**—Sets the authentication and encryption key for all RADIUS communications between the Mobility Agent and RADIUS server.

Example 5-1 shows a sample Mobile IP configuration using RADIUS as the default group to retrieve security associations from the AAA server.

Example 5-1   *Home Agent Configuration Using a RADIUS AAA Server*

```
aaa new-model
aaa authorization ipmobile default group radius
radius-server host 192.168.162.173 auth-port 1645 acct-port 1646
radius-server key itsasecret
ip mobile host 10.0.0.1 10.0.0.5 virtual-network 10.0.0.0 255.0.0.0 aaa
```

NOTE   You must ensure that your RADIUS ports match on both the NAS and the server. Request for Comment (RFC) 2138 defines ports 1812 and 1813 as the default authentication and accounting ports, respectively, replacing the widely used ports 1645 and 1646.

TACACS+

TACACS+ is another AAA protocol that provides authentication and authorization services. Although TACACS+ is considered to be heavier-weight than RADIUS, it provides more flexibility because it separates the functions of AAA. TACACS+ uses TCP as the transport layer protocol and encrypts the entire packet. Use of TACACS+ is not recommended with Mobile IP because many features are only supported with RADIUS. TACACS+ can only receive the Mobile Node-Home Agent security association. Advanced features, such as dynamic addressing, are not supported.

Use the following TACACS+ configuration commands to specify the TACACS+ server and authentication keys:

- **tacacs-server host** *host*—Specifies a TACACS+ host.

- **tacacs-server key** *key*—Sets the authentication encryption key that is used for all TACACS+ communications between the access server and the TACACS+ daemon.

Example 5-2 uses TACACS+ to retrieve security associations from the AAA server.

Example 5-2 *Home Agent Configuration Using a TACACS+ AAA Server*

```
aaa new-model
aaa authorization ipmobile tacacs+
tacacs-server host 192.168.3.4
tacacs-server key mykey
ip mobile host 10.0.0.1 10.0.0.5 virtual-network 10.0.0.0 255.0.0.0 aaa
```

Cisco Zero Configuration Client

As described in Chapter 3, "Mobile IP Security," the dynamic security association and key distribution protocol, introduced in IOS Release 12.3(4)T, is designed to provide dynamic Mobile Node-Home Agent key generation by integrating with the commonly deployed Windows authentication infra-structure. This can be coupled with other protocol features to enable a Mobile IP solution to be deployed that does not require configuration of the Mobile Node client. Commonly referred to as Cisco ZeCC, or ZeCC, this solution enables the Mobile IP client to be installed through a standard operating system image that is replicated to every new mobile computer. Users need only to log in to the Windows domain to establish a Mobile IP session. This simplifies the overall deployment of a Mobile IP solution.

The goal is to not only simplify the Mobile Node deployment but also to design a Mobile IP implementation that provides optimized connectivity for all users. To this end, the Zero Configuration solution uses Collocated Care-of Address (CCoA), Dynamic Host Configuration Protocol (DHCP)-assigned Home Agent addresses, and a dynamically allocated home address for the Mobile Node. For authentication, the Zero Configuration solution integrates with existing Microsoft Windows domain authentication services and transparently generates the necessary keys when the user performs Windows authentication on the Mobile Node. A loopback interface is used as the home network because the proxy DHCP client cannot be used with virtual networks. (The proxy DHCP client requires an interface IP address to be used as the relay address, or *giaddr*. Because virtual networks do not have an address, they cannot be used.) The call flow for power-up registration in a zero-config environment is shown in Figure 5-4. The steps of the call flow are as follows:

1 DHCP is used to acquire a Care-of Address (CoA).

2 The Mobile Node learns the IP address of a local Home Agent through DHCP option 68.

3 The Mobile Node computes the authentication tokens as described in Chapter 3.

4 The Mobile Node sends a RRQ to the Home Agent, with the home address set to 0.0.0.0.

5 When the Home Agent receives the RRQ, it forwards the authentication request to the RADIUS server.

6 In turn, the RADIUS server queries the Windows domain controller or active directory.

7 User is authenticated.

8 Windows Domain Controller or active directory returns the authentication results and secure key to the RADIUS server.

9 The RADIUS server relays the result and key to the Home Agent.

10 Upon an acknowledgment from the AAA infrastructure, the Home Agent derives the session key, authenticates the Mobile Node, and allocates a home IP address for the Mobile Node.

11 The Home Agent returns the home address, home network prefix length, DNS server, DHCP server, and DHCP client ID to the Mobile Node in the RRP.

12 The Mobile Node authenticates the RRP.

13 Registration is complete.

ZeCC solutions are based heavily on AAA and DHCP infrastructure configuration, and as such, no specific configuration is required on the Home Agent. The Home Agent configuration, which is the same as for MN-AAA, requires the use of Point-to-Point Protocol (PPP) authentication and Mobile IP authorization. Example 5-3 shows a Home Agent configuration for Zero Client Configuration. In this example, the **radius domain-stripping** command removes the realm portion of the NAI from the username. Depending on the AAA architecture, this might be necessary. Finally, the configuration uses a loopback for the home network and specifies a DHCP server in the **ip mobile host** statement. Configuration of the Mobile Node is also simple—none is required, but then that is the point! Server configurations are not laid out because they are specific to AAA and DHCP servers, but the following steps need to be taken to configure the servers:

Step 1 A Mobile IP Home Agent router with software supporting the Dynamic security association and Key Distribution feature should be configured. The proper image can be found using Feature Navigator on Cisco.com (http://www.cisco.com/go/fn). Access to Feature Navigator requires a valid Cisco.com account.

Step 2 A ZeCC-compliant Mobile Node client must be installed on the end device. See http://www.cisco.com/go/mobile_ip for a list of clients.

Step 3 A RADIUS server and Windows domain controller must be configured to return the Microsoft Challenge Handshake Authentication Protocol (MS CHAP) Microsoft Point-To-Point Encryption (MPPE) keys to the Home Agent in RADIUS authentication response. Some RADIUS servers can support this without a domain controller. Look for information on setting up MS CHAPv2 in the RADIUS server documentation.

Step 4 A DHCP server is needed to return the Home Agent IP address in option 68.

Figure 5-4 *ZeCC Call Flow*

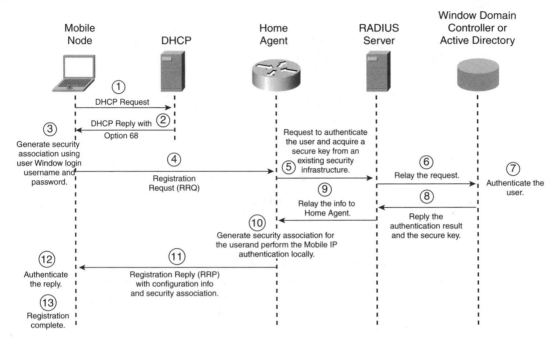

Example 5-3 *Home Agent Configuration for a ZeCC Network*

```
hostname HA
!
aaa new-model
!
interface Loopback1
 ip address 192.168.101.1 255.255.255.0
!
router mobile
!
ip mobile home-agent
ip mobile host nai @example address pool dhcp-proxy-client dhcp-server 192.168.2.2
interface Loopback1 aaa
!
radius-server host 172.19.192.100 auth-port 1645 acct-port 1646
radius-server domain-stripping
radius-server key skeleton
```

Home Agent Redundancy

The Home Agent is an important entity in the successful operation of the Mobile IP process. Recall that upon receiving a successful RRQ from the Mobile Node, the Home Agent creates a mobility binding entry that tracks the association of the Mobile Node's home address with its current CoA. The Home Agent maintains all associations in a mobility binding table, which is essentially the heart of the Mobile IP process. If the Home Agent fails for any reason, the mobility binding table is lost, and all Mobile Nodes registered with the Home Agent lose connectivity. The Mobile Nodes usually experience a noticeable lapse in service during outage, which can lead to some unhappy customers.

The Cisco Mobile IP Home Agent Redundancy feature is designed to provide scalable high availability with near-instantaneous failover support. When a Home Agent fails, another Home Agent takes over immediately to maintain all sessions to the Mobile Nodes. With this mechanism, the mobility binding table is fully replicated on each Home Agent in the redundancy group, and thus, no downtime occurs for any Mobile Node. The high availability not only ensures that all mobility bindings survive a Home Agent failure but also ensures minimal packet loss, which leads to happy customers!

The Home Agent Redundancy mechanism leverages the Hot Standby Router Protocol (HSRP) (described in RFC 2281), which designates one router as active and another as standby. HSRP determines redundancy peers and is used as a first-hop routing protocol for the Home Agent address. HSRP can be defined as follows:

NOTE	HSRP is a router redundancy protocol developed by Cisco that provides network resilience in a way that ensures that user traffic will immediately and transparently recover from "first hop" failures in network edge devices and access circuits. By sharing a virtual IP address and a MAC (Layer 2) address, two or more routers can act as a single "virtual" router or default gateway to the hosts on a LAN. The members of the router group continually exchange status messages to detect when a peer goes down. This router group is referred to as the HSRP group, and the virtual IP address is known as the HSRP group address.

The Cisco Home Agent Redundancy functionality then specifies the behavior of these routers in the HSRP group to provide backup Home Agent service in Mobile IP. The *preemption* and *priority* capabilities of HSRP can be configured to prefer one Home Agent to another, that is, one Home Agent can be given preference to become the main Home Agent by configuring these options appropriately.

The main idea in this mechanism is that the Home Agents in the redundancy group all have the necessary information to provide Mobile IP service to the Mobile Nodes, and can seamlessly take over for one another. However, to the Mobile Node, the redundancy group looks like one Home Agent. The Cisco Home Agent Redundancy feature supports two main configurations: an active-standby configuration and a peer-peer configuration. Active-standby and peer-peer only refer to how Mobile IP signaling is handled. Actual forwarding of data traffic to Mobile Nodes is handled by integration with routing. Both Home Agents in the redundancy group bring up the Mobile IP tunnels and have a full copy of the mobility binding table. Thus, either one can forward data traffic to the Mobile Node based on which one receives the Mobile Node's traffic via the IGP routing protocol. When virtual networks are redistributed into dynamic routing, all data traffic, and as such tunneling, is load balanced. (This is because both Home Agents can advertise equal cost reachability to the virtual networks to their neighbors. This can be disabled by tweaking redistribution metrics.)

A particular Home Agent Redundancy group can either support Mobile Nodes residing on a physical network or Mobile Nodes residing on a virtual network (see Chapter 4, "IOS Mobile IP in the Lab"), but not both. In the case of virtual networks, if the Home Agent address is the HSRP virtual address, the active-standby configuration is used. If the Home Agent address is configured on a loopback interface and the same address is configured on both Home Agents, peer-peer mode is used.

Regardless of the formation, the following two main functions are accomplished with the Mobile IP Home Agent Redundancy mechanism, as shown in Figure 5-5:

- **Updating/creating a mobility binding**—When an RRQ is accepted by the active/peer Home Agent, the binding is updated or created on the standby/peer Home Agent. This process keeps the mobility binding table synchronized between the Home Agents. Note that this also includes updating a mobility binding by deleting the binding upon a deregistration. If a mobility binding expires on the active/peer Home Agent, it also expires on the standby/peer Home Agent, and as such, no messaging is needed.

  Note that an active Home Agent assumes the lead Home Agent role and receives all the RRQs from Mobile Nodes. It then updates the standby Home Agent with the necessary binding information. (A particular Home Agent in the redundancy group can be preferred as the active Home Agent by appropriately configuring the *priority* option in HSRP. More information on HSRP can be found on Cisco.com.)

  In the case of the peer configuration model, the peer Home Agents share the lead Home Agent role and either of them can receive the RRQs from the Mobile Nodes. They update each other accordingly. The peer Home Agent configuration allows load balancing of the incoming RRQs because either Home Agent can receive the RRQs.

- **Downloading the mobility binding table**—A Home Agent downloads the mobility binding table from the active/peer Home Agent immediately upon assuming the standby/ peer Home Agent role. The standby/peer Home Agent ensures that it has downloaded the entire mobility binding table through a reliability mechanism. This process ensures that the standby/peer Home Agent has a copy of the current mobility binding table before providing backup Home Agent service.

The Home Agents participating in the redundancy group should be configured similarly, with the exact configuration depending on the formation model, as outlined in the next section. Because the Home Agents are sharing their mobility binding table with one another, a trust relationship must exist between the agents. The Home Agents, therefore, must be configured with a security association, and all redundancy-related messages must be secured by this security association.

Figure 5-5   *Overview of Home Agent Redundancy Mechanism*

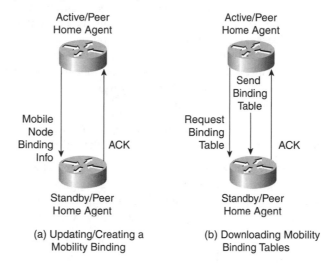

Configuration Commands

Home Agent redundancy is a critical component of a high-availability network and, as such, is not a configuration to be taken lightly. The redundancy mechanism supports numerous complex options and configurations, many of which are designed for use in specific topologies. Often times, configuration options that can seem beneficial do not benefit users in their particular environment. Home Agent redundancy is a perfect example of a "less is more" configuration. If you don't need it, don't use it. If you need it, make sure that you understand what you are doing and validate the expected outcome.

Configuration for Home Agent Redundancy must be identical on all Home Agents within the redundancy group, as follows:

Step 1   Configure HSRP on the Home Agents using the following commands (see Cisco.com for more details on HSRP):

- **standby** [*group-number*] **ip** *ip-address*—This command enables HSRP on the router and sets the HSRP group address.

- **standby** [*group-number*] **name** *hsrp-group-name*—This command sets the name of the standby group. A group name must be used because it is used by the Home Agent process to identify the standby group.

- **standby** [*group-number*] **priority** *priority* [**preempt** [**delay** [**minimum** | **sync**] *delay*]]—This command sets the hot standby priority used in choosing the active router.

By default, the router that comes up later becomes standby. When one router is designated as an active Home Agent, the priority is set highest in the HSRP group and the preemption is set. Configure the **preempt delay sync** command so that all mobility bindings are downloaded to the router before it takes the active role. The router becomes active when all bindings are downloaded or when the timer expires, whichever comes first. You should generally use the maximum value of 3600 seconds for the sync timer.

Step 2 Configure the Home Agent process to support redundancy using the specified HSRP group, which is accomplished with the following command:

```
ip mobile home-agent redundancy hsrp-group-name [virtual-network]
```
The *hsrp-group-name* is the same HSRP group that is configured during HSRP configuration on the interface in Step 1. The **virtual-network** option is used if the redundancy group is supporting virtual networks.

Step 3 Configure the security association between the Home Agents using the following command:

```
ip mobile secure home-agent address spi spi key [hex | ascii] string
```
This command sets up the security association between the Home Agents. Each Home Agent in the redundancy group must have a security association with every potential peer.

Active-Standby Home Agent Configuration

The most common Home Agent Redundancy configuration is the active-standby model because of its effectiveness and simplicity. The active-standby Home Agent configuration specifies one Home Agent in the lead role, and is the implicit formation. That is, no extra configuration is needed to specify this formation other than that presented in the previous section.

The Home Agent Redundancy formation is best illustrated by reviewing Figure 5-6. In this figure, you find two Home Agents (Home Agent1 is 1.0.0.1 and Home Agent2 is 1.0.0.2) in the redundancy group. They are supporting Mobile Nodes on a physical home network and are in the active Home Agent–standby Home Agent configuration. The HSRP group name is SanJoseHome Agent, and the HSRP group address is 1.0.0.10. Example 5-4 shows simple configurations of the Home Agents for this redundancy network. Note that the two Home Agents are configured to share a mandatory security association.

Figure 5-6   *Home Agent Redundancy Supporting Mobile Nodes on Physical Networks*

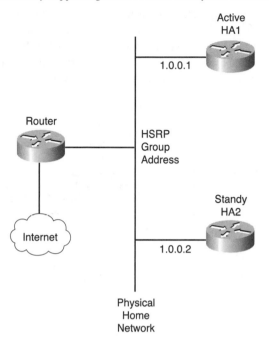

Example 5-4   *Home Agent Redundancy Configuration of Active-Standby Formation*

```
HA1 Configuration
interface ethernet0
 ip address 1.0.0.1 255.0.0.0
 standby ip 1.0.0.10
 standby name SanJoseHA
 standby preempt delay sync 3600
 standby priority 110
ip mobile home-agent redundancy SanJoseHA
ip mobile host 1.0.0.10 1.0.0.20 interface ethernet0
ip mobile secure home-agent 1.0.0.2 spi 100 key hex 00112233445566778899001122334455

HA2 Configuration
interface ethernet0
 ip address 1.0.0.2 255.0.0.0
 standby ip 1.0.0.10
 standby name SanJoseHA
ip mobile home-agent redundancy SanJoseHA
ip mobile host 1.0.0.10 1.0.0.20 interface ethernet0
ip mobile secure home-agent 1.0.0.1 spi 100 key hex 00112233445566778899001122334455
```

Peer-Peer Home Agent Configuration

In the peer-peer formation, the Home Agents share the lead role and update one another accordingly. This behavior is achieved by configuring a *loopback* interface on both Home Agents with the same Home Agent address(es). (Reachability of the loopback interface on the Home Agents must be achieved.) Thus, RRQs destined to an address on the loopback interface can then be received by either Home Agent, as shown in Figure 5-7.

Figure 5-7 *Virtual Network Support Using One Physical Network (Peer Home Agent–Peer Home Agent Configuration)*

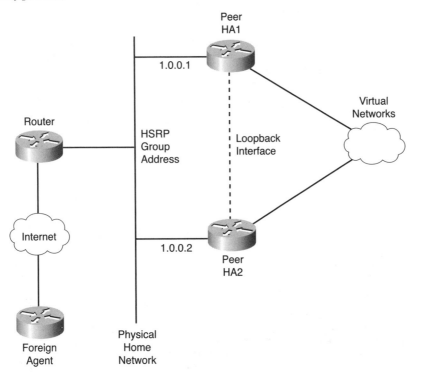

Before we look more closely at the peer-peer formation, it seems our duty to issue a slight health warning: This formation can seem purposefully confusing and designed to induce headaches. It is not purposeful, but it is indeed confusing! To help mitigate the confusion, we first explain a particular configuration concept, and then we present the configuration command(s).

The peer-peer Home Agent configuration is beneficial when using virtual networks (refer to Figure 5-7). With physical home networks, the Home Agent cannot accept bindings if the home network is down. (This can also be accomplished with the active-standby Home Agent configuration.)

Multiple virtual networks can be supported by the same Home Agent redundancy group. For example, a Home Agent redundancy group can support virtual networks 20.0.0.0/24, 30.0.0.0/24, and 40.0.0.0/24.

A main concern when supporting virtual networks is the proper configuration of the Home Agent address that a Mobile Node should use to register with its home network. Essentially, the following two scenarios are possible:

- **Scenario I**—Mobile Node and Home Agent must reside on the same network subnet.
- **Scenario II**—Mobile Node and Home Agent can reside on different network subnets.

The category into which a Mobile Node falls is usually based on home network and roaming policy. To satisfy Mobile Nodes falling under Scenario I, an Home Agent address is configured on the particular virtual network, for example, virtual network 40.0.0.0/24 supported with Home Agent address = 40.0.0.1. For all Mobile Nodes that fall under Scenario II, a global Home Agent address is configured on the Home Agents, for example, virtual networks 20.0.0.0/24 and 30.0.0.0/24 supported with a single Home Agent address = 10.0.0.1. All the Home Agent addresses are then configured *identically* on the loopback interface of each of the Home Agents. Thus, because the RRQ is received on the *loopback* interface of the Home Agents, either Home Agent can end up receiving the message. (Note that which Home Agent is to receive the RRQ is determined by the underlying routing protocol.) Upon receipt of an authenticated RRQ, the receiving peer Home Agent updates the other peer Home Agent.

Hopefully, you don't have a migraine now and are ready to continue with the Home Agent Redundancy configuration steps needed to achieve the peer-peer formation. We continue with the steps presented in the previous section, as follows:

Step 4 Configure the virtual networks that are to be supported by the redundancy group using the **ip mobile virtual-network** command introduced in Chapter 4. If a Home Agent address is required on a particular virtual network, use the **address** option of this command as follows:

```
ip mobile virtual-network address mask address HA-address
```
The *Home Agent-address* value is the Home Agent address on the same subnet as the virtual network being configured.

Step 5 Configure a global Home Agent address, if needed, using the **address** option of the **ip mobile home-agent** command, as follows:

```
ip mobile home-agent address HA-address
```
The *Home Agent-address* value is the global Home Agent address that can be used by any roaming nodes that do not require a Home Agent address on their particular subnet.

Step 6 Configure all Home Agent addresses from Step 4 and Step 5 on the *loopback* interface as follows:

```
interface Loopback interface-number
    ip address address mask [secondary]
```

In this case, *interface-number* is the name of a loopback interface. There are as many **ip address** subinterface commands as there are Home Agent addresses, with the **secondary** option specified for any addresses configured after the first.

It will probably be the most helpful to see how these commands materialize into a configuration. Example 5-5 shows the configuration added to Example 5-4 to make the Home Agents support virtual networks in the peer-peer Home Agent formation. In this example, RRQs from Mobile Nodes residing on virtual network 40.0.0.0/24 are sent to Home Agent address 40.0.0.1, while RRQs from all other Mobile Nodes are sent to the global Home Agent address 10.0.0.1.

Example 5-5 *Home Agent Redundancy Additional Configuration for Peer-Peer Formation*

```
HA1 Configuration
! Configure loopback to receive RRQ from Mobile Nodes
interface loopback0
  ip address 10.0.0.1 255.255.255.255
  ip address 40.0.0.1 255.255.255.255 secondary

! Configure global Home Agent address
ip mobile home-agent address 10.0.0.1

! Configure virtual-networks and Home Agent address for 40.0.0.0/24
ip mobile virtual-network 20.0.0.0 255.0.0.0
ip mobile virtual-network 30.0.0.0 255.0.0.0
ip mobile virtual-network 40.0.0.0 255.0.0.0 address 40.0.0.1

HA2 Configuration
! Configure loopback to receive RRQ from Mobile Nodes
interface loopback0
  ip address 10.0.0.1 255.255.255.255
  ip address 40.0.0.1 255.255.255.255 secondary

! Configure global Home Agent address
ip mobile home-agent address 10.0.0.1

! Configure virtual-networks and Home Agent address for 40.0.0.0/24
ip mobile virtual-network 20.0.0.0 255.0.0.0
ip mobile virtual-network 30.0.0.0 255.0.0.0
ip mobile virtual-network 40.0.0.0 255.0.0.0 address 40.0.0.1
```

Just in case you are still headache-free, we have more configurations to add to the mix. The virtual networks configured in Step 4 can be supported by one or more physical connections between the Home Agents (see Figure 5-8). Each physical network connection is configured as a separate HSRP group, for example, HSRP-group1 and HSRP-group2, and Home Agent Redundancy is tied to each of the HSRP groups. With multiple physical connections, even if one network connection fails, the Home Agents can still communicate through the other physical net-work, that is, the other HSRP group. This provides another level of redundancy against network failures and leads to the next step.

Figure 5-8   *Virtual Network Support Using Multiple Physical Networks (Peer Home Agent–Peer Home Agent Configuration)*

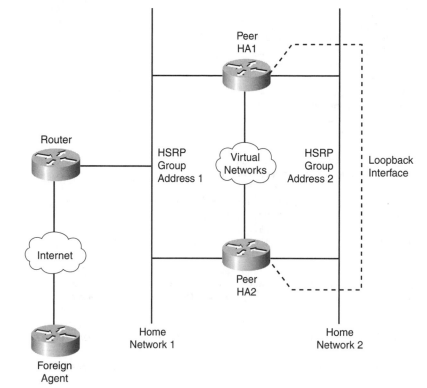

Step 7   If you are using multiple physical connections between the Home Agents, configure the other HSRP group as defined in Step 1. Configure the HSRP group to support Mobile IP and Home Agent Redundancy as defined in Step 2.

Example 5-6 shows the final configuration for two peer Home Agents using all the configuration steps outlined. In this example, Home Agent Redundancy is provided by two HSRP Groups: SanJoseHANet1 and SanJoseHANet2. Mobile Nodes are configured on virtual networks 20.0.0.0/24, 30.0.0.0/24, and 40.0.0.0/24. Mobile Nodes on virtual network 40.0.0.0/ 24 must register with a Home Agent address on the virtual network (that is, 40.0.0.1), while the Mobile Nodes on the other two virtual networks can use the global Home Agent address 10.0.0.1.

Example 5-6   *Home Agent Redundancy in Peer-Peer Formation Using Multiple Physical Networks*

```
HA1 Configuration
interface ethernet0
 ip address 1.0.0.1 255.0.0.0
 standby ip 1.0.0.10
```

continues

Example 5-6 *Home Agent Redundancy in Peer-Peer Formation Using Multiple Physical Networks (Continued)*

```
 standby name SanJoseHANet1

interface ethernet1
 ip address 2.0.0.1 255.0.0.0
 standby ip 2.0.0.10
 standby name SanJoseHANet2

! Configure loopback to receive RRQ from Mobile Nodes
interface loopback0
 ip address 10.0.0.1 255.255.255.255
 ip address 40.0.0.1 255.255.255.255 secondary

! Configure global Home Agent address
ip mobile home-agent address 10.0.0.1

! Configure virtual-networks and Home Agent address for 40.0.0.0/24
ip mobile virtual-network 20.0.0.0 255.0.0.0
ip mobile virtual-network 30.0.0.0 255.0.0.0
ip mobile virtual-network 40.0.0.0 255.0.0.0 address 40.0.0.1

! Used to map to the HSRP groups SanJoseHANet1 and SanJoseHANet2
ip mobile home-agent redundancy SanJoseHANet1 virtual-network
ip mobile home-agent redundancy SanJoseHANet2 virtual-network

! Configure security association with Peer Home Agent
ip mobile secure home-agent 1.0.0.2 spi 100 key hex 00112233445566778899001122334455

ip mobile secure home-agent 2.0.0.2 spi 100 key hex 00112233445566778899001122334455

HA2 Configuration
interface ethernet0
 ip address 1.0.0.2 255.0.0.0
 standby ip 1.0.0.10
 standby name SanJoseHANet1

interface ethernet1
 ip address 2.0.0.2 255.0.0.0
 standby ip 2.0.0.10
 standby name SanJoseHANet2

! Configure loopback to receive RRQ from Mobile Nodes
interface loopback0
 ip address 10.0.0.1 255.255.255.255
 ip address 40.0.0.1 255.255.255.255 secondary

! Configure global Home Agent address
ip mobile home-agent address 10.0.0.1

! Configure virtual networks and Home Agent address for 40.0.0.0/24
```

Example 5-6   *Home Agent Redundancy in Peer-Peer Formation Using Multiple Physical Networks (Continued)*

```
ip mobile virtual-network 20.0.0.0 255.0.0.0
ip mobile virtual-network 30.0.0.0 255.0.0.0
ip mobile virtual-network 40.0.0.0 255.0.0.0 address 40.0.0.1

! Used to map to the HSRP groups SanJoseHANet1 and SanJoseHANet2
ip mobile home-agent redundancy SanJoseHANet1 virtual-network
ip mobile home-agent redundancy SanJoseHANet2 virtual-network

! Configure security association with Peer Home Agent
ip mobile secure home-agent 1.0.0.1 spi 100 key hex
  00112233445566778899001122334455
ip mobile secure home-agent 2.0.0.1 spi 100 key hex
  00112233445566778899001122334455
```

When to Use Peer-Peer Home Agent Redundancy

On the surface, peer-peer configuration looks like an ideal way to improve network capacity and performance. When you look closer, however, you can see that this might not be the case. First, it does not afford extra capacity; the memory used by each Home Agent is the same because the binding table is replicated. Second, minimal gains are found in signaling capacity because the processing necessary to add a binding on the active Home Agent is only slightly more than that for adding a binding on a standby Home Agent.

Peer-peer redundancy adds value in two deployment scenarios. In networks where AAA server latency is high, peer-peer redundancy can provide added capacity because processing a binding on just the active Home Agent takes far longer than sharing the responsibility. The second case is in networks where Home Agents must use more than one interface for redundancy. This can mitigate some failure scenarios in networks where both Home Agents could be up and accepting bindings when a single link is down.

Summary

The campus mobility model is the simplest of Mobile IP deployments, and it provides us with a chance to look at some of the key features of IOS Mobile IP.

In this chapter, integration with AAA was discussed, and RADIUS was identified as the optimal protocol for AAA services. The details surrounding the Cisco ZeCC should have made it clear that this is an ideal solution for enterprise deployment because of the simplified client rollout and the integration with existing backend systems.

Home Agent Redundancy was introduced as a critical component to a high-availability Mobile IP solution. The use of Home Agent Redundancy in its simplest form—the active-standby mode—is the ideal deployment in most cases. The added complexity of peer-peer redundancy is only necessary in a few deployment scenarios. Remember, when discussing active-standby mode, it is for processing of RRQs only. Even in active-standby mode (unless static or connected routing is used to reach the Home Agent), standard equal-cost multipath routing always loads balance data traffic between Home Agents.

The next chapter adds the complexity of roaming across multiple autonomous systems and introduces the specifics of Internet deployment.

Review Questions

1 What does *campus mobility* mean*?*

2 What is a AAA server? How does it help in a Mobile IP deployment?

3 When using a AAA server in the home network, which of the following statements is true?

   a The Mobile Node shares a security association with the AAA server and not the Home Agent, and thus the AAA server authenticates the RRQ and informs the Home Agent whether the request should be accepted or denied.

   b The AAA server allows administrative functions to be streamlined.

   c The MHAEs are stored on the AAA server, and the Home Agent consults the AAA server to retrieve a security association upon receiving a RRQ.

   d The AAA server and Home Agent must share a security relationship.

4 What is RADIUS? Why is RADIUS recommended over TACACS+ for use in a Mobile IP deployment?

5 Describe the Cisco IOS feature that mitigates the latency involved in processing a Mobile Node's RRQ when the Home Agent must consult the AAA server for the Mobile Node's security association.

6 What is ZeCC?

7 What are the two Home Agent formations in the Cisco Home Agent Redundancy feature?

8 Briefly describe the updating function in the Cisco Home Agent Redundancy feature.

9 Briefly describe the downloading function in the Cisco Home Agent Redundancy feature.

10 Which of the following statements are true about the Cisco Home Agent Redundancy feature?

   a The active Home Agent and standby Home Agent both receive an incoming RRQ and set up the mobility binding. Only the active Home Agent responds with the RRP.

   b One of the Home Agents in the redundancy group receives the incoming RRQ and updates the standby Home Agent with the mobility binding.

   c All Home Agents in the redundancy group must share a security association.

   d The standby Home Agent keeps track of all active mobility bindings, but it only sets up the Mobile IP tunnels upon becoming the active Home Agent.

CHAPTER 6

Metro Mobility:
Client-Based Mobile IP

Metro Mobility Model

The previous chapters addressed mobility within a single private network. However, during the course of a business day, most mobile workers move beyond the confines of a single private network. These workers traverse multiple public and private networks and thereby exhibit *metro mobility*. For example, delivery personnel, service workers, and public safety officers spend their days traveling across a metropolitan market and would benefit greatly from a seamless "always on" mobility solution. Imagine how productivity would increase if employees could access just-in-time training, real-time work order systems, procurement systems, and other job-related systems while on the go.

The proliferation of in-vehicle computers with multiple wireless links makes metro mobility and access to these capabilities a reality. However, placing the burden of managing metro mobility on the end user is not cost effective and is almost counterproductive. For example, service technicians or sales personnel should not need extensive information technology training to do their jobs, but should be able to leverage on-the-go capability outside their private networks. Deploying Mobile IP in the network easily accomplishes this.

NOTE   Mobile IP–enabled systems do not require an end user to be aware of the networking capabilities of his or her computer. Rather, the Mobile IP client automatically selects the most cost-effective link and provides the user with the most appropriate level of connectivity while enabling real-time applications such as voice, video, and data.

Metro mobility adds a new set of challenges to Mobile IP deployment, most of which are easily overcome. Many of the challenges stem from the security implications of Internet routing. Although the basic requirements of roaming remain the same, the challenges of traversing multiple autonomous systems require a greater integration effort than roaming in a private intranet.

Figure 6-1 shows the different environments that a Mobile Node might encounter in a metro mobility deployment. This chapter explores Mobile IP features that can be used in these different environments. When roaming on a public network, Mobile Nodess can encounter asymmetric routing problems because of firewalls and ingress filtering that can be addressed with reverse tunneling. Network Address Translation (NAT) traversal, as seen in the public hot spot at the coffee shop, also presents a problem and requires a new type of tunneling. Virtual private network (VPN) integration and public and private roaming is also explored. Finally, the chapter discusses the Registration Revocation mechanism that efficiently manages mobility bindings.

Figure 6-1   *High-Level Metro Roaming Topology*

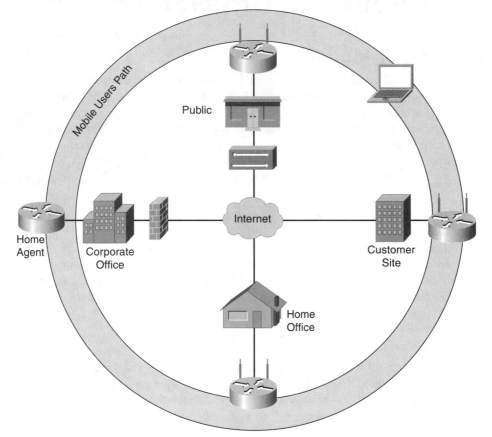

Reverse Tunneling

As you saw in Chapter 2, "Understanding Mobile IP," Mobile IP uses triangle routing for the Mobile Nodes's communication while it is roaming in a Foreign Network. That is, Mobile IP relies on tunneling to deliver all data-plane traffic to the Mobile Nodes while it is roaming, but by default, the traffic from the Mobile Nodes is sent directly to the Correspondent Node (CN).

As shown in Figure 6-2, the Mobile Nodes sources traffic with its Home Address from the visiting network, which works well within a trusted autonomous system. However, when crossing autonomous system boundaries and traversing public networks, as in the metro mobility model, this traffic is difficult to distinguish from "source address spoofed" traffic.

Figure 6-2   *Direct Delivery (Triangle Routing)*

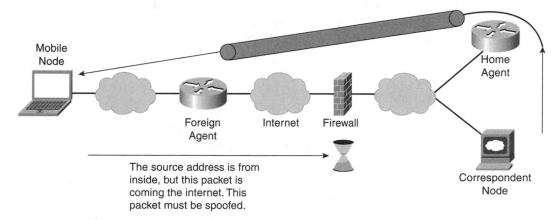

NOTE   Spoofing is a malicious attempt to make traffic appear as if it is coming from a node other than the one from which it originated. Spoofing is possible because the connectionless nature of an IP network means that each packet is forwarded independently to the destination with no consideration of its origin. Spoofing can obscure the source of large denial-of-service attacks and other security exploits.

These types of attacks and the growth of IP networking and the Internet have brought about an increased requirement for security. To eliminate spoofing, many edge networks deploy ingress filtering to block incoming packets with a source address from inside the network. Furthermore, most public networks implement an enhanced version of ingress filtering called *unicast Reverse Path Forwarding (uRPF)*. uRPF checks the source address of each inbound packet at the edge of the public network to ensure that traffic destined for the source address would be routed out the same interface that the traffic came in on. If no return route exists, the router assumes that the packet is spoofed and discards it.

Ingress filtering and uRPF spell a bit of trouble for Mobile IP. Ingress filtering and uRPF can prevent Mobile Nodess from communicating while they are in a Foreign Network—"they can hear, but they cannot speak" (which, by the way, is not always a bad thing in life!). The return routability check in uRPF discards all traffic originated by a Mobile Nodes while it is not in its

Home Network. Thus, if ingress filtering and uRPF are deployed in the network, a Mobile Nodes might not be able to communicate with its peer.

To overcome the antispoofing mechanisms, Mobile IP uses a technique called *reverse tunneling*, as defined in Request For Comment (RFC) 3024. With reverse tunneling, traffic sourced from the Mobile Nodes is sent from the CoA back to the Home Agent through a reverse tunnel, and then forwarded to its final destination from the Home Network. Now the source address of the traffic is topologically correct. Figure 6-3 shows how reverse tunneling solves the problem represented in Figure 6-2 by presenting a topologically correct source address at the ingress interface of the firewall. Although specified in a separate RFC than core Mobile IP, reverse tunneling is becoming mainstream in Mobile IP deployments.

Figure 6-3   *Reverse Tunneling*

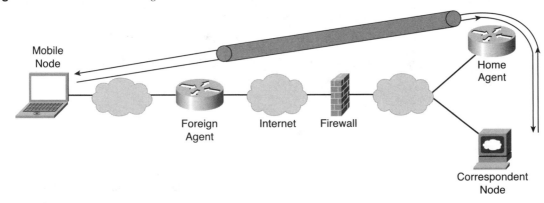

In addition to providing topological correctness, reverse tunnels also allow Mobile Nodess to now participate in multicast groups on their Home Networks. That is, a Mobile Nodes can be a source in a multicast group in its Home Network, and while it is in a Foreign Network, reverse-tunnel any multicast packets for the group back to the Home Network. This way, the multicast packets look as though they emanated from the Home Network before they are forwarded.

Another implicit advantage of reverse tunnels is that the TTL on a packet traversing a reverse tunnel is only decremented by one, as with most tunnel mechanisms. Without reverse tunnels, the TTL on a packet from a Mobile Nodes to another node still on the Home Network can be too low, and thus, the TTL can expire before the packet reaches the Home Network.

Reverse-Tunnel Delivery Style

Reverse tunneling can use either the *direct delivery style* or *encapsulated delivery style* method of delivery. The type of delivery style to use depends on the type of traffic that needs to be reverse-tunneled. Direct delivery style is the simpler form but can only be used for unicast packets. In the direct delivery style, the Mobile Nodes sends its packets without encapsulation to the Foreign Agent (FA), with the IP source as its Home Address and the IP destination as the CN's address. The FA intercepts such a packet and encapsulates it with the IP source as the Care-of Address (CoA) and the IP destination as the Home Agent's address. When the Home Agent receives the packet, it decapsulates it to retrieve the original packet from the Mobile Nodes and sends the packet to the CN.

With the encapsulated delivery style, the Mobile Nodes sends encapsulated traffic to the FA. The FA decapsulates the packets and then reencapsulates the packets in the reverse tunnel to the Home Agent. The Mobile Nodes must use the encapsulating delivery style for the reverse tunnel for multicast or broadcast traffic. This is because a multicast or broadcast packet for the Home Network should not be transmitted in the clear on the Foreign Network directly. If such packets are sent directly on the Foreign Network, nodes on the foreign link incorrectly think that the multicast or broadcast traffic is intended for them. Thus, the Mobile Nodes encapsulates the multicast or broadcast traffic into a packet destined for the FA. The FA decapsulates the packet and then reverse-tunnels the original multicast or broadcast packet to the Home Agent.

The Mobile Nodes can request the encapsulating delivery style from the FA by appending the Encapsulating Delivery Style Extension, defined in RFC 3024, to its Registration Requests (RRQs). The extension is consumed by the FA and not forwarded to the Home Agent.

Using the encapsulating delivery style method also allows the Mobile Nodes to use selective reverse tunneling, as follows:

- If the Mobile Nodes does not want a particular packet to be reverse-tunneled, it sends the packet using the direct delivery style. In this case, the FA treats the packet as regular traffic and routes the packet normally (because the reverse tunnel is set up with the encapsulating delivery method).

- For traffic that should be reverse-tunneled to the Home Agent, the Mobile Nodes uses the encapsulating delivery style for the packets.

Reverse-Tunnel Signaling

To use reverse tunneling, the Home Agent and the CoA endpoint must both support the technique. The Mobility Agents indicate support for reverse tunneling in their Mobile IP agent advertise-ments through the T bit. By setting the T bit in the advertisement extension, the Mobility Agent is saying that it offers reverse-tunneling service, and in the case of the FA, it necessarily supports the direct delivery style.

Using this information from the agent advertisement, a Mobile Nodes can now choose to register through a FA that supports reverse tunneling. The T bit in agent advertisements is backward compatible, in the sense that it is not required to be understood by Mobile Nodess. If a Mobile Nodes does not understand the T bit, it simply ignores the bit and parses the rest of the agent advertisement as usual.

A Mobile Nodes explicitly requests reverse-tunneling service by setting the T bit in its RRQ. (At the risk of stating the obvious, this is different from the T bit in the agent advertisement. Refer to Chapter 2 for the various option bits in the agent advertisement and RRQ messages.)

This requests the FA to reverse-tunnel all the Mobile Nodes's packets to the Home Agent, and requests the Home Agent to accept a reverse tunnel from the CoA. The default method of delivery for the reverse tunnel is the direct delivery style, and thus, the Mobile Nodes must take care to use this FA as its default router to ensure that its packets are indeed reverse-tunneled to the Home Agent.

If a Mobility Agent receives a RRQ with the T bit set and it cannot provide the reverse-tunneling service, it rejects the RRQ with an appropriate failure code. In addition to this failure, a RRQ can fail for other reasons with reverse tunnels. The following self-explanatory failure codes for reverse tunneling are used in Registration Reply (RRP) messages to the Mobile Nodes:

- Reverse-tunneling service denied by the FA:

```
74 requested reverse tunnel unavailable
75 reverse tunnel is mandatory and 'T' bit not set
76 Mobile Node too distant
79 delivery style not supported
```

- Reverse-tunneling service denied by the Home Agent:

```
137 requested reverse tunnel unavailable
138 reverse tunnel is mandatory and 'T' bit not set
139 requested encapsulation unavailable
```

If a Mobile Nodes is operating in Colocated Care-of Address (CCoA) mode directly with its Home Agent, it can perform its own reverse tunneling.

Reverse-Tunnel Configuration

Configuration for the reverse-tunnel feature is possible on both the Home Agent and FA as follows:

- **Configuration on the Home Agent**—The Cisco IOS Home Agent is configured to allow reverse tunneling by default, which goes back to the point of reverse tunneling becoming mainstream in Mobile IP deployments. Reverse-tunneling support in the Home Agent can be disabled with the following command:

```
ip mobile home-agent reverse-tunnel off
```

- **Configuration on the FA**—The IOS FA supports both encapsulating and direct delivery style. On the FA, reverse tunneling is not enabled by default. Reverse tunneling at the FA is not currently supported in the Cisco Express Forwarding (CEF) path and requires extra resources. Use care before enabling reverse tunneling. Reverse tunneling is enabled on a per-interface basis using the following command:

```
ip mobile foreign-service reverse-tunnel
```

For cases in which reverse tunneling is a known requirement, for example, in domains where ingress filtering is deployed, the FA can be configured to force all Mobile Nodess connected through an interface to use reverse tunneling with the following command:

```
ip mobile foreign-service reverse-tunnel mandatory
```

Tunnel Path MTU

Although not specific to Mobile IP, it makes sense to discuss path maximum transmission unit (MTU), because it has implications on the tunnel soft state and encapsulation methods. This is especially significant in the metro mobility model, because the tunnel path can traverse multiple autonomous systems with varying MTU capabilities. Further discussion of path MTU discovery as it relates to Mobile IP is presented in Chapter 8, "Deployment Scalability and Management."

Usually, an upper limit exists on the size of a frame that can be sent over a link, and this limit is called the *link MTU*. An IP packet that is larger than the link MTU is fragmented (broken into smaller portions or fragments) and sent over the link. When considering an entire path to the destination, the path MTU is then the smallest link MTU among all links in the path. The path MTU represents the largest amount of data that can be sent along the entire path without having to be fragmented. To prevent fragmentation, devices usually determine the path MTU of the route between a source and destination by using the Path MTU Discovery mechanism, which works as follows:

- The sender sets the DF (don't fragment) bit in the IP header for all IP packets to a destination, and initially assumes the path MTU to be the outgoing link MTU.

- Any router along the path that cannot forward the packet on the next outgoing link—because the link MTU is less than the total length of the packet—instead forwards the sender an Internet Control Message Protocol (ICMP) Destination Unreachable message with code conveying that "fragmentation is needed, but the DF bit is set." This message usually includes an extension that specifies the MTU of the link requiring fragmentation. The packet is then dropped.

- Upon receipt of such an ICMP Destination Unreachable message, the sender decreases the path MTU estimate to the destination and sends smaller IP packets along the path.

- Discovery is complete when the sender receives no more ICMP Destination Unreachable messages.

When using tunnel encapsulation, the DF bit must be copied onto the outer tunnel header. This ensures that the path MTU discovery can still be used. However, the sender might have to adjust the size of the IP packet to account for the extra tunnel header in meeting path MTU requirements.

NOTE   Path MTU discovery can be problematic in open Internet scenarios. Many firewalls are configured to discard all ICMP messages, and encountering a PTU MTU discovery black hole is therefore possible. That is the case, for example, when ICMP messages are being generated but not returned to the source. Some operating systems include black-hole discovery mechanisms that disable path MTU discovery after multiple retransmissions fail. Without black-hole discovery, users often see odd behavior on their computers, such as web pages that start to load but never finish.

The black-hole problem is more common when Mobile IP is used because the added header of the tunnel might be detectable in only one direction. Typically the smallest MTU seen in the Internet is 1500 bytes, so one common workaround is to lower the maximum MTU on the Mobile Nodes to account for the 20-byte tunnel header. Users often round down and choose an MTU of 1400 bytes.

Impact of Network Address Translation

Network Address Translation (NAT) is another technology commonly deployed at the edge of private autonomous systems that can conflict with the delivery of encapsulated traffic. Network Address Translation, which comes in two basic flavors—NAT and Network Address and Port Translation (NAPT)—is designed to allow networks with private addressing schemes to exchange traffic with public networks. NAT works by translating the address used by the node in the private autonomous system to an address that is valid in the global network. NAT typically relies on statistical multiplexing to allow a large pool of private addresses to share a smaller pool of public addresses. NAPT goes one step further and allows many nodes to use a single public address by translating the IP address and the Transmission Control Protocol (TCP) or User Datagram Protocol (UDP) port.

In Mobile IP, usually IP-in-IP tunneling or generic routing encapsulation (GRE) tunneling sends data traffic between the Home Agent and Mobile Nodes, either directly or through a FA. When the CoA tunnel endpoint is behind an NAT gateway, the IP-in-IP tunneling cannot pass through the NAT gateway. Specifically, the IP layer encapsulations do not carry transport layer (TCP/UDP port numbers) to permit unique translation of the private CoA into the public address. For NAPT gateways, the problem is worse because IP-in-IP and GRE tunneling do not use ports to identify sessions and, thus, the tunnel cannot traverse an NAPT gateway.

Note that NAT and NAPT traversal is not an issue with Mobile IP RRQs and RRPs because they are UDP datagrams that originate from behind the NAT. Hence, when these Mobile IP messages pass through the NAT or NAPT gateway on their way to the Home Agent, they are translated into a public address and UDP port mapping that the RRP can pass back through.

NAT Traversal UDP Tunneling

To solve the problems that occur when the tunnel needs to terminate behind NAT and NAPT gateways, the Internet Engineering Task Force (IETF) Mobile IP working group standardized RFC 3519, which defines a UDP tunneling protocol to be used for both the forward and reverse Mobile IP tunnels. The new protocol defines extensions to the registration and agent advertisement portions of the Mobile IP protocol. A key feature of this NAT–Mobile IP solution is that data packets are now also sent to the UDP ports that set up the Mobile IP registration, that is, UDP port 434 on the Home Agent and the UDP source port used for the RRQ on the Mobile Nodes. To this end, a new format for encapsulating data packets is also defined. A basic assumption in the solution is that the NAT gateway allows UDP datagrams from the Mobile Nodes destined to UDP port 434 on the Home Agent to pass through.

The fundamental design of the NAT–Mobile IP solution follows the standard Mobile IP implementation with the following specifics:

- The FA advertises support for UDP tunneling. This is accomplished by setting a newly defined U bit in the Mobile IP agent advertisement. (The U bit in agent advertisements is backward compatible; if a Mobile Nodes does not understand the U bit, it simply ignores the bit.)

- A UDP tunnel is requested in the RRQ. To accomplish this, either the FA or the Mobile Nodes appends the UDP Tunnel Request Extension, defined in RFC 3519, to the RRQ. (Although the Mobile Nodes or FA might not know whether the RRQ will traverse an NAT or NAPT gateway, by appending the extension, they are conveying support for UDP tunneling if in fact it is needed.)

- The Home Agent sends a RRP, either accepting the registration with UDP tunneling or denying the registration if it cannot establish a UDP tunnel. To accomplish this, the Home Agent appends the UDP Tunnel Reply Extension, as defined in RFC 3519, to the RRP.

So, how does the Home Agent know whether the Mobile Nodes's RRQ did, in fact, pass through an NAT or NAPT gateway? It doesn't know for sure, but rather it infers as such—a bit of detective work! The Home Agent evaluates the RRQ and compares the source IP address of the packet to the CoA inside the request. If the two addresses differ, the Home Agent deduces that an NAT gateway exists in the middle and enables the use of UDP tunneling. The UDP Tunnel Request Extension has an F bit to allow the Mobile Nodes to forcefully request UDP tunneling for cases in which the NAT detection algorithm does not work. For example, this can be used to traverse firewalls and other filter devices that allow only TCP and UDP traffic, but do not necessarily perform address translation.

After the UDP tunnel is established between the CoA and Home Agent, all the data traffic is encapsulated within a new format as defined in RFC 3519. Basically, a new Mobile IP Tunnel Data Message header is defined. This header differentiates data traffic that is sent in the tunnel to port 434 on the Home Agent from other Mobile IP messages, for example, RRQs and RRPs.

Although the Mobile IP tunnel has been established for the lifetime granted in the RRQ, the actual life of the tunnel depends on the NAT state information being current on the tunnel. To this end, *keepalive* messages are sent to ensure that the UDP tunnel through the NAT gateway retains the NAT translation state information if traffic has not been sent down the tunnel in a specified amount of time. Essentially, the keepalive serves as a message saying, "Although traffic hasn't been sent down this tunnel in a while, it is still valid. Please keep it up." The keepalive message is a properly UDP-encapsulated ICMP echo request sent by the Mobile Nodes or FA and directed to the Home Agent. The frequency of the keepalive messages is configurable.

NAT on the Home Agent

In the metro mobility model in which the Mobile Nodes roams outside its autonomous system, the Home Agent must have a global IP address. Usually, the Mobile Nodes is configured with its Home Agent address, and if that address is from a private address space, when the Mobile Nodes leaves its home autonomous system, it cannot reach the private Home Agent address. (A good analogy is using your boss's internal extension when calling him from within the company. As soon as you go outside your company, that extension has no meaning and your boss's full "global" phone number must be known and dialed.)

In these metro mobility models, the Home Agent can reside on the edge of the private network and act as an NAT gateway for its Mobile Nodess. By straddling the public and private networks, the Home Agent address can be global, and the Mobile Nodess can use private addresses. For the most part, configuration of NAT on the Home Agent is similar to standard NAT configuration in IOS. The main difference is the additional configuration needed to address the fact that the egress interface is dynamic.

Remember that the Home Agent uses standard IOS tunnel interfaces and adds a route to the Mobile Nodes through the tunnel interface. Thus, every time the Mobile Nodes changes its CoA, the egress interface changes on the Home Agent. However, the standard IOS NAT protocol requires that inside and outside interface pairs be defined for address translation to take place.

Mobile IP NAT Configuration

Configuration for the Mobile IP NAT feature is needed on both the Home Agent and FA in Cisco IOS.

Configuration on the Home Agent

The first configuration task is to enable the NAT traversal feature on the Home Agent, as follows:

```
(i) ip mobile home-agent nat traversal  [keepalive time] [forced {accept | reject}]
```

This command enables Network Address Translation-User Datagram Protocol (NAT-UDP) encapsulation support on the Home Agent. The **keepalive** option allows the Home Agent to configure the frequency of keepalive messages. The **forced accept** option configures the Home

Agent to allow forced UDP tunneling. Conversely, the **forced reject** option configures the Home Agent to reject forced UDP tunneling. Forced UDP tunneling occurs when the Mobile Nodes requests UDP tunneling, even when the Home Agent does not detect an NAT in the path. Forced tunneling can be useful for firewall traversal as well.

The next step is to configure NAT traversal on the tunnel interface as follows:

```
(ii) ip mobile tunnel nat {inside | outside}
```

The **inside** option sets the dynamic tunnel as the inside interface for NAT. Conversely, the **outside** option sets the dynamic tunnel as the outside interface for NAT.

Configuration on the FA

The FA must be configured to support the NAT traversal feature as follows:

```
ip mobile foreign-agent nat traversal  [keepalive  time]  [force]
```

This command enables NAT-UDP encapsulation on the FA. The **keepalive** option allows the FA to use this keepalive time for the messages when the Home Agent does not provide a specific value. The force option allows the FA to force the Home Agent to allocate an NAT UDP tunnel without performing detection presence of NAT along the Foreign Agent-Home Agent (FA-HA) path.

VPN Integration

In metro mobility, Mobile Nodess usually have an added requirement of maintaining a secure tunnel into their private/corporate network as they roam. Although the techniques for traversing secured and NATed networks allow Mobile IP to be deployed in public networks, they do nothing to secure the communications of the Mobile Nodes. In fact, Mobile IP provides no security for the traffic of Mobile Nodess. While it might have been acceptable to send certain traffic in the clear to the Mobile Nodes while it was at home, it might not be acceptable to tunnel that traffic in the clear to the Mobile Nodes while it is in a Foreign Network.

Throughout the course of this book, Mobile IP has been treated as a routing protocol, and this is a clear example that helps identify Mobile IP as a routing protocol and not an application protocol. Consistent with that, Mobile IP integrates well with existing data-plane security protocols like IP Security (IPSec). Mobile IP provides a significantly improved user experience for Mobile IPSec users because the sessions need not be reestablished when the access link changes. This eliminates the need for the long setup times associated with most IPSec implementations.

Almost all Mobile IP clients support some level of integration with IPSec clients; some even come integrated. However, you must ensure that the two clients interoperate. Mobile IP and IPSec both require extensive integration with the host IP stack, and this integration can cause interference between Mobile IP and IPSec. Furthermore, some of the changes that Mobile IP clients make to the host stack can be construed as security violations, causing some VPN clients to prohibit the changes or tear down sessions. Specific client configuration is not included because it varies from client to client.

Placement of the Home Agent for mobile roaming clients is important and critical to the proper operation of the network. Figure 6-4 shows the two most common deployments. Option A is viable for clients that always connect through the public network and do not require roaming between the public and private networks. Option B shows how two Mobile IP sessions can be coupled with a single VPN session to allow roaming between public and private networks.

Figure 6-4   *Options for Integrating Mobile IP and IPSec*

Option A: IPSec over Mobile IP

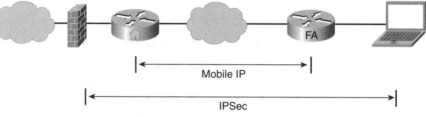

Option B: Mobile IP over IPSec over Mobile IP

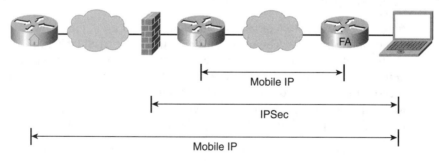

IPSec and Mobile IP

Although there are no specific configuration requirements to allow Mobile IP and IPSec to interoperate, you should follow certain rules. The most important rule is that neither tunnel can interrupt the other, as shown in Figure 6-5. Said another way, one tunnel must contain the other tunnel.

The first two examples show scenarios in which the tunnels interfere with one another and, thus, are unacceptable. In the first example, the traffic is first IPSec encapsulated and then Mobile IP encapsulated. When the traffic hits the remote IPSec peer first, it is an IP-in-IP packet, and the

IPSec peer has no idea what to do with it because no IPSec credentials are present. Similarly, in the second example, the traffic is first Mobile IP encapsulated and then IPSec encapsulated. When the traffic hits the FA, the FA cannot retrieve the internal IP-in-IP packet to deliver it to the Mobile Nodes.

Figure 6-5   *Possible Placement of Mobility Agents and VPN Concentrators*

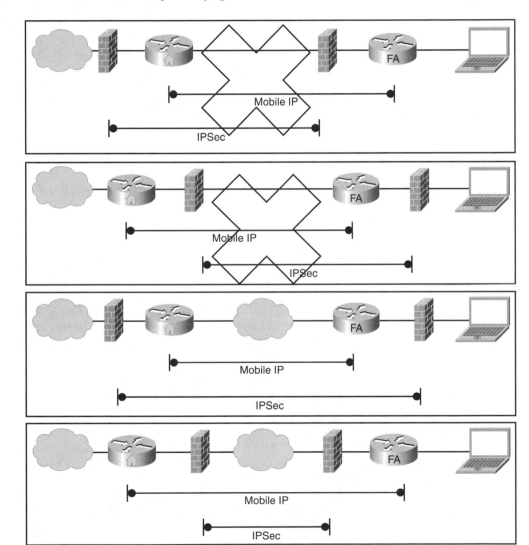

The last two examples in Figure 6-5 depict acceptable integration scenarios. In these examples, a particular protocol tunnel is contained within the other, that is, Mobile IP over IPSec or IPSec over Mobile IP, and encapsulation is always removed in the order opposite to the order in which it was added. A single device can perform both Mobile IP and IPSec functions. However, you must make sure that the device is performing the encapsulation in the expected order. You must also ensure that the MTU setting on the Mobile Nodes supports both the overhead from Mobile IP and IPSec.

Both Mobile IP over IPSec and IPSec over Mobile IP have advantages and disadvantages. Running IPSec over Mobile IP allows the user to roam without needing to reestablish the VPN after each access link change. However, this configuration allows the Mobile Nodes to roam only outside the private network. This solution works well for users who never roam into the private network. For users who need to roam into the private network, running Mobile IP over IPSec can allow sessions to be maintained within the private network. Unfortunately, with Mobile IP over IPSec, the IPSec session needs to be reestablished every time the access link changes. This can be acceptable in configurations in which the Mobile Nodes has only one single public network connection and the IP address does not change, such as with a cellular network. However, for many cases, it does not provide an ideal solution.

Mobile IP over IPSec over Mobile IP

Another viable deployment solution is Mobile IP over IPSec over Mobile IP. Before you groan too much, we present a little history.

When the Mobile IP working group in IETF first looked at solving the problem of having the Home Agent on a private network and allowing a Mobile Nodes to securely roam on public networks, some elegant proposals were presented. These proposals required new features to be implemented on VPN concentrators and firewalls. However, given that Mobile IP was an emerging technology at the time, the likelihood of mainstream adoptions of these ideas did not seem likely. Mobile IP/VPN/Mobile IP is not the most efficient solution; however, it can be deployed without making changes to existing infrastructure.

The basic premise of Mobile IP/VPN/Mobile IP is that inside a private Home Network, the Mobile Nodes can reach its Home Agent, but from outside that network, it can only reach that Home Agent through a VPN tunnel. However, to keep that VPN session alive as the Mobile Nodes roams in the network, it needs to be anchored outside the VPN concentrator. This basic topology is shown in Figure 6-6. The Mobile Nodes can detect when it has roamed out of the Home Network because it can no longer reach its Home Agent. At this point, it registers with the external Home Agent. When the registration is established, the Mobile Nodes initiates a VPN session over the Mobile IP session, allowing it to access its private network. From there, the Mobile Nodes then renews the registration with the internal Home Agent, allowing internal sessions to be maintained.

Resource Revocation

A mobility binding can be viewed as a contract between the Home Agent and CoA endpoint, which is either a FA or a colocated Mobile Nodes. In the metro mobility model, the contract is across different administrative domains because the Home Agent and FA are in different autonomous systems. During the lifetime of this contract, either Mobility Agent might want to prematurely terminate the binding, for example, for administrative reasons, and thus revoke the contract.

Figure 6-6   *Mobile IP over IPSec over Mobile IP Topology*

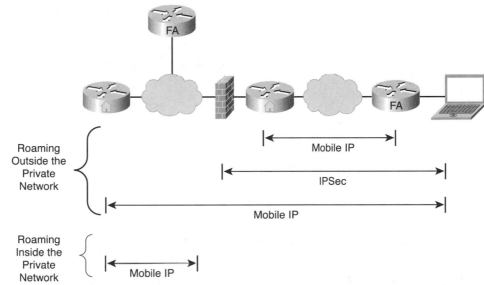

Now, instead of waiting for the binding to expire on the peer Mobility Agent, wouldn't it be nice if the revoking Mobility Agent could somehow tell the peer agent that the binding is gone? This allows the peer agent to reclaim resources that it was using to service the Mobile Nodes. Wouldn't it be nice if resources could also be reclaimed when a Mobile Nodes moved from one FA to another FA? In base Mobile IP, the Home Agent would obviously learn about the new FA through a RRQ and, thus, update the mobility binding. However, the previous FA would have to maintain the visitor entry until it expired because it has no way of knowing that the Mobile Nodes moved on.

Registration Revocation, as defined in RFC 3543, is an enhancement to Mobile IP that allows more efficient management of Mobile IP resources and services. It is an unobtrusive, yet proactive, feature that allows more timely communication between the different Mobile IP entities. Basically, Registration Revocation solves all the mobility problems. Okay, not really, but with Registration Revocation, you can accomplish the following:

- **Timely release of Mobile IP resources**—Resources being consumed to provide Mobile IP services for a Mobile Nodes that has stopped receiving Mobile IP services by one agent can be reclaimed by the peer agent in a more timely fashion than if it had to wait for the mobility binding to expire.

- **Early adoption of domain policy changes with regard to services offered/required of a Mobile IP binding**—For example, the home domain might now require reverse tunneling, yet existing mobility bindings do not use them. Without a revocation mechanism, new services can be put in place or removed only as bindings are reregistered.

- **Timely notification to a Mobile Nodes that it is no longer receiving mobility services**—This significantly shortens any black-hole periods to facilitate a more robust recovery.

- **Accurate accounting**—This has a favorable impact on resolving accounting issues with respect to the length of mobility bindings in both domains, because the end of the registration is relayed.

Resource Revocation Overview

Resource revocation has a negotiation phase and a revocation phase. During the negotiation phase, the Mobility Agents agree to inform one another of revocations and exchange their clock timestamps so that they can be used during the revocation phase. They also negotiate whether the Mobile Nodes is to be informed of a revocation of its binding. During the revocation phase, the Mobility Agents inform one another when a mobility binding is revoked.

The Mobile IP signaling that is involved in the negotiation phase and revocation phase can be summarized into the following four main components:

- The Mobility Agents advertise support for the revocation feature. This is accomplished by setting a newly defined X bit in the Mobile IP agent advertisement message. This allows Mobile Nodess to choose FAs that support revocation, if so desired. The X bit in agent advertisements is backward compatible, and if a Mobile Nodes does not understand the X bit, it simply ignores the bit.

- The Mobility Agents convey to one another that they are interested in receiving revocation messages upon early termination of a binding. They accomplish this by appending the Revocation Support Extension, as defined in RFC 3543, to the RRQ and RRP messages. Specifically, a FA can append the extension to a RRQ to start the negotiation phase. When the Home Agent receives the RRQ, it knows that the FA supports the revocation mechanism. In turn, if the Home Agent wants to participate in the revocation mechanism, it appends the extension to the RRP. When the FA receives the reply, revocation support is considered to be negotiated and the Mobility Agents have agreed to inform one another upon revocation (or early termination) of a binding. In the revocation extension, the Mobility Agent can also express whether it wants the Mobile Nodes to be informed upon revocation (or early termination) of the binding through the I bit in the extension.

- After negotiating and establishing use of the revocation mechanism for mobility binding(s), the Mobility Agents send reliable revocation messages that must be authenticated to one another upon revocation (or early termination) of a mobility binding. Revocation messages are sent reliably through an acknowledgment mechanism in an earnest effort to notify the peer agent so that the peer can also release the resources consumed in supporting the Mobile Nodes. Upon receiving a revocation message, the peer agent responds with a revocation acknowledgment message.

- If the Mobile Nodes should be notified that its binding has been revoked, the FA simply unicasts an agent advertisement with a [re]set sequence number of 0 to the Mobile Nodes. The Mobile Nodes understands that its mobility binding has been reset and that it must reregister, as discussed in Chapter 2.

If a colocated Mobile Nodes is registering directly with its Home Agent, with the D bit set in its RRQ and not registering through a FA, the Mobile Nodes can participate in a "one-sided" revocation mechanism. In this case, the Mobile Nodes and Home Agent negotiate the revocation mechanism as previously described. However, in the revocation phase, the Mobile Nodes can receive revocation messages from the Home Agent upon early termination of its binding by the Home Agent, but it does not send revocation messages in the reverse case.

Revocation Support Extension and Messages

All the messaging associated with the revocation mechanism must be secure because it is altering the status of mobility bindings. Otherwise, you can imagine that there would be some unhappy Mobile Nodess if their bindings were rudely revoked without proper authorization! To this end, the revocation messages and revocation support extension must be protected. If the communication is between Mobility Agents, a HA–FA security association is used. If, however, the communication is being sent from a Home Agent to a "direct" colocated Mobile Nodes, a MN–HA security association is used. In either case, another security mechanism at least as secure, and agreed upon by the home and foreign domains (for example, IPSec), can also be used. The important point is that the messages must be secured.

In addition to authentication protection, the revocation messages are also protected against replay attacks and reflection attacks. Such protection is crucial to prevent denial-of-service attacks by *rogue repeaters*—those who store packets with the intent of replaying them at a later time, or by *rogue reflectors*—those who reflect packets at their original source.

So, how is all of this, coupled with revoking a mobility binding, accomplished with the revocation extension and messages? We now look into the relevant fields.

The Revocation Support Extension has the following main fields:

- **Timestamp**—This is the current timestamp of the Mobility Agent (or direct colocated Mobile Nodes). It identifies the offset between the clocks of the Mobility Agents providing support for this binding. The timestamp offset is used later during the revocation phase to provide replay and reflection attack protection.

- **I bit**—This bit negotiates whether the Mobile Nodes is informed upon revocation (or early termination) of its binding during the revocation phase.

The following fields in the revocation messages uniquely identify mobility bindings and provide replay and reflection protection:

- **A bit**—This bit identifies the role of the Revoking Agent. Specifically, it is set to 0 if the Revoking Agent is serving as the FA, and set to 1 if the Revoking Agent is serving as the Home Agent.

- **I bit**—This bit is used only if it was negotiated in the revocation extension messages. It specifies whether the Mobile Nodes should be informed of the revocation, with the exact meaning depending on the role of the Revoking Agent, as specified in RFC 3543.

- **Home Address**—This field specifies the home IP address of the Mobile Nodes whose registration is being revoked.

- **Foreign Domain Address**—This field specifies the relevant IP address in the foreign domain to identify which binding is being revoked. This is one of the following:

  — FA's IP address

  — Mobile Nodes's CCoA

- **Home Domain Address**—This field specifies the IP address of the Home Agent to identify which binding is being revoked.

- **Revocation Identifier**—This field protects against replay and reflection attacks. The Revoking Agent must insert its current 4-byte timestamp running off the same clock as it is using to fill in the timestamp in its revocation extensions.

A subset of these fields is found in revocation acknowledgment messages, namely, the Home Address and Revocation Identifier, to uniquely map acknowledgment messages to revocation messages. Specific details and format of the Revocation Support Extension and revocation messages can be found in RFC 3543.

Registration Revocation Example

Consider an example that illustrates the revocation mechanism. In this example, a Mobile Nodes is registering through a FA that shares a security association with the Home Agent. Both Mobility Agents support the revocation mechanism:

1 The FA sends an agent advertisement with the X bit set.

2 The Mobile Nodes sends a RRQ through the FA.

3 The FA appends the Revocation Support Extension to the RRQ and secures it with the FA–Home Agent Authentication Extension. The FA sets the I bit in the extension to 1, indicating that it will let the Home Agent decide whether the Mobile Nodes should be notified if the binding is revoked.

4   Upon receiving the RRQ containing a revocation extension, the Home Agent includes a Revocation Support Extension in the RRP. Because the FA set the I bit to 1 in its revocation extension, and the Home Agent supports the use of the I bit, the Home Agent sets the I bit in its registration extension to 1. The Home Agent appends the revocation extension to its RRP and secures it with a HA–FA Authentication Extension.

5   Upon receiving the authenticated RRP, the FA checks the Revocation Support Extension and notes that the Home Agent wants to decide whether the Mobile Nodes should be notified in the event that this registration is revoked, that is, because the Home Agent set the I bit in the return revocation extension.

6   At a later time, the FA revokes the Mobile Nodes's binding and generates a revocation message to be sent to the Mobile Nodes's Home Agent. Because the I bit was negotiated in the revocation extensions and the FA is still willing to let the Home Agent indicate whether this Mobile Nodes should be informed about the revocation, it sets the I bit to 1 in the revocation message. The FA sets the A bit to 0, places the address of the Mobile Nodes whose registration it is revoking in the Home Address field, places the address that the Mobile Nodes registered as the CoA in the foreign domain field, and places the address registered as the Home Agent in the home domain address field. The FA sets the revocation identifier to the current 32-bit timestamp and appends the FA–HA Authentication Extension.

7   Upon receiving the above revocation message, the Home Agent uses the address specified as the foreign domain address to identify the security association and authenticates the revocation message. After authenticating the message, the Home Agent verifies that the A bit and revocation identifier indicate that this revocation is not a replay. The Home Agent then uses the Mobile Nodes Home Address field, the foreign domain address field, and home domain address field to locate the Mobile Nodes whose registration is being revoked. It deletes the mobility binding.

8   Upon processing a valid registration revocation message, the Home Agent generates a revocation acknowledgment message. Because the I bit was set to 1 in the revocation message and the Home Agent wants the identified Mobile Nodes to be informed of the revocation, it sets the I bit in the revocation acknowledgment to 1. The Home Agent then copies the Home Address and the revocation identifier field into the revocation acknowledgment. The Home Agent protects the revocation acknowledgment with a HA–FA Authentication Extension.

9   Upon receiving a valid revocation acknowledgment (in which the authenticator and identifier fields are acceptable), the FA checks the state of the I bit.

10 Because the I bit is set to 1, the FA notifies the Mobile Nodes of the revocation by unicasting an agent advertisement with a reset sequence number.

Registration Revocation Configuration

All the configuration specific to Registration Revocation is performed on the Home Agent, with the exception of the FA–HA security association. After a security association is configured, revocation is configured with the following command:

```
ip mobile home-agent revocation [timeout number] [retransmit number]
```

The optional **timeout** and **retransmit** parameters control how long the Home Agent must wait for a reply to the revocation message and how many times the revocation message is to be retransmitted.

NOTE   Some versions of IOS support a prestandard version of revocation that is referred to as *bindupdate*. You should use the standards-based revocation wherever possible. This Binding Update is not related to the Binding Update functionality in Home Agent Redundancy.

Bringing It All Together Through an Example

Figure 6-1 presents a basic topology for metro mobility, and the subsequent sections of this chapter present individual components that play a roll in the overall solution. Figure 6-7 pulls the pieces together into an example. The goal here is to allow a user to establish and maintain sessions while roaming within and between multiple networks with no interruption. Reverse tunneling and UDP NAT traversal are used on the Home Agent. Finally, Registration Revocation allows efficient communication between the various Mobile IP entities as the Mobile Nodes roams across different autonomous systems. The configurations for these devices are shown in Example 6-1.

Figure 6-7   *Metro Mobility Example*

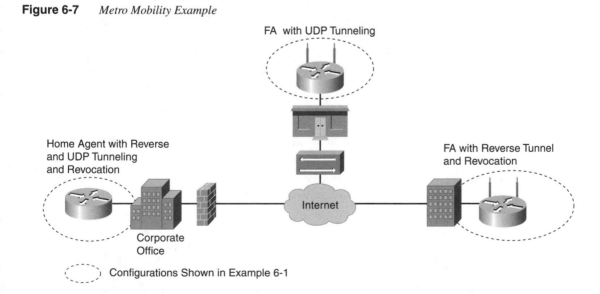

Example 6-1   *Configurations for a Metro Mobility Solution*

```
Home Agent Configuration
!
hostname Home Agent
!
interface Ethernet0/0
 ip address 192.168.1.2 255.255.255.0
!
router mobile
!
router ospf 1
 redistribute mobile subnets
 network 192.168.0.0 0.0.255.255 area 1
!
ip mobile home-agent nat traversal keepalive 20
ip mobile home-agent revocation
ip mobile virtual-network 192.168.100.0 255.255.255.0
ip mobile host 192.168.100.10 192.168.100.20 virtual-network 192.168.100.0
255.255.255.0
ip mobile secure host 192.168.100.10 spi 100 key hex 1234567890abcdef1234567890abcdef
algorithm md5 mode prefix-suffix
ip mobile secure foreign-agent 192.168.5.1 spi 100 key ascii bindupdatekey algorithm
md5 mode prefix-suffix
!
end
```

```
Foreign Agent Configuration with reverse tunnel and revocation
hostname FA1
!
interface Ethernet0/0
 ip address 192.168.3.2 255.255.255.0
!
interface Ethernet1/0
 ip address 192.168.5.1 255.255.255.0
 ip irdp
 ip irdp maxadvertinterval 4
 ip irdp minadvertinterval 3
 ip irdp holdtime 9
 ip mobile foreign-service reverse-tunnel mandatory
!
router mobile
!
router ospf 1
network 192.168.0.0 0.0.255.255 area 1
!
ip mobile foreign-agent care-of Ethernet1/0
ip mobile secure home-agent 192.168.1.2 spi 100 key ascii bindupdatekey algorithm md5
mode prefix-suffix
!
end
```

continues

Example 6-1 *Configurations for a Metro Mobility Solution (Continued)*

```
Foreign Agent Configuration with UDP Tunneling
hostname FA2
!
!
interface Ethernet0/0
 ip address 192.168.4.2 255.255.255.0
 ip mobile foreign-service
!
interface Ethernet1/0
 ip address 192.168.6.1 255.255.255.0
 ip irdp
 ip irdp maxadvertinterval 4
 ip irdp minadvertinterval 3
 ip irdp holdtime 9
 ip mobile foreign-service reverse-tunnel
!
router mobile
!
router ospf 1
 network 192.168.0.0 0.0.255.255 area 1
!
ip mobile foreign-agent care-of Ethernet1/0
ip mobile foreign-agent nat traversal keepalive 20
!
end
```

Evaluating the Metro Mobility Example

A Mobile Nodes operating in the environment shown in Example 6-1 can have many different states than those seen in Chapter 4, "IOS Mobile IP in the Lab." Cisco IOS **show** commands can determine the states for the feature presented in the chapter.

To determine whether a Mobile Nodes is using reverse tunneling, look under the routing options section of the **show ip mobile binding** command, as follows. If "(T)Reverse-tunnel" is listed, the Mobile Nodes is using reverse tunneling.

```
HA#show ip mobile binding
Mobility Binding List:
Total 1
192.168.100.10:
    Care-of Addr 192.168.5.1, Src Addr 192.168.5.1
    Lifetime granted 10:00:00 (36000), remaining 09:40:54
    Flags sbdmg-T-, Identification C5C75C51.A5787D48
    Tunnel1 src 192.168.1.2 dest 192.168.5.1 reverse-allowed
    Routing Options - (T)Reverse-tunnel
```

The path MTU supported by a tunnel is listed in the output of the **show ip mobile tunnel** command, as follows. The configured MTU of the tunnel is listed as "IP MTU." The discovered MTU is listed under "Path MTU Discovery"; if this value is 0, the configured value can transit the path.

```
HA#show ip mobile tunnel
Mobile Tunnels:
```

```
Total mobile ip tunnels 1
Tunnel1:
    src 192.168.1.2, dest 192.168.5.1
    encap IP/IP, mode reverse-allowed, tunnel-users 1
    IP MTU 1480 bytes
    Path MTU Discovery, mtu: 980, ager: 10 mins, expires: 00:08:52
    outbound interface Ethernet0/0
    HA created, fast switching enabled, ICMP unreachable enabled
    10 packets input, 7700 bytes, 0 drops
    20 packets output, 9723 bytes
```

UDP tunneling can be seen in the output of the **show ip mobile tunnel** command under "encap." A value of "MIPUDP/IP" indicates UDP tunneling. To determine which tunnel a Mobile Nodes is using, look at the output of the **show ip mobile binding** command, as follows. You can also see that "NAT detect" is in effect for this Mobile Nodes.

```
HA#show ip mobile binding
Mobility Binding List:
Total 1
192.168.100.10:
    Care-of Addr 192.168.6.1, Src Addr 192.168.60.1
    Lifetime granted 02:00:00 (7200), remaining 01:42:49
    Flags sbdmg-T-, Identification C5C7702D.E9FD2C7C
    Tunnel0 src 192.168.1.2 dest 192.168.60.1 reverse-allowed
    Routing Options - (T)Reverse-tunnel
    Service Options:
        NAT detect
HA#show ip mobile tunnel
Mobile Tunnels:

Total mobile ip tunnels 1
Tunnel0:
    src 192.168.1.2, dest 192.168.60.1
    src port 434, dest port 434
    encap MIPUDP/IP, mode reverse-allowed, tunnel-users 1
    IP MTU 1468 bytes
    Path MTU Discovery, mtu: 0, ager: 10 mins, expires: never
    outbound interface Ethernet0/0
    HA created, fast switching disabled, ICMP unreachable enabled
    0 packets input, 0 bytes, 0 drops
    52 packets output, 3120 bytes
```

Summary

In this chapter, we looked at mobility in the metro mobility environment. To this end, we examined real-world tunneling issues that arise and Mobile IP solutions that overcome these challenges. We saw how reverse tunneling overcomes ingress filtering and uRPF checks in the network. We discussed NAT and VPN (IPSec) traversal, and finally, we showed how Registration Revocation can improve the efficiency of communication between the Mobile IP entities.

In the next chapter, the PC-based client is replaced with a router, allowing many IP devices to share a single set of links without regard to mobility. The features and configurations build on the Home Agent/FA topologies shown in this and previous chapters and focus on the specifics of the mobile router.

Review Questions

1 What does the term *metro mobility* mean?

2 What are the challenges or concerns for Mobile IP in the metro mobility model?

3 What feature is necessary for a network to overcome ingress filtering?

   a GRE tunneling

   b Reverse tunneling

   c Mobile Agent–FA security association

   d Firewall on the home network

   e IP-in-IP encapsulation

4 Draw a diagram showing how packets travel when using reverse tunneling.

5 What is tunnel path MTU, and why is it sometimes an issue when using Mobile IP?

6 Describe the Path MTU Discovery mechanism.

7 What is NAT and why is it a challenge when using Mobile IP?

8 How is the coexistence of NAT with Mobile IP achieved?

9 How does the Home Agent infer that a Mobile Nodes is roaming behind an NAT gateway?

10 Mobile IP and IPSec can coexist with proper configuration and placement of the devices. Draw a diagram that shows Mobile IP over IPSec and IPSec over Mobile IP.

11 In the previous question, a particular protocol tunnel is contained within the other, that is, Mobile IP over IPSec or IPSec over Mobile IP. In these cases, in what order is the encapsulation removed?

12 What are the advantages and disadvantages of IPSec over Mobile IP?

13 What are the advantages and disadvantages of Mobile IP over IPSec?

14   Registration Revocation allows for which of the following?

    a   Timely release of Mobile IP resources

    b   Early adoption of domain policy changes with regard to services offered/required of a Mobile IP binding

    c   Timely notification to a Mobile Nodes that it is no longer receiving mobility services, thereby significantly shortening any black-hole periods to facilitate a more robust recovery.

    d   Accurate Mobile IP and resource accounting

    e   All of the above

15   What are the four main components of resource revocation?

CHAPTER 7

Metro Mobility:
Cisco Mobile Networks

As the name suggests, Cisco Mobile Networks allows entire networks to be mobile while maintaining IP connectivity. In a nutshell, a router is used as a Mobile Node to enable mobility for all its attached networks. The advantage of Mobile Networks is that because the router is the Mobile Node, all the devices attached to the mobile network inherit the mobility without having to be Mobile IP aware. A good example of network mobility is an airplane outfitted with a mobile router, allowing the passengers to stay connected to the Internet as they fly to their destination. Just imagine being able to surf the Internet, trade stocks, or even connect to your corporate virtual private network (VPN) while flying in the sky! Now, that would take the world of business travel to a new level! Or, imagine being the chief of police and having complete intranet access to criminal records and database information as you drive in your police vehicle outfitted with a mobile router.

Typically, the nodes that reside on the mobile network are not even aware that IP mobility is transpiring right under their noses. The nodes need not have any Mobile IP client software, although they could. In essence, the mobile router shields mobility and roaming from the nodes; as far as the nodes are concerned, they are directly attached to a fixed network. As shown in Figure 7-1, a mobile network comprises the three main Mobile IP entities: Home Agent, Foreign Agent (FA), and mobile router (the Mobile Node in this case is a router).

Cisco Mobile Networks is standard Mobile IP with a few additions to enable network mobility. Most of the information presented in previous chapters applies to a mobile router just as it would to any other Mobile Node, with a few exceptions. Before we get into the details, lets look at a few questions we need to address:

- How does the Home Agent know that the Mobile Node is actually a mobile router supporting mobile networks?

- How does the Home Agent know which networks are reachable through the mobile router?

- How is traffic delivery different for mobile networks?

- How does a mobile router perform move detection, and what Mobile IP handover policies are supported?

Figure 7-1 *Key Components of a Cisco Mobile Networks Solution*

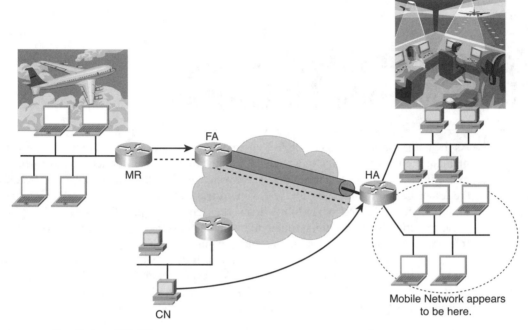

As we answer each of these questions in this chapter, you will see that a mobile router is primarily a standard Mobile IP Mobile Node. As with a Mobile Node, it follows the Mobile IP phases as outlined in Chapter 2, "Understanding Mobile IP," namely, move detection and agent discovery, Mobile IP handover, registration, and deregistration. However, because the mobile router has mobile networks attached to it, additional features are designed to ensure that traffic is properly delivered to nodes on the mobile networks. To this end, a key feature of Cisco Mobile Networks is *dual* Mobile IP tunnels—inside the tunnel from the Home Agent to the CoA is another tunnel from the Home Agent to the mobile router, as depicted in Figure 7-2.

Figure 7-2 *Key Feature of Cisco Mobile Networks (Dual Tunnels)*

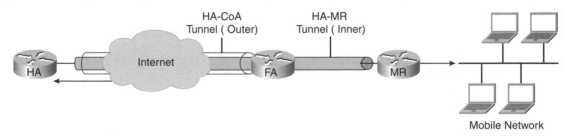

In the first part of the chapter, we examine the three Mobile IP entities, the Mobile Node (Router), Home Agent, and FA and see the behavior and additional features involved with Cisco Mobile Networks. We introduce the IOS configuration for the different features. In the latter part of the chapter, we look at IOS enhancements to support Cisco Mobile Networks that arose from the type of environments in which a mobile router is typically deployed. Specifically, we examine how the mobile router operates in fault-tolerant mode, with asymmetric links, and in Colocated Care-of Address (CCoA) mode. Finally, we consider the integration of Cisco Mobile Networks with quality-of-service mechanisms and IP Security (IPSec).

Mobile Router

As described in the previous section, the mobile router provides and maintains IP connectivity to its mobile networks as it roams. The functionality and configuration of a mobile router can be broken down into the following components:

- Basic Mobile Node functionality
- Roaming interface features
- Mobile networks
- Handover policy
- Routing

Each of these components is discussed in the following sections. Although the mobile router is an IOS router just like any other in your network, restrictions and limitations exist as to which IOS features are supported and how they interact with Cisco Mobile Networks. Several of these cases are directly described in this chapter and can be extrapolated to see the impact on other features.

Mobile Networks (Static or Dynamic)

For network mobility to work, the Home Agent must be aware of the mobile networks connected to a mobile router. This information can be provided either through static configuration of the mobile networks or through dynamic updates during the Mobile IP registration process, as shown in Figure 7-3. These mobile networks are generally *stub networks*, that is, packets are not routed through the network. A statically configured mobile network takes precedence over the same dynamically registered mobile network.

Figure 7-3   *Static and Dynamic Mobile Network Registration*

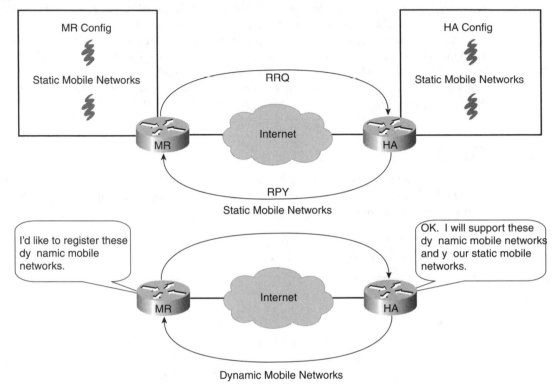

Static mobile networks require static configuration on the Home Agent of the mobile networks associated with a specific mobile router. Each network is configured with the network prefix and mask. When the mobile router registers, the Home Agent automatically processes the mobile networks, as described in section "Home Agent Enhancements," later in this chapter.

A Home Agent will most likely support many mobile routers. A priori knowledge of the mobile networks requires configuration for every mobile router and every mobile network, as shown in Figure 7-4. This practice does not lend itself well to network changes, or even scalability for that matter.

On the contrary, dynamic mobile network registration allows significant flexibility because the Home Agent learns the mobile networks at registration time. Specifically, with dynamic networks, the mobile router tells the Home Agent which mobile networks it is supporting and their current status in RRQs. This allows easier administration and initialization because minimal configuration is needed on the Home Agent, that is, the Home Agent need not be statically configured with the mobile networks.

Figure 7-4   *A Single Home Agent Often Supports Many Mobile Routers*

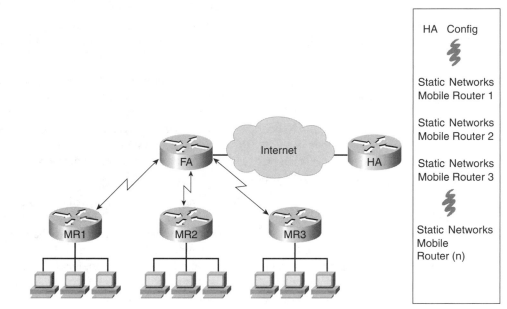

HA   Config

Static Networks
Mobile Router 1

Static Networks
Mobile Router 2

Static Networks
Mobile Router 3

Static Networks
Mobile
Router (n)

NOTE   Cisco Mobile Networks does not allow dynamic routing protocols such as Open Shortest Path First (OSPF) and Border Gateway Protocol (BGP) to be run between the mobile router and the Home Agent for a number of reasons, the most important of which is to maintain stability. Because the Home Agent injects mobile networks into the Interior Gateway Protocol (IGP), it is less likely that instability in the wireless network will impact the IGP. This method also minimizes traffic between the Mobile Node and the Home Agent, which is often important on pay-per-byte wireless links.

To this end, the Mobile IP registration process is extended with the following Mobile Network Non-Critical Vendor Specific Extension (NVSE) [RFC 3115]:

- Mobile Router Dynamic Mobile Network NVSE (used in the Registration Requests [RRQs] and Registration Reply [RRP])

- Mobile Router Static Mobile Network NVSE (used in the RRP)

These extensions convey the mobile network prefix and mask, and in the case of the Dynamic Mobile Network NVSE, specify whether the network is being added or deleted.

When a mobile router registers, it appends the Mobile Router Dynamic Mobile Network NVSE and notifies its Home Agent of the mobile networks that it is currently supporting. After successful registration with its Home Agent, the mobile router does not need to include the NVSE in reregistrations if the status of the mobile networks has not changed. However, if there are any changes to the status of the dynamic mobile networks registered with the Home Agent, the mobile router sends a RRQ with an NVSE, either deleting or adding the appropriate mobile networks.

In response to a RRQ with the Mobile Router Dynamic Mobile Network NVSE appended, the mobile router expects to receive a RRP from its Home Agent acknowledging all the mobile networks associated with the mobile router. Specifically, it expects to see a RRP with the Mobile Router Dynamic Mobile Network NVSE describing its dynamic mobile networks, and a Mobile Router Static Mobile Network NVSE describing its static mobile networks, if any exist. Such a RRP serves as an acknowledgment to the mobile router that the Home Agent has indeed processed its mobile networks properly.

If the mobile network is a routed network, that is, other routers are attached to the mobile network interface, it requires static network configuration. When examining the configuration, it will be clear that this is the case because dynamic networks are learned from the interface configuration. It might seem odd to have a routed network attached to a mobile router, but it is not unheard of. For example, a large cruise ship might already have a routed network infrastructure on board and might be retrofitted with a mobile router to take advantage of multiple link types to provide passengers with optimal connectivity at a minimal cost.

Configuration of Mobile Router and Its Mobile Networks

The mobile router must first be configured as a Mobile Node. Its mobile networks are then either statically configured, or the mobile router is configured to send its mobile networks dynamically during the Mobile IP registration process.

Because the mobile router is a Mobile Node, it requires the same basic configuration as we have previously seen with Mobile Nodes. The mobile router requires the use of a static Home Address and does not support the use of a Network Access Identifier (NAI) or dynamic addressing. This Home Address must be configured on an interface and then identified in the mobile router configuration. Although you can configure the Home Address on a physical interface and use a physical Home Network, numerous problems arise. For example, physical interfaces do not allow a 32-bit subnet mask to be configured. Thus, when the mobile router is not attached to its physical Home Network, it cannot reach other devices on its Home Network because it identifies them as being directly connected. Also, if the Home Address is on a physical interface and that interface is down, the mobile router cannot receive tunneled packets.

The Home Address should be configured on a loopback interface, and a 32-bit mask should be applied to the address. The mask of the Home Network is identified in the mobile router configuration section. The Home Network should be configured as a virtual network on the Home Agent.

The **router mobile** command must first be used to invoke the Mobile IP process on the router, and the mobile router must be configured to share a security association with its Home Agent, as described in Chapter 4, "IOS Mobile IP in the Lab." Configuration of the mobile router and its mobile networks is then accomplished through the **ip mobile router** command. This enables the Mobile Node client and enters the *mobile router configuration mode*.

Within the *mobile router configuration mode*, the home IP address and the mobile networks of the mobile router are configured using the following commands:

- **address** *address mask*—This sets the home IP address and network mask of the mobile router. This address should be configured on a loopback interface, as previously described.

- **home-agent** *ip-address*—This specifies the Home Agent that the mobile router uses during registration.

- **mobile-network** *interface*—This specifies that the mobile router can support dynamic mobile networks and, in particular, specifies the interface on which the dynamic mobile networks are to be connected. The mobile router's registrations contain these dynamic mobile networks. More than one mobile network can be configured on a mobile router. However, a specific mobile network prefix can be configured or registered by only one mobile router at a time.

- **register** {**extend expire** *seconds* **retry** *number* **interval** *seconds* I **lifetime** *seconds* I **retransmit initial** *milliseconds* **maximum** *milliseconds* **retry** *number*}—This command controls the registration parameters of the mobile router.

- **reverse-tunnel**—This enables the reverse-tunnel function.

Mobile Router Service on an Interface

Because the mobile router is serving as a roaming router, several interface-level considerations are important. Interfaces serve one of two purposes: They are either used as roaming interfaces or mobile networks. Roaming interfaces are used for uplink between the mobile router and the rest of the network. Mobile network interfaces attach devices to the mobile router. Although an interface can be used for both roaming and mobile networks, this is not generally recommended.

NOTE   If the roaming interface is used with an IP-managed radio, this dual configuration is necessary. For example, consider a mobile router that has a wireless local-area network (WLAN) bridge that needs an IP address for management, connected through Ethernet. For the bridge to be remotely managed, it must be given an IP address from a mobile network.

The mobile router must consider the fact that it might obtain Layer 2 connections on different interfaces, and therefore must decide on which interface to roam and register. For example, the mobile router might be connected through satellite on one interface and through an 802.11 WLAN on another interface. To this end, the notion of *preferred path* is introduced to allow the mobile router to select the best interface on which to roam and register based on a priority, as depicted in Figure 7-5.

Figure 7-5   *Preferred Path Selection by a Mobile Router*

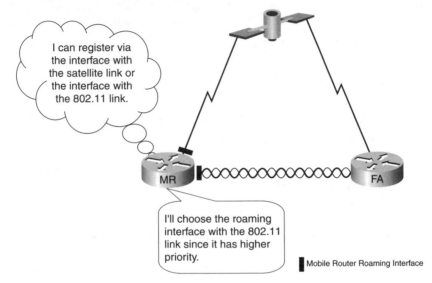

When multiple interfaces have the same priority, the interface with the highest bandwidth is preferred. If a tie still results, the interface with the highest IP address is preferred.

Typically, a mobile router is configured to wait for a hold down period before using a FA. That is, after hearing a FA's advertisement, the mobile router waits for the duration of the hold down period before deciding to use the agent. The hold down period allows the mobile router to be sure that a link is reliable enough to hear the agent for a period of time before committing to using the agent. If the interface transitions from the up state or if regularly scheduled agent advertisements are missed, the hold down timer is reset. Thus, the mobile router avoids prematurely registering with a FA on a lossy wireless link.

In addition to interface-level configuration for preferred path, configuration is also needed to determine whether the mobile router should solicit Mobile IP agent advertisements, and if so, how often it should solicit. Typically, this decision is based on the ratio of mobile routers to FAs in the network deployment. If many mobile routers and few FAs exist, you should disable periodic solicitation and defer to frequent agent advertisements. Otherwise, the network is flooded with periodic solicitations. Using frequent advertisements, the mobile router can detect movement faster and can better evaluate roaming options. Conversely, if few mobile routers and many FAs exist, periodic solicitation is typically enabled. The basic idea is that sending frequent advertisements when only a few mobile routers exist can be a waste of radio bandwidth. Thus, it is better to let the mobile routers solicit for advertisements when they need them.

Regardless of the configured periodic solicitation interval, the mobile router always sends a solicitation when an interface transitions to the *up state*. This allows fast agent discovery as a link comes up by not waiting for an advertisement from the FA. Unfortunately, many radio devices keep their fixed interface up, even when the radio link is down, to allow IP-based management of the device. When possible, this should be disabled to improve Mobile IP handover performance.

Mobile Router Interface-Level Configuration

The following two steps are involved in configuring a roaming interface on a mobile router:

- Assigning an IP address
- Enabling mobile router service

It might seem obvious that the interface needs to be configured with an IP address, but by this point in the book, you should understand why it isn't obvious. If you recall, after the FA has removed the encapsulation header, it delivers traffic to the Mobile Node using the home IP address and a Layer 2 address. As described previously, the Home Address should be configured on a loopback, and even if it is on a physical interface, it can only be configured on one interface at a time.

So what purpose does the interface IP address serve? Unless it is being used as a CCoA or it is part of a mobile network, it does not serve a purpose. Unfortunately, it is still required, because IOS cannot receive IP packets on an interface without an IP address configured. What address should you use? That is hard to say; first, we look at what not to use. You should make sure that the address is not used anywhere else in the network. Otherwise, nodes on the mobile network can never reach that address because all traffic is delivered locally. Also, if two devices have the same IP address, Address Resolution Protocol (ARP) problems could ensue. So, what do you do? Well, the standards people will surely flame us, but the authors generally use addresses from the IPv4 link-local space. Why? These addresses are only used for link-local traffic delivery and of the nodes that implement zeroconf, most do a good job of resolving address conflicts. What is the link-local address range? You don't want us to get into trouble by telling you, do you?

After the addressing problem has been solved, the interface can be configured for roaming. To enable mobile router service on an interface, use the following command in interface configuration mode:

```
ip mobile router-service {hold-down seconds | roam [priority value] | solicit
[interval seconds] [retransmit initial min maximum seconds retry number]}
```

This command enables various services on the mobile router. Furthermore, it allows the following relevant parameters to be changed:

- **hold-down** *seconds*—This specifies the time (in seconds) that the mobile router should wait before registering to agents that are heard on an interface.

- **roam**—This enables the mobile router to use the interface on which it is configured to establish a registration with its Home Agent. This is the key piece necessary to make an interface a roaming interface.

- **priority** *value*—This sets the priority value that is compared among multiple configured interfaces to select the interface on which to send the RRQ.

- **solicit**—This instructs the mobile router to send agent solicitation messages periodically.

- **interval** *seconds*—This specifies the interval (in seconds) that the mobile router waits before it sends the next agent solicitation message after an advertisement is received on an interface.

- **retransmit initial**—This specifies the wait period (in seconds) before a RRQ is retransmitted when no reply is received.

- **maximum** *seconds*—This is the maximum wait period (in seconds) before a RRQ is retransmitted when no reply is received. Each successive retransmission timeout period is twice the previous period, as long as that is less than the maximum value.

- **retry** *number*—This is the number of times to retry sending the RRQ. Retransmission stops after the maximum number of retries are attempted. The range is from 0 to 10; the default is 3. A value of 0 means no retransmission.

Agent Selection and Mobile IP Registration

A mobile router learns about Mobility Agents on its interfaces configured for roaming through the same agent discovery process as for Mobile Nodes. It is highly conceivable that the mobile router can hear advertisements from multiple agents at the same time, as depicted in Figure 7-6.

If the mobile router does not choose its agent in an intelligent manner, it could continually toggle between different agents, leading to inefficient communication, not to mention excess overhead and processing.

So, what happens when a mobile router hears multiple FA advertisements? How does it select which of these agents to register through? For FAs heard on the same interface, the mobile router selects the Mobility Agent from which it has most recently learned about. That is not to say that if it is currently hearing from two FAs, it can flip-flop between them each time it hears an advertisement. Changes only occur when a new FA is heard (and its hold down timer has expired.) For FAs heard on different interfaces, the mobile router selects the agent on the preferred interface, that is, the preferred path as described previously. Keep in mind that a FA is selected only after the hold down period, as described in the previous section. If the mobile router does change FAs, it sends a Mobile IP RRQ to its Home Agent.

Figure 7-6   *Mobile Router with Multiple Active Foreign Agents*

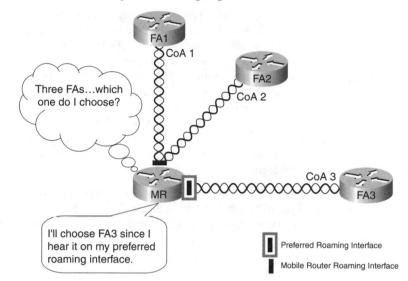

In addition to moving from one FA to another, and the typical reregistration to extend a mobility binding's lifetime, several other events trigger a mobile router to send a Mobile IP registration to its Home Agent. If the mobile router detects that its FA has rebooted, as described in Chapter 2, and thus has lost all its visitor information, the mobile router initiates a RRQ. If the mobile router doesn't hear from its current FA for a period of time and thus ages out, the mobile router registers through another FA, if one exists. Similarly, if the interface that is connected to the current FA goes down, the mobile router registers with another FA, if one exists. If the mobile router does not have a usable CoA, it transitions to an isolated state. If the mobile router is in an isolated state and then hears an advertisement from a FA, it also initiates a RRQ. The final way that registration is triggered is with the **clear ip mobile router registration** exec command. The following events trigger a RRQ:

- Roam to new FA
- FA ages out
- FA is rebooted
- Interface goes down
- Isolated MR hears FA
- **clear ip mobile router registration**

Regardless of the scenario, it is the mobile router's responsibility to maintain a valid mobility binding with its Home Agent whenever possible. Note that just as in standard Mobile IP, when the mobile router roams back home, it deregisters its mobility binding with its Home Agent and resumes standard operation.

Routing to and from the Mobile Router

At a risk of stating the obvious, the mobile router serves as the first-hop router for nodes that reside on mobile networks associated with the mobile router. For traffic that is originating on its mobile networks, the mobile router can either reverse-tunnel traffic to the Home Agent or forward traffic through the default gateway on the Foreign Network. To this end, the mobile router establishes a default route to its FA and sends all outgoing traffic through the FA. However, for traffic that must be reverse-tunneled, the mobile router first encapsulates the packets to the Home Agent, as shown in Figure 7-7(a). Specifically, for reverse tunneling, the mobile router creates a default route through a tunnel between itself and its Home Agent, and a host route to its Home Agent through the FA. Reverse tunneling should be used if the mobile network uses private addressing or if any routers between the mobile router and Home Agent use ingress filtering, and thus can drop packets that are not topologically correct.

For packets that are destined for nodes on its mobile networks, the mobile router receives an encapsulated packet from its Home Agent through the FA. The mobile router then decapsulates the tunneled packet to retrieve the original packet and forwards the packet to the appropriate node on its mobile network, as shown in Figure 7-7(b).

Figure 7-7   *Mobile Router Routing*

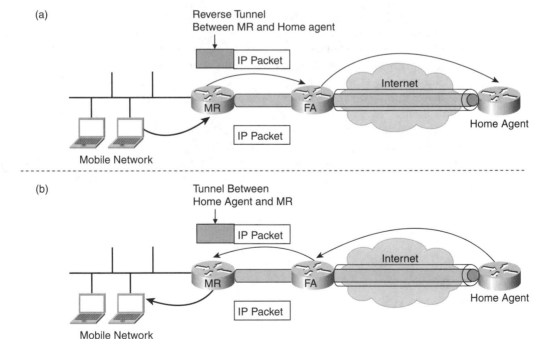

Home Agent Enhancements

The Home Agent receives and processes Mobile IP RRQs from the mobile router in the same way that it does for standard Mobile Nodes. Specifically, the Home Agent validates the RRQ and, upon validation, it establishes a mobility binding. In addition to the standard Mobile IP processing, the Home Agent must also "process" the mobile networks associated with the mobile router. Recall that a mobile network can either be statically configured on the Home Agent or dynamically learned in the RRQ. In either case, the Home Agent injects the mobile networks into its forwarding table so that routing protocols configured on it can redistribute these mobile routes.

If the mobile router registered dynamic mobile networks with the Home Agent, the Home Agent acknowledges proper processing of all the mobile networks to the mobile router. This is accomplished by the Home Agent appending the Mobile Router Dynamic Mobile Network NVSE to convey dynamic mobile networks and Mobile Router Static Mobile Network NVSE to convey static mobile networks to its RRP to the mobile router. If the Home Agent shares a security association with the FA, it also appends the FA–Home Agent Authentication Extension (FHAE) to the RRP. The Home Agent does not append all the NVSEs in a RRP for a deregistration message.

In addition to injecting the mobile networks, the mobile router also creates an additional tunnel to the mobile router's Home Address and adds routes to the mobile networks through this tunnel. The Home Agent then advertises reachability to these mobile networks through the Interior Gateway Routing Protocol (IGRP), thereby attracting packets that are destined to nodes on the mobile networks, as shown in Figure 7-8.

Thus, a key feature of network mobility is that inside the Home Agent CoA tunnel is another tunnel from the Home Agent to the mobile router. This second tunnel is required because if a FA is in use, it has a route only to the Home Address. Packets destined to the mobile networks would follow the standard routing back to the Home Agent and end up in a routing loop. Pictorially, this can be seen in Figure 7-9 and is described as follows. Consider a packet that is sent from a Correspondent Node (CN) to a node on one of the mobile router's networks. Because the Home Agent is injecting the mobile networks into the IGP, the packet is routed to the Home Agent using standard IP routing. The Home Agent receives the packet and realizes that it is destined for a node on a mobile network. Thus, the Home Agent encapsulates the packet in a tunnel from itself to the mobile router. For this tunneled packet to reach the mobile router, the packet must be encapsulated again to the mobile router's CoA. Figure 7-10 shows the IP header of a double-encapsulated packet from the Home Agent to the mobile router.

Figure 7-8 *Home Agent Advertises Reachability*

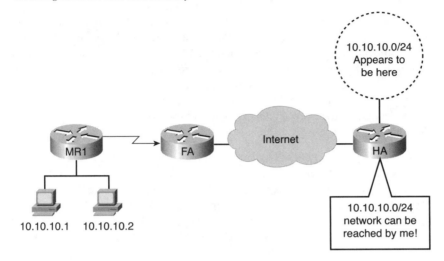

Figure 7-9 *Dual Tunnels Deliver Traffic to the Mobile Networks*

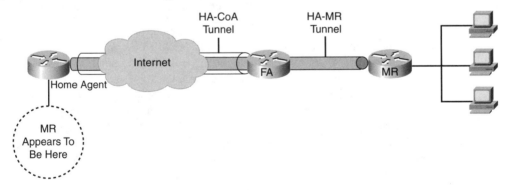

Figure 7-10 *Two Layers of Encapsulation*

HA-FA Tunnel		HA-MR Tunnel		Original Packet	
IP Sec= HA	IP Dest= FA CoA	IP SRC= HA	IP Dest= MR	IP SRC	IP Dest

HA double encapsulates original packet destined for node on mobile network.

NOTE	The Cisco Home Agent Redundancy feature, which provides fault tolerance on the Home Network is enhanced so that the Home Agents in the redundancy group are kept in sync with respect to dynamic mobile networks. Specifically, the active Home Agent updates the standby Home Agent with mobile networks that are registered dynamically.

Home Agent Configuration for Network Mobility

The Home Agent must first be configured to provide Home Agent services, as described in Chapter 4. In addition, the Home Agent must be configured appropriately for it to support the mobile networks associated with mobile routers. This includes configuring the Home Agent with the following command:

```
ip mobile host lower [upper] {interface name | virtual-network net mask} [lifetime
    number]
```

This configures the mobile router as a mobile host. This is the same configuration that would be used for a Mobile Node with a static Home Address. *lower* and *upper* are a range of IP addresses on the Home Network that are allowed to register as Mobile Nodes. The interface *name* option configures a physical connection from the Home Agent to the mobile router. The following command establishes that the mobile host (or range of hosts) is a mobile router:

```
ip mobile mobile-networks lower [upper]
```

The command enters the Home Agent into mobile networks configuration mode, where details about the mobile networks associated with the mobile router are configured. The *upper* range can be used only with dynamically registered networks and allows multiple mobile routers to be configured at once. This range does not need to match the range in the **ip mobile host** statement. This is useful if the network includes Mobile Nodes and mobile routers.

Within the mobile networks configuration mode on the Home Agent, the following configuration commands can be used to configure the mobile networks:

- **description** *string*—This optional command adds a description to the mobile router configuration.

- **network** *net mask*—This optional command statically configures a mobile network on the mobile router. Specifically, it configures a network that is attached to the mobile router as a mobile network.

- **register**—This optional command allows the mobile router to dynamically register mobile networks with the Home Agent. That is, the Home Agent is configured to accept RRQs with a Mobile Network Prefix Critical Vendor Specific Extension (CVSE) from the mobile router to learn about the mobile networks. When the mobile router registers its mobile networks on the Home Agent, the Home Agent looks up the mobile network configuration and verifies that the **register** command is configured before adding forwarding entries to the mobile networks. If the **register** command is not configured, the Home Agent rejects an attempt by the mobile router to dynamically register its mobile networks.

The Home Agent must be configured to share a security association with the mobile router and redistribute routes into its routing protocol.

Priority Home Agent Assignment

Although not an enhancement to the Home Agent per se, the Cisco Mobile Networks–Priority Home Agent Assignment feature allows a mobile router to select a "closer" Home Agent when it is roaming. However, the mobile router doesn't just choose a random Home Agent. Rather, the mobile router can select a preferred Home Agent from a set of configured Home Agents based on a combination of existing Home Agent priority configurations on the mobile router and CoA access lists configured on the Home Agent, as shown in Figure 7-11. Although this feature might sound like a dream come true, some caveats also need to be discussed.

Figure 7-11 *Priority Home Agent Assignment*

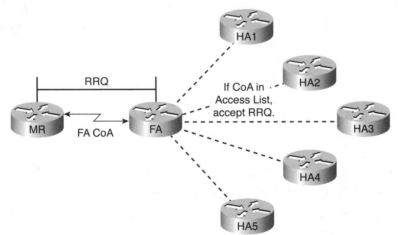

Each participating Home Agent is configured with an access list that contains the FA CoAs in its region. When a mobile router sends a RRQ to the selected Home Agent, the Home Agent consults its access list and either accepts or denies the request based on the CoA in the request. If the Home Agent denies the request because the CoA is outside its "domain," that is, the CoA is not in the access list, the mobile router tries to register with the next-best Home Agent, and so on. By doing so, the mobile router is able to register with a geographically closer Home Agent, thereby improving latency on the network.

A number of things must be considered when deploying priority Home Agents. Routing updates don't come free. When the mobile router registers with the new Home Agent, the new Home Agent injects the mobile networks associated with the mobile router into the IGP. Following the successful registration with the new Home Agent, the mobile router attempts to deregister from the old Home Agent so that the old Home Agent can withdraw the redistributed mobile network routes from the IGP. At this point, the IGP must converge before the forwarding path is optimized. While the IGP is reconverging, packets can bounce around the network following stale routes. In some cases, these packets can be lost.

With priority Home Agents, the Home Address of the mobile router must also not be used. The same Home Network needs to be configured on all Home Agents. However, you cannot make the Home Address reachable through the Home Agent that is in use without injecting host routes into the network. Host routing would defeat the purpose of Mobile IP. Use a route map to prevent the Home Network from even being redistributed into the IGP, and use an address from the mobile network for management of the mobile router.

Deployment of priority Home Agents on a large scale also requires careful evaluation of the impacts to the IGP. When large numbers of mobile routers are used in conjunction with many Home Agents, frequent routing updates can cause instability in the IGP. Try to avoid changing Home Agents too frequently. For example, if a train operator has many trains in several cities, but only a few trains ever cross from city to city, having one Home Agent per city would be ideal. In the same example, if multiple Home Agents were used in the same city, frequent Home Agent changes would force the IGP to reconverge frequently.

Foreign Agent Details

The FA does not need to be enhanced to support network mobility per se. However, a few minor enhancements can be made to the FA to provide more efficient communication.

Agent Discovery—Tuning IRDP Options

Mobile routers discover FAs using the same agent discovery process as described in Chapter 2. Recall that the Mobile IP agent discovery and move detection process is through ICMP Router Discover Protocol (IRDP). The IRDP parameters determine how often a FA sends out Mobile IP agent advertisements, and impact the behavior and efficiency of the network. Thus, you should tune the IRDP advertisement interval and holdtime to allow the expected behavior. The advertisement interval is configured by setting the minimum amount of time and maximum amount of time between a FA's advertisements.

If the desired behavior is to send agent advertisements only in response to a solicitation by a mobile router, set the advertisement interval and holdtime to 0 seconds. In contrast, the IRDP parameters can be tuned to optimize move detection by the mobile router. Tuning the advertisement interval can also preempt advertisement solicitations by the mobile router in this case.

The FA should be configured as described in Chapter 4. The IRDP parameters on an interface can then be tuned using the following interface-level subcommands:

- **ip irdp maxadvertinterval** *seconds*—This optional command specifies the maximum interval (in seconds) between FA advertisements. Typically, it is set at 10 seconds and adjusted accordingly.

- **ip irdp minadvertinterval** *seconds*—This optional command specifies the minimum interval (in seconds) between FA advertisements.

- **ip irdp holdtime** *seconds*—This optional command specifies the length of time (in seconds) that FA advertisements are considered valid. The default value is three times the maxadvertinterval period.

NOTE   A basic mobile router example showing most of the features discussed thus far, as well as basic troubleshooting techniques, can be found in Chapter 4.

Local Routing to Mobile Networks

In standard Mobile IP, traffic from a CN to a Mobile Node must traverse the Home Agent, as described in Chapter 2, as *triangle routing*. Said another way, a CN cannot communicate directly with the Mobile Node in its visiting location. Translated further to network mobility, it means that a CN cannot communicate directly with a mobile router or any of the nodes on the mobile networks even if the CN is directly connected to the FA.

An example clarifies our point. Consider the video surveillance camera of a bank that is being robbed. Police arrive on the scene in their vehicles equipped with a mobile router. The mobile router discovers a local FA and registers back to its police headquarters (Home Agent) through this FA. The mobile router connects to the video surveillance camera (CN) that is inside the bank. This scenario is depicted in Figure 7-12. As the video camera transmits its live streaming feed through its first-hop router (the FA), the packets are routed to the police headquarters and then tunneled back to the mobile router on the police car. Not only does this result in triangle routing, but it also consumes valuable bandwidth and ultimately provides the police officers with a lower-quality solution. If another police officer arrives and connects to the video camera, the bandwidth between the FA and Home Agent is even further strained. Now, it would be great if the FA (also the first-hop router of the surveillance camera) could somehow know that the video feed is being sent to a node on a mobile network of one of its visiting mobile routers.

Figure 7-12 *Police Headquarters Communicating with a Bank*

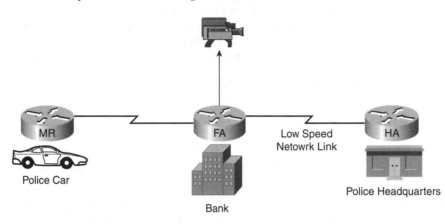

By using the Cisco FA Optimized Routing for Mobile Networks, the FA can directly send traffic from a CN that is directly connected to it to a node on a mobile network of one of its visiting mobile routers. Going back to the previous example, this means that because the video camera is directly connected to the FA, the FA could simply forward the video feed to the police officers, saving valuable time! Essentially, this feature is useful in scenarios in which the bandwidth between the Home Agent and the FA is limited, or in scenarios in which the mobile router receives high-bandwidth or time-sensitive traffic from a device on the Local Area Network (LAN) of the FA.

So, what does this need to work? It requires the FA to have knowledge of the mobile networks that are associated with a visiting mobile router. How is this accomplished? The FA cavesdrops as the mobile router registers its mobile networks, paying particular attention to a successful RRP from the Home Agent. This has the following implications:

- The FA can trust what the Home Agent is saying in the RRP.
- The FA can understand what the Home Agent is saying in the RRP.

Trust is easily obtained by the FA and Home Agent sharing a security association. Then, in addition to the Mobile Node–Home Agent Authentication Extension (MHAE), the Home Agent also secures such a RRP with the FHAE. When the FA receives the RRP, it can confidently trust information that it extracts from the reply. If the FA receives a RRP without the FHAE, it does not extract the information and, thus, does not provide the local optimized routing. Okay, one part down; now the FA needs to understand the information.

To this end, the FA needs to be enhanced to understand the Mobile Network NVSEs that are appended by the mobile router and Home Agent during the registration process. Specifically, the FA must parse the Mobile Router Static Mobile Network NVSE and Mobile Router Dynamic Mobile Network NVSE in a successful RRP to extract the network prefix and mask of the mobile networks associated with the visiting mobile router. After the FA gains knowledge of the mobile networks, it injects the mobile network routes into its forwarding table. Upon receiving a deregistration message, the FA can remove the routes from the forwarding table and any local data structures. The FA must associate the local routes (through local data structures) to the visitor entry for the mobile router. Moreover, because the FA is injecting the routes to the mobile networks into its forwarding table, the mobile networks must necessarily be nonoverlapping. Figure 7-13 shows the message flow for this local optimization.

Figure 7-13 *Foreign Agent Local Routing Message Flow*

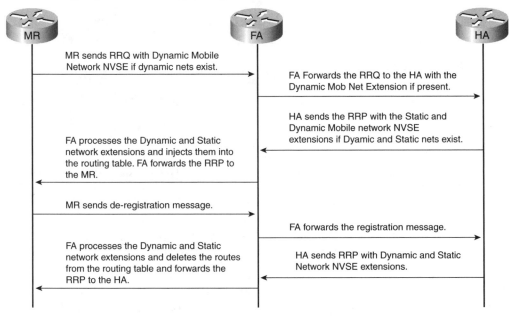

Configuration for Local Routing to Mobile Networks

The FA must first be configured to provide FA services, as described in Chapter 4. The FA can then be configured for the local route optimization as follows:

```
ip mobile foreign-agent inject-mobile-networks [mobnetacl access-list-identifier]
```

This command enables the local route optimization on the FA. The **mobnetacl** optional parameter allows an access control list (ACL) (simple or named) to be specified for controlling the mobile networks that the FA provides to the route optimization. Without an ACL, all learned mobile networks are injected into the local forwarding table.

Note that the FA and Home Agent must also be configured to share a security association, as described in Chapter 3, "Mobile IP Security."

Mobile Router Redundancy

A mobile router is the all-important "outdoor" link to the Internet for the nodes on its mobile networks. If the mobile router fails, the mobile networks are left in a precarious situation— without Internet connection and without another first-hop router with which to connect. Thus, it seems prudent that the mobile router should have the capability to be "backed up" in some way. Mind you, it is highly unlikely that a Cisco mobile router will fail, but it's better to be safe than sorry!

The Cisco Mobile Networks feature provides full redundancy capability for its mobile routers, as shown in Figure 7-14. Just like the Home Agent Redundancy feature, the Mobile Router Redundancy feature also uses the Hot Standby Router Protocol (HSRP) to provide the backup mechanism. A brief description of HSRP is given in Chapter 6, "Metro Mobility: Client-Based Mobile IP."

Figure 7-14   *Mobile Router Redundancy*

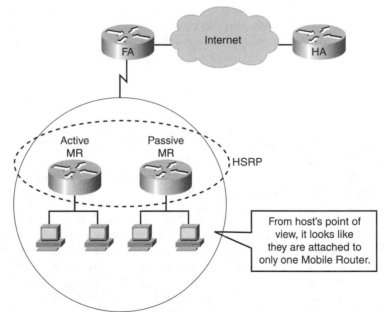

Recall that HSRP assigns one router in the HSRP group as the active router, and the other router in the group is considered a standby. The HSRP group attributes are defined on the interfaces of each mobile router in the redundancy group, enabling this selection. The active mobile router is the router responsible for registering with the Home Agent and maintaining an active mobility binding. If the active mobile router fails, the standby mobile router is selected as the new active mobile router. The new active mobile router seamlessly takes over with no loss of connectivity or traffic by the mobile networks. Specifically, upon becoming the active mobile router, a mobile router sends an agent solicitation out of its roaming interfaces to learn about the existing FAs, and it registers with its Home Agent.

The router must first be configured to provide mobile router service, as described in the section "Mobile Router Interface-Level Configuration," earlier in this chapter. While in mobile router configuration mode, the following configuration is needed to provide the redundancy feature:

```
redundancy group name (state)
```

This subcommand enables the Mobile Router Redundancy feature.

The HSRP does not need to be configured on both the mobile router's roaming interface and the interface attached to the physical mobile networks. It is enough to configure HSRP on one of the interfaces and the **standby track** command on the other interface.

Asymmetric Links

Mobile routers can be deployed on a number of entities, such as "planes, trains, and automobiles." Hey, sounds like a movie! Seriously though, because the range of deployment scenarios for mobile routers varies, some can find themselves in varied environments, including an asymmetric link situation in which one link sends traffic and another link receives traffic. This arises, for example, with some satellite links in which an uplink transmits traffic while a downlink receives traffic. The implication is that each link supports only one-way traffic, as shown in Figure 7-15.

If a mobile router and FA communicate through a satellite, this means that the FA receives the mobile router's RRQ on an interface that is *different* from the one on which it sent its agent advertisement. Also, it means that the FA forwards the RRP to the mobile router on an interface that is *different* from the one on which it received the RRQ. Because this is a departure from the way that Mobile IP normally works, modifications to the mobile router and FA are necessary to support these asymmetrical links. The modifications are what comprise the Cisco Asymmetric Link Support feature for network mobility.

The first issue to decide in designing the Asymmetric Link Support feature is where the FA should be located: on the path from the mobile router or on the path to the mobile router. Going back to the roots of network mobility and Mobile IP makes this question easy to answer. Because the Home Agent tunnels the mobile router's traffic to the FA, which in turn forwards the traffic to the mobile router, it's seams clear that the FA should be on the receiving path of the mobile router. In other words, because the FA is the tunnel endpoint with the Home Agent, it should be on the uplink path to the mobile router. The FA does not need to be on the mobile router's sending path, because the downlink router can always forward the packets to the FA.

Figure 7-15 *Asymmetric Links*

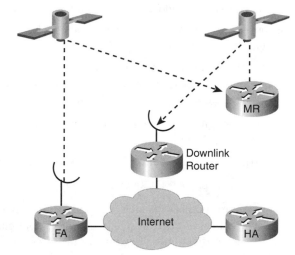

The FA maps a CoA to the interface that is connected to an uplink, and sends its periodic agent advertisements on the uplink. Note that a FA can have multiple uplinks. If a mobile router hears the agent advertisements on its uplink, it registers with that (CoA (FA) by sending a RRQ on its downlink. The downlink router then forwards the RRQ to the FA. Because the FA maps the CoA to the advertising interface, it treats the RRQ as if it received the request on that interface. The FA then processes the RRQ and forwards it to the Home Agent as normal. Upon receiving a RRP from the Home Agent, the FA forwards the reply to the mobile router out the proper CoA interface (or, uplink).

The special behavior just described does not preclude the standard Mobile IP and network mobility behavior. This means that the FA and mobile router can support any combination of symmetric (bidirectional) and asymmetric (unidirectional) links.

Configuration Needed for Asymmetric Links

The FA and mobile router must be configured appropriately to support asymmetric link behavior. This is largely accomplished with existing serial interface commands to configure unidirectional interfaces.

On the mobile router, the serial interfaces for the uplink (receive-only) and downlink (transmit-only) are configured as follows:

- **interface type** *number*—This command configures an interface type for the uplink. It enters interface configuration mode, where the matching downlink interface is specified.

- **transmit-interface** *type number*—This interface subcommand assigns a transmit interface (downlink) to the receive-only interface (uplink) to use.

- **ip address** *ip-address mask*—This command sets the primary IP address for the interface for the uplink. This is the IP address of the roaming interface.

- **ip mobile router-service roam**—This command enables the mobile router to discover FAs on this interface for the uplink.

The receive-only interface (uplink) is not configured to solicit for agent advertisements. The **transmit-interface** command must then be configured with the usual interface commands, for example, IP address and so on.

A new interface-level configuration option is introduced on the FA to map the CoA to the advertising uplink interface, as follows:

```
ip mobile foreign-agent [care-of interface [interface-only transmit-only]]
```

This interface subcommand enables FA service on the interface.

The **interface-only** keyword causes the interface type specified in the interface argument to advertise only its own address as the CoA. Other interfaces configured for FA service do not advertise this CoA. The **transmit-only** keyword informs Mobile IP that the interface acts as an uplink. Thus, for the registration process, RRQs received for this CoA are treated as having arrived on the **transmit-only** interface. Note that any CoA can be configured as **interface-only**, but only serial interfaces can be configured as **transmit-only**.

Typically, the advertising interface on the FA is configured to advertise more often to reduce latency when the mobile router roams to a new FA. This is accomplished with the IRDP interface-level commands detailed in the section "Agent Discovery—Tuning IRDP Options," earlier in this chapter. This becomes more important because the mobile router is configured to *not* solicit for advertisements in this environment.

Example of Asymmetric Link Behavior

Although the asymmetric link support might sound confusing and visions of a ball bouncing up and down might be floating in your head, an example should help to clarify things. Review Figure 7-16 to see how the Cisco Asymmetric Link Support feature for network mobility works. The mobile router and FA in Figure 7-16 are configured as described in Example 7-1.

Example 7-1 *Mobile Router Example Configuration*

```
!
interface Loopback1
 ip address 20.0.4.1 255.255.255.0
!
interface Serial3/0
! Uplink interface
 transmit-interface Serial3/1
 ! Specifies the matching transmit interface as Serial3/1
 ip address 11.0.0.1 255.255.255.0
 ip mobile router-service roam
!
```

Example 7-1   *Mobile Router Example Configuration (Continued)*

```
interface Serial3/1
! Downlink interface
 ip address 12.0.0.1 255.255.255.
 ip mobile router-service roam
!
router mobile
!
ip mobile secure home-agent 43.0.0.3 spi 100 key hex 11223344556677881122334455667788
ip mobile router
address 20.0.4.1 255.255.255.0
home-agent 43.0.0.3
```
Foreign Agent Example Configuration:
```
!
interface Serial4/0
! Uplink interface
 ip address 11.0.0.2 255.255.255.0
 ip irdp
 ip irdp maxadvertinterval 10
 ip irdp minadvertinterval 5
 ip irdp holdtime 30
 ip mobile foreign-service
!
router mobile
!
ip mobile foreign-agent care-of Serial4/0 interface-only transmit-only
```

In this example, the FA sends agent advertisements with CoA 11.0.0.2 out the uplink interface 11.0.0.2. The mobile router receives the advertisement on interface 11.0.0.1. The mobile router sends its RRQ with CoA 11.0.0.2 out interface 12.0.0.1, which is then received by the downlink router. The downlink router forwards the RRQ using normal IP routing to the FA. The FA treats the RRQ as if it were received on the CoA interface 11.0.0.2 and then forwards the request to the Home Agent as usual. Upon receiving the RRP from the Home Agent, the FA forwards the reply to the mobile router on the uplink 11.0.0.2.

Figure 7-16 *Asymmetric Link Example*

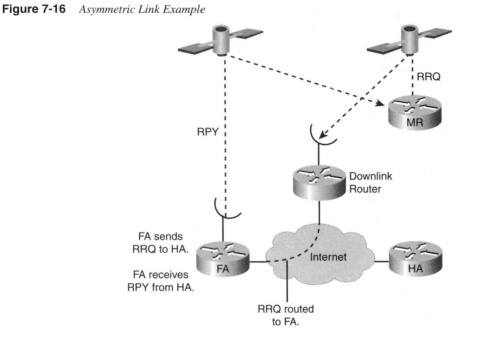

Colocated Care-of Address Support

Recall from Chapter 2 that two types of CoAs exist—a FA CoA and a CCoA. Thus far, this text has presented the network mobility model in which the mobile router roams with a FA CoA with the support of a FA. This section explores the situation in which FAs are not available, and thus, the mobile router can either wait for a FA or roam with a CCoA.

A CCoA is an IP address assigned to the interface of the mobile router itself. This address is usually dynamically obtained, for example, using Dynamic Host Configuration Protocol (DHCP) or Point-to-Point Protocol (PPP)/IP Control Protocol (IPCP), but can also be statically configured in special cases. The benefit of using a CCoA is that the mobile router can use Foreign Networks, where FAs are not available.

Static Colocated Care-of Address

The static CCoA is a special case and applies to networks in which the endpoint IP address is *always* fixed. Sometimes a static IP address can be acquired from mobile cellular service providers.

If you are using a static CCoA, the mobile router is configured with a static IP address (CoA) in the Foreign Network and a default gateway in the Foreign Network, if needed. This is accomplished with additional interface-level configuration on the interface, after the interface is configured to roam, as specified in the section "Mobile Router Interface-Level Configuration," earlier in this chapter. The following interface commands are needed on the roaming interface:

- **ip address** *ip-address mask*—This command sets a primary IP address for the interface. In this case, the IP address is the static CCoA.

- **ip mobile router-service roam**—This command enables roaming on an interface.

- **ip mobile router-service colocated** [**gateway** *ip-address*] —This interface subcommand enables static CCoA processing on the mobile router. The **gateway** IP address is the next-hop IP address for the mobile router to forward packets. The **gateway** IP address is required only on Ethernet interfaces, and must be on the same logical subnet as the primary interface address of this roaming interface.

- **ip mobile router-service colocated registration retry** *seconds*—This optional interface subcommand configures the time period that the mobile router waits before sending another RRQ after a registration failure.

Dynamic Colocated Care-of Address

This feature allows a mobile router to not only roam to a Foreign Network, where FAs are not available, but also allows the mobile router to dynamically obtain a CCoA. To accomplish this, the roaming interface on the mobile router is configured to allow the IPCP negotiation of the CCoA.

NOTE   Dynamic CCoAing on Ethernet using DHCP is supported on the Cisco Mobile Access Router (MAR) 3200 Series routers when using the WLAN Mobile Interface Card (WMIC). Generic support for DHCP CCoA is not available because, in most cases, Ethernet interfaces attach wireless bridging devices. When using bridging devices, no move detection information is available, and the router does not know when it needs to acquire a new address. The implementation on the 3200 Series routers uses Simple Network Management Protocol (SNMP) traps sent by the bridge for move detection. Documentation on this feature can be found in the 3200 section of Cisco.com.

The interface is first configured to roam as specified in the section "Mobile Router Interface-Level Configuration," earlier in this chapter, with additional subcommands as follows:

- **ip address negotiated**—This subcommand specifies that the IP address for a particular interface is obtained through IPCP address negotiation.

- **encapsulation ppp**—This subcommand enables PPP encapsulation on a specified serial interface.

- **ip mobile router-service roam**—This command enables roaming on an interface.

- **ip mobile router-service colocated**—This subcommand enables CCoA processing on a mobile router interface. The interface first solicits FA advertisements and registers with a FA CoA if an advertisement is heard. If no advertisements are received, the mobile router registers with the CCoA.

- **ip mobile router-service colocated registration retry** *seconds*—This optional subcommand configures the time period that the mobile router waits before sending another RRQ after a registration failure.

Dynamic CCoA using DHCP is a much harder problem to solve because it is often difficult for the router to determine when it has changed links. As discussed previously, when using many Ethernet-configured bridges, the interface is always up and the mobile router does not know when the bridge has associated with a new subnet. DHCP-based dynamic CCoA is supported on the Cisco 3200 Series routers when using the Wireless LAN Mobile Interface Card. The dynamic CCoA uses SNMP traps from the bridge to monitor the state of the radio interface. This feature receives *linkUp* and *linkDown* traps on the roaming interface from the Dot11Radio0 interface. A *linkUp* trap triggers to the interface to restart DHCP; a *linkDown* indicates that Mobile IP should select another interface. The following interface-level command, when coupled with the ip address dhcp command, causes the DHCP client to respond to Layer 2 information received through SNMP:

```
ip dhcp client mobile renew count count interval msec
```

Behavior Using Colocated Care-of Addresses

The mobile router can be configured to ignore FA advertisements on an interface with a CCoA, or it can be configured to use a CCoA only when a FA is not available.

In the latter case, when an interface comes up, the mobile router attempts to discover a FA on the link through the normal agent discovery process. If it succeeds in finding a FA, the mobile router registers using the advertised FA CoA and continues to do so as long as a FA is heard.

On the other hand, if a FA is not available, the mobile router enters into CCoA mode and the roaming interface registers its CCoA. If a FA is heard again, the mobile router reregisters with the FA CoA.

The desired behavior is accomplished through configuration. The roaming interface on the mobile router can be configured to register only its CCoA and ignore FA advertisements by using the following subinterface command:

```
ip mobile router-service colocated ccoa-only
```

This option defers to CCoA mode regardless of the availability of a FA.

The default behavior is for the mobile router to defer to a FA CoA, if one is available. Explicit configuration is required for the mobile router to ignore the FA advertisements.

When the mobile router registers back to its Home Agent with a CCoA, it registers in the same way that a Mobile Node would register. Specifically, it sets the D bit in its RRQ, as specified in Chapter 2.

When a mobile router is using a CCoA, only one tunnel transports all traffic, as opposed to the two tunnels needed when using a FA. The CCoA is then the remote endpoint of the tunnel between the Home Agent and mobile router. Upon decapsulation of a tunneled packet, the mobile router retrieves the original packet destined for a node on one of its mobile networks and forwards the packet. The mobile router uses this same tunnel to reverse-tunnel packets to the Home Agent, if configured.

Configuration Examples Using Colocated Care-of Addresses

Because examples serve us so well, we look at three sample configurations to obtain the desired CCoA behavior.

Example One: Mobile Networks with Static Colocated Care-of Address Only

In this configuration example, the mobile router is configured with a static CCoA. Furthermore, the mobile router is configured to use only the static CCoA and ignore FA advertisements heard on the interface.

```
! Static CCoA with CCoA-only option
interface Ethernet 1/0
 ip address 10.0.1.1 255.255.255.0
 ip mobile router-service roam
 ip mobile router-service colocated gateway 10.0.1.2 ccoa-only
 ip mobile router-service colocated registration retry 30
```

Example Two: Mobile Networks with Dynamic CCoA

In this configuration example, the mobile router is configured to dynamically obtain a CCoA through IPCP. However, the mobile router listens to FA advertisements heard on the interface and prefers a FA CoA, if one is available.

```
! Dynamic CCoA.
interface Serial 3/1
 ip address negotiated
 encapsulation ppp
 ip mobile router-service roam
 ip mobile router-service colocated
```

Example Three: Mobile Networks with Dynamic CCoA Only

In this example, the mobile router is configured to dynamically obtain a CCoA. Furthermore, the mobile router is configured to ignore FA advertisements and use only the dynamic CCoA.

```
! Dynamic CCoA with CCoA-only option
interface Serial 2/0
 ip address negotiated
 encapsulation ppp
 ip mobile router-service roam
 ip mobile router-service colocated ccoa-only
 ip mobile router-service colocated registration retry 30
```

Quality of Service

It is desirable to maintain quality of service (QoS) on traffic destined for nodes on a mobile router's mobile networks. In Mobile IP, the Home Agent copies the ToS (type of service) bits from the original IP header into the new Mobile IP tunnel header before forwarding the packet to the Mobile Node/mobile router. Theoretically, this should allow the QoS on the original packet to be maintained as the packet traverses the Mobile IP tunnel. However, theory is not always reality. In reality, the encapsulated packet looks different from the original packet and, thus, can cause transit routers to change the ToS/QoS bits in the tunnel header.

Here is a case and point: Consider a network in which voice traffic receives the highest priority, as shown in Figure 7-17. When such a voice packet arrives at the Home Agent and is forwarded to the Mobile IP tunnel interface, the ToS/QoS bits are copied into the encapsulated packet before being forwarded to the mobile router. But, unsuspecting transit routers can interpret the packets as IP-in-IP packets instead of the high-priority voice packets that they really are and, thus, can modify the ToS/QoS bits. Yes, it sounds a bit rude, but this is the reality. Moreover, during the encapsulation process, the Home Agent loses information that it needs to properly carry out QoS features that require flow information on the outbound interface. If only there were a way to preserve the QoS credentials across the Mobile IP tunnel...

Figure 7-17   *Integration of QoS and Mobile IP*

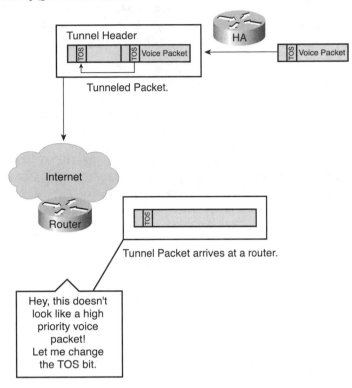

Because Mobile IP tunnels are created dynamically, QoS interface-level configuration on the tunnel interface is not feasible. Instead, tunnel interface templates, as shown in Figure 7-18, add the QoS features on the dynamic tunnels established between the Home Agent and FA, and the dynamic tunnels generated between the Home Agent and mobile router.

Figure 7-18   *Tunnel Template*

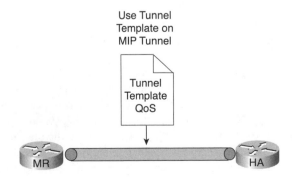

continues

NOTE	A tunnel template allows attributes to be applied to a particular tunnel when it is created. Essentially, a tunnel template is created, and a mapping is established with the tunnel template and a particular type of tunnel that says, "When this type of tunnel is created, apply this tunnel template to the tunnel."

In this manner, QoS preclassification (the **qos-preclassify** command) can be applied to the tunnel, allowing the original packet header to classify the packet on the outbound interface instead of the Mobile IP tunnel header. It lets the router peek into the original packet and use the QoS credentials of that packet, allowing certain traffic types to receive preferential treatment over the Mobile IP tunnel. The feature is applied dynamically to the Home Agent mobile router tunnel when it is created on the mobile router.

Example 7-2 shows how the tunnel template can be applied on the mobile router and Home Agent.

Example 7-2   *Tunnel Template Configuration on the Mobile Router*

```
interface Tunnel50
        no ip address
!Turn on Qos Pre-Clasification
        qos pre-classify
!
ip mobile router
!Tunnel template to use for Mobile IP Tunnels
        template Tunnel50
Tunnel Template Configuration on Home Agent:
interface Tunnel100
        no ip address
!Turn on Qos Pre-Clasification
        qos pre-classify
!
!Define Mobile Node 65.1.1.1 as a mobile router
ip mobile mobile-networks 65.1.1.1
!Define template to use when creating tunnel to MR
        template Tunnel100
```

IPSec and the Mobile Router

Last, but by no means least, is integration of IPSec into the mobile router solution. In Chapter 6, you learned that Mobile IP and IPSec complement each other and you saw some of the specific considerations for their deployment. Now it is time to address the piece that was previously not covered: the Mobile Node. In many mobile router deployments, the network is treated like a mobile branch office. In this case, all nodes attached to the mobile network would be expected to communicate with an enterprise-based application without each node establishing a VPN session. In a branch office scenario, the edge router would establish a VPN tunnel across the corporate network. The same can be done with a mobile router. Figure 7-19 shows how the mobile router runs IPSec over Mobile IP. The Home Agent is outside the private network, and the termination of the IPSec tunnel is handled by a VPN device that straddles the internal and external networks. This is a simplified example. In reality, this solution is easily integrated into standard DMZ architectures by placing the Home Agent on the Demilitarized Zone (DMZ) and using existing VPN concentrators.

Figure 7-19   *Mobile Router with IPSec*

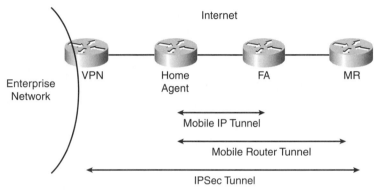

Configuration of IPSec on the mobile router is different from standard IPSec configuration. IOS IPSec encapsulation happens on the egress interface of the router. However, because the mobile router changes the interface on which packets are sent out, and those interfaces might not have valid addresses, you cannot configure IPSec directly. The trick is to use the loopback interface on which the Home Address is configured. Because the Home Address is constant and always available, it is the ideal address to use for the IPSec endpoint. To do this, however, all packets must egress that interface. Fortunately, loopback interfaces do just that; they loop traffic back. That is, traffic sent out a loopback interface comes back in and is passed through standard routing again. To take advantage of this functionality, the "set interface" target of policy routing takes all traffic coming in from the mobile network and "loops it back" through the loopback interface. With the crypto map applied to the loopback interface, all traffic is encrypted and then sent back in for standard forwarding. At this point, the encrypted traffic is forwarded through the FA or more likely through a reverse tunnel. From an inbound perspective, traffic is decrypted automatically when it reaches the mobile router.

Example 7-3 shows the configuration for a mobile router running IPSec. It is beyond the scope of this book to cover the configuration of IPSec, but the crypto map is applied to the loopback and the route map that is used for policy routing.

Example 7-3   *Mobile Router Running IPSec*

```
hostname MobileRouter
!
crypto isakmp policy 15
 hash md5
```

continues

Example 7-3 *Mobile Router Running IPSec (Continued)*

```
  group 2
  lifetime 5000
 !
crypto isakmp policy 20
 authentication pre-share
 lifetime 10000
crypto isakmp key 1234567890 address 192.168.101.1
 !
 !
crypto ipsec transform-set ts1 esp-des esp-sha-hmac
 !
crypto map tocorp 10 ipsec-isakmp
 set peer 192.168.101.1
 set transform-set ts1
 match address 101
 !
interface Loopback0
 description Home Address
 ip address 192.168.50.1 255.255.255.255
 no ip mroute-cache
 crypto map tocorp
 !
interface FastEthernet0/1
 decription Mobile Network
 ip address 192.168.30.1 255.255.255.0
 ip policy route-map cryptotraffic
 duplex auto
 speed auto
 !
interface FastEthernet1/0
 description Roaming Interface
 ip address 192.169.200.2 255.255.255.0
 ip mobile router-service roam
 ip mobile router-service solicit
 duplex half
 !
interface FastEthernet2/0
 description Roaming Interface
 no ip address
 ip mobile router-service roam priority 10
 ip mobile router-service solicit
 duplex half
 !
router mobile
 !
ip mobile secure home-agent 192.168.101.2 spi 100 key ascii cisco
ip mobile router
```

Example 7-3   *Mobile Router Running IPSec (Continued)*

```
 address 192.168.50.1 255.255.255.0
 home-agent 192.168.101.2
 !
 !
 access-list 101 permit ip 192.168.30.0 0.0.0.255 192.168.100.0 0.0.0.255
 !
 route-map cryptotraffic permit 10
  match ip address 101
  set interface Loopback0
 !
 end
```

Summary

This chapter introduced the notion of network mobility using an IOS Cisco mobile router. It looked at the basic mobile router functionality, including static and dynamic mobile networks. Roaming interface features were discussed, as well as agent selection and routing to/from the mobile router and its mobile networks. The chapter also considered enhancements to the Home Agent and FA to support network mobility. Furthermore, the chapter discussed some advanced features that optimize the behavior in network mobility, including local routing to the mobile networks and mobile router redundancy. Throughout, the chapter gave insights into the practical issues that can arise in deployment.

Thus far, the book has discussed IOS Mobile IP features in the context of specific deployment scenarios and applications, that is, campus mobility, metro mobility, and network mobility. In the next chapter, we look at some of the features that arc separate from a mobility scenario and present alternate deployment options. We look at the impacts of Home Address management and scalability in a Mobile IP deployment and discuss common troubleshooting techniques.

Review Questions

1   Cisco Mobile Networks is a mobility solution that provides which of the following? (Select three.)

   a   Dynamic host routing propagation to clients on the mobile router.

   b   The devices connected to the mobile router do not need to be Mobile IP aware because the MR is providing the roaming capabilities.

   c   FA redundancy for transparent FA failure between the mobile router and FA.

   d   Packets destined to the mobile router are double encapsulated. The Home Agent forwards packets destined to the mobile networks to the FA, which then forwards the packets to the mobile router, which then forwards to the devices on its networks.

   e   It allows entire network(s) to roam.

2 In network mobility, how does the Home Agent know which mobile networks are connected to a mobile router?

3 What is the roaming interface?

4 What is the preferred path feature, and why is it needed?

5 What is the hold down period? Describe its purpose.

6 Draw a diagram showing routing to and from a mobile router.

7 What additional processing over standard Mobile IP must the Home Agent do to support network mobility?

8 Draw a diagram depicting the dual tunnels used in network mobility.

9 For IOS Mobile Networks, why is another tunnel needed inside the standard Home Agent CoA tunnel?

10 What is the Priority Home Agent Assignment feature?

11 What caveats are involved with using the Priority Home Agent Assignment feature?

12 By using the Cisco FA Optimized Routing for Mobile Networks, the FA can do which of the following?

    a It can directly set up a visitor entry between a node on a visiting mobile router and a CN, and tunnel traffic to the CN.

    b It can directly receive traffic from a CN and tunnel the traffic to a visiting mobile router.

    c It can directly send traffic from a CN that is directly connected to it, to a node on a mobile network of one of its visiting mobile routers.

    d It can directly send traffic from a node on one of its visiting mobile routers to a node on another visiting mobile router.

13 Briefly describe the Mobile Router Redundancy feature.

14 Mobile IP traffic is sent on one link and received on another link in which of the following?

    a Nested Mobile IP tunnels

    b Asymmetric links

    c Bidirectional links

    d Simultaneous bindings

15 How are QoS features added to the dynamic tunnels established in network mobility, that is, the tunnel between the Home Agent and FA, and the tunnel between the Home Agent and mobile router?

CHAPTER 8

Deployment Scalability and Management

The previous chapters covered IOS Mobile IP deployment in the context of specific applications, for example, corporate intranet, client mobility, and network mobility. In those specific applications, we presented features that fit the need of the application. This chapter looks at some of the features separately, presenting various options that can be used in place of those discussed in previous examples.

Home Address management is one of the more flexible features of IOS Mobile IP and has been presented in parts thus far. Essentially, we know that a Mobile Node/router must have a Home Address to complete the registration process. But where did it come from, and who gave it to the Mobile Node? This chapter examines all the Home Address options and describes how they work together.

At some point, it was inevitable that the S word would come up—*scalability*. Just as you cannot discuss Lance Armstrong without mentioning the Tour de France, you cannot discuss networks without discussing scalability and management. To this end, this chapter addresses scaling issues as well as network management options. It also introduces the concept of a call model as a network-planning tool. Specific details related to both fault management and performance monitoring are presented. Finally, the chapter examines the common problems found in the deployment of Mobile IP and presents viable solutions.

Management of the Mobile Nodes Home Address

IOS Mobile IP supports the following methods of home addressing:

- Static addressing without Network Access Identifier (NAI)
- Static addressing with NAI
- Dynamic addressing with NAI

Static addressing is the original addressing style from Request For Comment (RFC) 2002. Static addresses are preconfigured on the Mobile Node and are the only unique identifier for the Mobile Node. The benefit of static addressing is simply that it provides a permanent reachable IP address, as discussed in the section "Static Home Addressing Without NAI," later in this chapter. However, as one would guess, static addresses do not lend themselves well to scalability, simply because each Mobile Node must be preconfigured with a Home Address.

However, static addresses can also be used with an NAI. You might be asking yourself, "Well, what's the benefit of using a static Home Address and an NAI?" The section "Static Home Addressing with NAI," later in this chapter, tackles this question, but here is a glimpse of the behavior. When used together, the NAI serves as the unique identifier for the Mobile Node, and the static Home Address is verified for use by that particular NAI. The Mobile Node proposes the configured Home Address as a nonzero Home Address in the Registration Request (RRQ) message, and the Home Agent verifies that the Mobile Node can indeed use the Home Address based on its NAI. The Home Agent can accept this address or return another address in the Registration Reply (RRP) message if that Home Address is not acceptable, for example, if it is currently in use by another Mobile Node.

Dynamic addressing with NAI is the most flexible and commonly used option. Dynamic addressing can be truly dynamic where the Mobile Node gets a random address upon initial registration. Dynamic addressing can also allocate the Mobile Node the same IP address all the time, which is commonly referred to as *fixed addressing*. This provides the benefits of static addressing, but leaves flexibility to change the address without making changes on the Mobile Node.

The flow chart in Figure 8-1 shows the order in which the different addressing options are evaluated for a RRQ with an NAI extension. The most commonly used home addressing mechanisms are the static Home Address with NAI, and dynamic addressing from Dynamic Host Configuration Protocol (DHCP) and local pool.

Virtual Networks

All Home Addresses, regardless of how they are allocated, must be associated with a Home Network that is attached to a Home Agent. The Home Network is the prefix that aggregates the Mobile Nodes. In IOS, the Home Network can be associated with an interface or it can be configured in Mobile IP as a virtual network.

It is often assumed that the Home Network should be a physical network. However, in many deployment cases, it does not make sense to have each Mobile Node attached to a physical network, because the two are never physically attached. Instead, it makes sense to have the Mobile Nodes reside on a virtual network, a "technical dreamland," if you will. When using virtual networks, the Mobile Node is always considered to be roaming; it can never be attached to its Home Network. In real-world deployments, this can cause some semantic problems. For example, in cellular deployment, users might be in their home calling area but are roaming from a Mobile IP perspective.

A virtual network is similar to a loopback interface, but it is owned by the Mobile IP process. Virtual networks are configured on the Home Agent and referenced by a network number and mask pair as follows:

```
ip mobile virtual-network net mask [address address]
```

Figure 8-1   *Home Address Processing Flow for Initial RRQ*

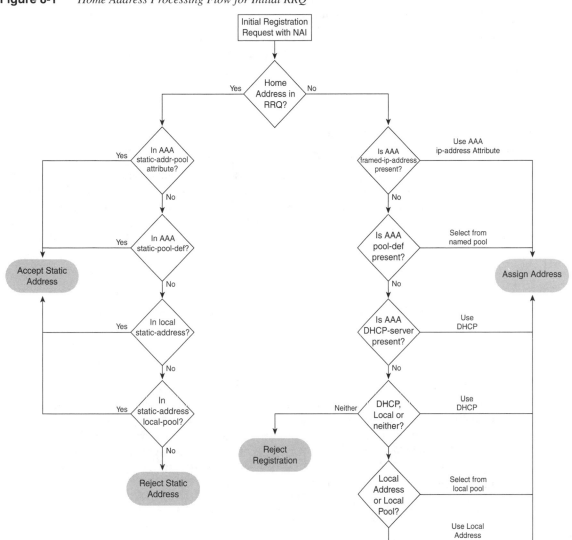

This Home Agent command defines the virtual network with IP address *net* and prefix mask ma*sk*. The optional parameter, *address*, specifies the IP address of a Home Agent on a virtual network and must also be configured on a loopback interface with a 32-bit mask.

After the virtual network is defined on the Home Agent, Mobile Nodes can be configured to reside on the virtual network using the following command. (The *ip mobile host* command has numerous options, and these options are presented in the appropriate sections throughout the chapter.)

```
ip mobile host {lower [upper]} virtual-network net mask
```

This Home Agent command configures one or more mobile hosts to reside in the specified virtual network on the Home Agent.

Virtual network routes are owned by the Mobile IP routing process and therefore must be redistributed into other routing protocols to be propagated. This can be accomplished with the following commands:

```
router rip
  redistribute mobile
```

Static Home Addressing Without NAI

The original Mobile IP specification supported only static addressing of Mobile Nodes. The Home IP Address served as the *user name* portion for the authentication when used with an IOS authentication, authorization, and accounting (AAA) server. Static addressing in itself is beneficial because it allows each device to keep the same address all the time, no matter where it is attached to the network. This allows the user to run mobile-terminated services without updating DNS or some other form of address resolution. Mobile Nodes are also easily managed with static addressing because the Home Address and the Home Agent always remain the same.

However, as a tradeoff, provisioning and maintenance are more difficult because address allocation must be handled manually, and both the Home Agent and Mobile Node must be updated when changes occur. Configuration of Mobile Node Home Addresses on the Home Agent can be done using either an individual address or a range of addresses to represent the Mobile Nodes as follows:

```
ip mobile host {lower [upper]} interface name
```

This Home Agent command configures a single Mobile Node or a group of Mobile Nodes on an interface. If only one address is specified, a single Mobile Node is configured; if *lower* and *upper* are configured, all addresses between and including *lower* and *upper* are configured as Mobile Nodes. The following Home Agent command sets up the mandatory security association between the Home Agent and the Mobile Nodes. It specifies the security parameter index (SPI) value and security key.

```
ip mobile secure host lower-address [upper-address]{inbound-spi spi-in outbound-
  spi spi-out | spi spi} key hex string
```

Dynamic Home Address Assignment

As with most things, real-world experience proved static Mobile Node addressing difficult to deploy. RFC 2794 specifies that if the Mobile Node uses an NAI extension in the RRQ, it can set its Home Address field to 0.0.0.0 or 255.255.255.255. In this case, the Home Agent assigns it an address to use for the duration of its Mobile IP session. The allocated Home Address is returned in the Home Address field of the RRP.

NOTE   A Mobile IP session begins with the first RRQ and ends either with the expiration of the binding lifetime or a deregistration message. When the session ends, the dynamic Home Address is returned. For this reason dynamic home addressing can only be used in scenarios where the Mobile Node is always roaming. Dynamic home addressing is often coupled with virtual networks to eliminate the possibility of returning home.

When the Home Agent receives a RRQ requesting a dynamic Home Address, it assigns a Home IP Address to the Mobile Node. IOS Mobile IP provides several options for address assignment by the Home Agent.

Fixed Addressing on the Command-Line Interface (CLI)

You can configure the Home Agent with a fixed Home IP Address for each NAI. The fixed address is assigned to the Mobile Node each time it starts a new session, as shown in Figure 8-2. It doesn't sound very dynamic because the same address is being assigned each time. It falls into somewhat the same category as "Have your cake and eat it too."

Figure 8-2   *Fixed Addressing with NAI*

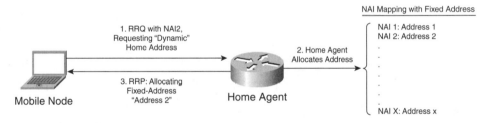

Fixed addressing with an NAI provides users all the benefits of static addressing, as described in the section "Static Home Addressing Without NAI," earlier in this chapter, while simplifying the configuration of the Mobile Node. The Mobile Node need only be configured with an NAI and security association, and any administrative changes to the address are transparent to the Mobile Node.

Fixed addressing on the CLI is ideal for lab environments because it is self-contained. However, it is not ideal for large-scale deployment because the Home Agent configuration must be updated to perform all maintenance.

A fixed Home Address is specified in the Home Agent configuration using the **address** keyword of the **ip mobile host** command, as follows:

```
ip mobile host nai string address addr interface name
```

This Home Agent command sets up a Mobile Node with an NAI and fixed Home Address on a particular interface. This command cannot be used when a group of nodes is being referenced.

Local Pool Address Assignment

Numerous IOS components, including Dial and Network Address Translation (NAT), use local pools to specify a group of addresses available for dynamic assignment. The same concept can be used with Mobile IP. Local pool assignment requires that one or more address pools be configured on the Home Agent. The Home Agent then allocates addresses from the pool on a first come, first served basis, as shown in Figure 8-3(a).

Figure 8-3   *Home Address Allocation Through Local Pool*

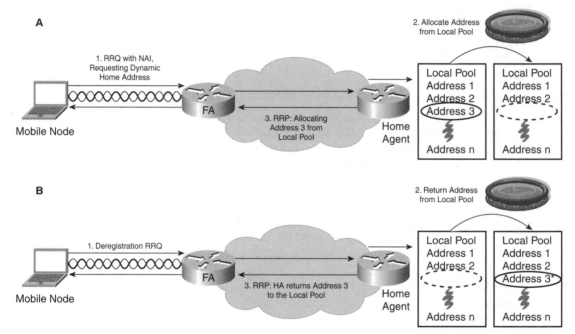

The Mobile Node keeps the address as long as it has an active mobility binding on the Home Agent. The Mobile Node can update its binding by sending a RRQ with either the allocated address or 0.0.0.0 as its Home Address. When the binding expires or the Mobile Node deregisters, the address is immediately returned to the local pool so that it can be assigned again, as shown in Figure 8-3(b). The number of local pools that can be configured on the Home Agent is limited only by the available memory on the router. Configuration is as follows:

```
ip local pool poolname low-ip-address [high-ip-address]
```

This Home Agent command defines the local pool and the range of IP addresses in the pool. All addresses between and including low-ip-address and high-ip-address are part of the local pool. If the high-ip-address parameter is missing, the pool consists of a single IP address, as follows:

```
ip mobile host nai string address pool local name {interface name | virtual-network
  network-address mask}
```

This Home Agent command instructs the Home Agent to accept registrations for a Mobile Node with the specified NAI. The Mobile Node is allocated a Home Address from a local pool. The Mobile Node can reside on an interface or reside on a virtual network.

NOTE   Currently, local pool allocation cannot be used with the Home Agent Redundancy feature.

DHCP-Based Address Assignment

The DHCP is already widely used in allocating IP addresses for desktop computers. IOS Mobile IP leverages the existing DHCP proxy client in IOS to allow the Home Address to be allocated by a DHCP server, as shown in Figure 8-4. Essentially, the Home Agent obtains an address through DHCP on behalf of the Mobile Node.

Figure 8-4   *Home Address Allocation Through DHCP*

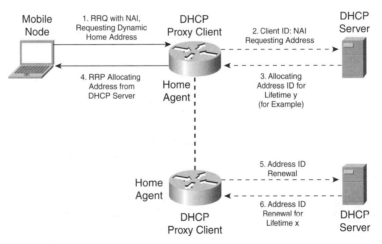

*Home Agent renews address while Mobile Node has an active mobility b

The DHCP proxy client allows the Home Agent to maintain the DHCP lease by tracking the lease time for each Mobile Node and renewing the lease while that Mobile Node still has an active binding. The NAI is sent in the Client-ID option and can provide dynamic DNS services. Proxy DHCP configuration on the Home Agent is as follows:

```
ip mobile host nai string address pool dhcp-proxy-client dhcp-server addr
    interface name
```

This Home Agent command sets up a Mobile Node with an NAI on an interface. A Home Address is allocated through DHCP.

AAA

Dynamic addressing from a AAA server allows the operator to support fixed and/or per-session dynamic addressing for Mobile Nodes without the trouble of maintaining addressing at the Mobile Node or Home Agent. The AAA server can return either a specific address, a local pool name, or a DHCP server address. If the AAA server is being used to return a specific address, the Home Address can either be configured as an attribute on the user entry in the Remote Authentication Dial-In User Service (RADIUS) database or can be allocated from a pool, depending on the capabilities of the AAA server. Not all RADIUS servers support per-session allocation, but fixed addressing should be available in all servers.

Configuration and use of a AAA server at the Home Agent is covered in detail in Chapter 5, "Campus Mobility: Client-Based Mobile IP." However, we reiterate the difference between authentication and authorization in IOS. The home addressing attributes are sent as authorization attributes. Before authorization attributes are returned, AAA authentication must be achieved for each request. The three ways this can be accomplished are through MN-authentication, authorization, and accounting (MN-AAA) authorization, authentication with the default password, or null password authentication.

AAA Address Assignment

When the AAA server allocates a specific Home IP Address for the Mobile Node, it must return the IP address in a RADIUS Framed-IP-Address attribute, as shown in Figure 8-5(a). The Framed IP Address attribute is commonly used in other protocols, including dial-up, and should be widely supported. If the RADIUS server assigns a dynamic per-session Home IP Address, RADIUS accounting for Mobile IP must be enabled. The accounting start/stop records are required to ensure that addresses can be returned to the pool after the Mobile IP session is torn down.

The configuration for accounting shown here allows the Home Agent to send session start and session stop messages to the AAA server so that it knows when the address can be returned to the pool:

```
aaa accounting ipmobile
ip mobile home-agent accounting
```

AAA-Based Local Pool Selection

AAA servers often track service subscriptions or groups of users. Using this information, you can then assign a specific type of IP address to a Mobile Node without the need for IP address pool configuration to be synchronized between the Home Agent and AAA server. The AAA server is configured to return the name of a specific local pool from which the Mobile Node's Home Address should be allocated, as shown in Figure 8-5(b). The Home Agent then allocates the Home Address from the specified local pool.

Figure 8-5   *Home Address Allocation Through AAA*

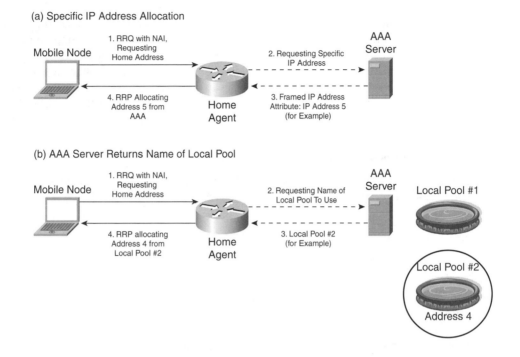

(a) Specific IP Address Allocation

(b) AAA Server Returns Name of Local Pool

A common example would be if users had the option of paying for a private address or a public address. The AAA server keeps track of this information and simply informs the Home Agent of the name of the local pool from which to allocate the Home Address. Each local pool can be configured as follows:

```
ip local pool poolname low-ip-address [high-ip-address]
```

This Home Agent command sets up the local pool and range of IP addresses in the pool, as described in the section "Local Pool Address Assignment," earlier in this chapter.

A RADIUS attribute is defined as follows:

```
Cisco-AVPair = "mobileip:pool-def=poolname"
```

This RADIUS attribute allows the AAA server to return a local pool name in the AV pair.

AAA-Assigned DHCP Server

The AAA server can also assign a DHCP server IP address. This is the same attribute that is configured as part of the **ip mobile host dhcp-proxy-client** command. When using this attribute, all mobiles nodes that share a Home Network must use the same DHCP server so that no conflict exists in address assignment.

```
Cisco-AVPair = "mobileip:dhcp-server=10.1.5.10"
```

Static Home Addressing with NAI

A static Home Address that is preconfigured on the Mobile Node can also be used in conjunction with NAI to support NAI-based authorization and other services. You can also allow an NAI to use multiple static IP addresses, either on the same device or multiple devices, while maintaining only one AAA record and security association. If the Home Agent receives a RRQ with a static Home Address and NAI, it authorizes the use of that address using either local or AAA-based authorization attributes, as depicted in Figure 8-6. If a Mobile Node requests an address for which a binding is already associated with a different NAI, the Home Agent attempts to return another address from the pool, unless the **reject-static-addr** command is set, as follows:

```
ip mobile home-agent reject-static-addr
```

This command configures the Home Agent to reject RRQs from Mobile Nodes if the Home Address in the request is already in use by another Mobile Node. Not all Mobile Nodes support this behavior.

Local Authorization of Static Home Addresses

A static address can be authorized on a per-Mobile Node or per-realm basis using configuration commands. Per-Mobile Node configurations require a specific NAI, in the form user or user@realm, to be defined and allow up to five addresses or a pool per NAI. The Mobile Node is authorized to use any address specified either explicitly or in the local pool. The following Home Agent command sets up a Mobile Node with an NAI on an interface:

```
ip mobile host nai string [static-address {addr1 [addr2] [addr3] [addr4] [addr5]
 | local-pool name}] interface name
```

The Mobile Node is allocated one of the static addresses that is configured or is allocated an address from the local pool specified.

Per-realm configurations require a generic NAI to be configured in the form @realm and allow only the specification of a local pool. The configuration for per-realm and per-NAI local pool is the same, except for the NAI specification, as shown here:

```
ip local pool poolname low-ip-address [high-ip-address]
```

The following command defines the local pool and the range of IP addresses in the pool, as described in the section "Local Pool Address Assignment," earlier in this chapter:

```
ip mobile host nai string static-address local-pool name interface name
```

This command associates a Mobile Node with an NAI on an interface. The Mobile Node is allocated a static address from a local pool.

Figure 8-6   *Static Home Address Authorization with NAI*

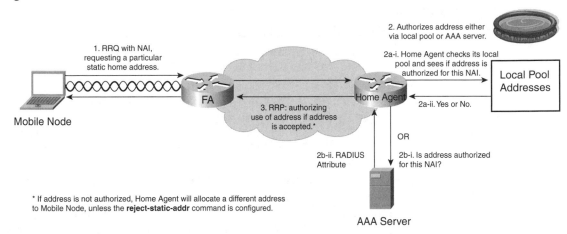

AAA Authorization of Static Home Addresses

You can also store either the authorized addresses or local pool name in a AAA server. Each user must have either the **static-addr-pool** attribute or the **static-pool-def** attribute configured in the AAA server. Unlike the static address configuration on the command line, the **static-addr-pool** attribute is not limited in the number of addresses that can be returned.

The configuration on the Home Agent is as follows:

ip local pool poolname *low-ip-address* [*high-ip-address*]

The following Home Agent command defines the local pool and the range of IP addresses in the pool, as described in the section "Local Pool Address Assignment," earlier in this chapter:

ip mobile host nai *string* **interface** *name* **aaa**

The following Home Agent commands associate a Mobile Node with an NAI on an interface. The Mobile Node is allocated a static address through AAA.

Cisco-AVPair = "mobileip:static-addr-pool = address(es) "
Cisco-AVPair = "mobileip:static-pool-def = poolname"

These RADIUS attributes allow the AAA server to return an authorized address for the Mobile Node or a local pool name.

To make it clearer, we present Examples 8-1 and 8-2.

Example 8-1   *Home Agent Configuration*

```
ip local pool static-pool 10.0.0.5 10.0.0.10
ip mobile host nai user@staticuser.com interface FastEthernet0/0 aaa
ip mobile host nai @static.com interface FastEthernet0/0 aaa
```

Example 8-2 *Radius Attributes*

```
Cisco-AVPair = "mobileip:static-addr-pool=10.0.0.1 10.0.0.2 10.0.0.3"
Cisco-AVPair = "mobileip:static-pool-def=static-pool"
```

Scaling Issues

Some of the most commonly asked questions about IOS Mobile IP are directly related to the scalability of Mobility Agents. As luck would have it, these questions are also the most difficult to answer. Seemingly simple questions such as "How many users can platform X support?" cannot be answered until numerous other questions are asked and answered. Scalability of Mobility Agents is best thought of like a balloon, as shown in Figure 8-7. An uninflated balloon can be stretched far in any direction, but when you inflate the balloon, it can never stretch so far. The same goes for Mobility Agents. For example, you can max out the number of bindings on a Mobility Agent (Mobility Agent or you can max out traffic forwarding, but when you put everything together, each piece impacts the other, and you never see the isolated maximums. Mobility Agent scaling in IOS depends on the following four main factors:

- Number of Mobile Nodes
- Frequency of movement of the Mobile Nodes
- Number of tunnels
- Amount of traffic that is being forwarded

Building a Call Model

The best approach to addressing scalability concerns is to build a call model and then apply it in lab testing. *Call model* is a term borrowed from the voice world that is similar to a traffic model, but more encompassing. A traffic model would simply identify how many bits each user would pass across the network in a given period of time. Although this is an important factor in the call model, you must also take other factors into account.

Call models are generally built toward the busy hour. The idea is that humans are creatures of habit, and in many cases, our habits are similar to those around us. The hour when all users are at their most active is referred to as the *busy hour*. From a network engineering perspective, if enough capacity exists in the busy hour, enough capacity is available all day long. A one-hour window is chosen because with a large number of users, it provides a good tradeoff between instantaneous and average use.

NOTE   The tradeoff between instantaneous and average use is a common problem in systems analysis. It is often seen in link utilization. For example, consider quantifying the percentage utilization of a specific link between two routers. If the measurement interval is instantaneous, the link is either in use (100%) or not in use (0%). These are not useful numbers. Because link speed is expressed as a quantity (bits) over time, the ideal measurement is to count bits that are sent in a specific interval and compare that to the maximum.

The problem is that if the interval is too long, information is lost in the average. However, as the interval gets smaller, it becomes more binary, which is also difficult to interpret. Specifically, looking at a link over a 24-hour interval clearly highlights the problem. A link that is full for the entire eight-hour business day, but otherwise unutilized, would show up as 33% utilization. No hard-and-fast rule exists for selecting intervals.

Figure 8-7   *Scalability of Balloons and Home Agents*

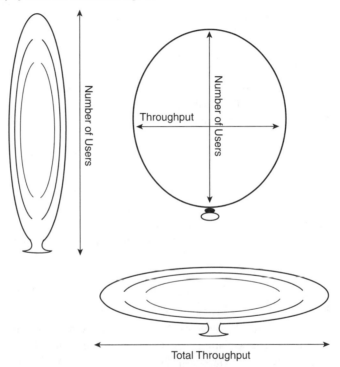

A busy-hour profile for one or more classes of users needs to encompass all four factors, as discussed in the sections that follow. You can generally classify users based on the application. For example, a mobile sales force and a service team likely have different busy-hour usage profiles, but within each class, the profile is similar. After the classes are established and the profiles are defined, the two can be merged based on the quantity of users in each profile.

Number of Nodes

The most often asked scalability question is "How many Mobile Nodes are supported by a specific platform?" This needs to be looked at as a foundation for scalability and not the entire answer. This number is not only the root of the call model development discussed in the sections that follow, but a scaling factor on its own. From a simple "maximums" perspective, this number is typically limited by the amount of available random-access memory (RAM) on the agent platform. Mobile IP visitors on the Foreign Agent (FA) and mobility bindings on the Home Agent each require a fixed amount of available memory on the agent. Unfortunately, no specific number quantifies memory usage. The number varies with each release and is based on which features are used. Although memory use is the largest factor in relation to the number of Mobile Nodes, it isn't the only factor impacted. The number of nodes also impacts features such as routing table lookup speed and other specific services. The more services, the more impact the total number of nodes has on the performance of the agent. It might be hard to imagine, but Home Agents have some of the largest routing tables because of the use of host routes.

Frequency of Mobility

Processing each RRQ also requires a specific amount of resources, this time from the CPU. Routers, on which Mobility Agents run, are designed to get data traffic in and out of the box as fast as possible. Control-plane operations are not as speed critical. Thus, whereas custom hardware is put in the forwarding path, routing protocols are not hardware assisted. Mobile IP, although designed to handle routing updates extremely efficiently, is still limited by the CPU's capabilities.

The frequency of routing updates, or RRQs as they are specifically called in Mobile IP, is determined by several factors. Each Mobile Node sends a RRQ when it powers on and possibly when it powers off. It also sends a RRQ when the lifetime expires and each time it changes its access link. In most networks, the power-on and power-off registrations are of negligible impact. Access-link changes are the hardest to quantify, especially when the roaming network is not completely known, as is the case with public network roaming. This is easiest to quantify with data from a real-world trial, but can be derived if physical movement habits can be correlated to network deployment.

Mobility binding lifetime is a controllable factor but one that is often difficult to address. What lifetime should be used? Generally, the longer the better, but failures must be detected and resources reclaimed in a timely fashion. One factor to consider is setting lifetimes in relation to roam frequency. If roaming is frequent, reregistration because of lifetime should be greater than the average plus the first standard deviation. This means that 68% of the reregistrations occur because of roaming and not lifetime expiration.

Amount of Data Traffic

The amount of data traffic the agent must forward is also an important factor, but not as important as in other routing applications. In a mobile environment, data traffic is often limited by the capabilities of the end device and the speed of the access links. As mobile solutions mature, forwarding rate is becoming more of a concern, but as with the slow-access networks of the past, it has not been a limiting factor. In terms of a call model, this should be expressed as the number of packets or bytes in the busy hour.

For devices in which forwarding occurs in software, the tunnel encapsulation adds a significant amount of overhead when compared to unprocessed packet forwarding. Newer platforms offer support for encapsulation in hardware but ensure that the tunnel type being used is explicitly supported.

Number of Tunnels

The final scaling factor, the number of tunnels used, might seem odd, but given that users sharing the same Care-of Address (CoA) share the same tunnel, it can have an impact on rollout. Each tunnel that the router builds contributes to the amount of memory used and the amount of processing required. The maximum number of tunnels supported in IOS is limited per platform and varies from release to release. Each tunnel requires the use of an interface description block (IDB), which is a key component of IOS. The maximum number of IDBs supported on a specific platform is documented on Cisco.com. Use care when Colocated Care-of Address (CCoA) mode is used because each Mobile Node requires a tunnel. Also, remember that a Mobile Router uses two tunnels when attached to a FA. The number of free IDBs on the Home Agent typically limits the number of mobility bindings.

NOTE   According to Cisco.com, an IDB is a special control structure internal to the Cisco IOS software that contains such information as the IP address, interface state, and packet statistics. Cisco IOS software maintains one IDB for each interface present on a platform and one IDB for each subinterface (http://www.cisco.com/en/US/partner/products/sw/iosswrel/ps1835/products_tech_note09186a0080094322.shtml).

An Example Call Model

Consider the two user classes that we identified previously, a mobile sales force and a mobile service team. Table 8-1 shows the profile for each class and indicates how that profile can be combined into a call model. We first determine that an equal number of sales and service workers exist, so each profile is weighted at 50% of the total call model.

Table 8-1   *Example Call Model*

	Sales Force	Service Team	Per User	Busy-Hour Total (MB)
Number of Users	100	100	—	200
Registrations	2	1	(2 * 50%) + (1 * 50%) = 1.5	300
Data Traffic	200 KB	900 KB	(200 * 50%) + (900 * 50%) = 550 KB	107
Tunnels	1	1	(1 * 50%) + (1 * 50%) = 1	200

Next, the mobility and traffic profiles are quantified. Each member of the sales team visits eight to ten customers a day. At each customer, either public wireless local-area network (LAN) or public wireless wide-area network (WAN) connectivity queries the order-entry system. Enterprise applications such as e-mail and web browsing can also be used. These can all be quantified in terms of bandwidth and total data utilization.

Each service worker visits four customers a day and uses public wireless LAN and WAN connectivity. The service applications include work-order management, streaming video for just-in-time training, and the download of highly detailed service manuals. Although the work-order management system is used often, it has very low data usage. Conversely, the video and service manuals use large quantities of data but are used less frequently.

Assigning specific numbers to these profiles requires estimation, but after the application is understood, this should be relatively easy. For this example, you can assume that each user performs two registrations per customer site, one when entering the site and one when leaving.

This is an example call model that cannot be generalized to all applications. For example, the registration rate in this example is 1.5 registrations per user in the busy hour. If the example involved delivery people in a campus environment using only wireless LAN, the registration rate might be significantly higher. If a Layer 2 (and Layer 3) handover occurs on every floor of every building and the delivery person visits 12 floors an hour, the registration rate would be 12 events in the busy hour. This makes registration rate a much larger factor in the call model.

Network Management

Although the call model provides a good estimation for initial deployment, you must monitor the network and quantify real-world utilization after the deployment is complete. Performance monitoring should encompass the same factors as the call model, plus traditional router health metrics. These metrics are not covered here but should include CPU and memory utilization. Performance monitoring is an important tool for network planning, but a comprehensive network management strategy also needs to encompass fault management.

Centralized fault management in Mobile IP is generally limited to the health and availability of Mobility Agents. Some capabilities for user monitoring are available, but because Mobile IP is an edge-intelligent routing protocol, the Mobile Node is the ideal to place to begin troubleshooting when something goes wrong. Remote management in the situation is not possible because the node is usually unreachable. The Simple Network Management Protocol (SNMP) is an ideal and established tool for networking and is ideal for monitoring and managing Mobile IP agents. Specific management objects related to Mobile IP are discussed in the sections that follow, but you should also monitor non–Mobile IP objects such as Hot Standby Router Protocol (HSRP) and AAA, when those services are in use.

RFC 2006 Management Information Base (MIB)

RFC 2006 provided the original definition of management objects for Mobile IP. The objects in the RFC 2006 MIB provide detailed counters that are related to the basic features and error message in the original definition of Mobile IP in RFC 2002. Objects that you should watch include the registration acceptance and failure counters. How these objects are used depends largely on the overall management strategy and is generally beyond the scope of this book. Fault management systems should look at failed registrations and analyze specific error codes to help determine minor failures with individual nodes from systemic problems. Performance management with the RFC 2006 MIB should include monitoring registration rate by evaluating the number of registrations over a given monitoring interval.

Cisco Enterprise MIB

The RFC 2006 MIB has some significant shortcomings when dealing with modern Mobile IP implementations. Management of Mobile Nodes identified by NAI is difficult because the NAI is not part of the original MIB and, as such, must be translated to the Home Address externally. Proposals to update the RFC 2006 MIB have been made, but to date, no new standard has been adopted. In the interim, Cisco IOS has adopted an enterprise-specific (vendor-specific) MIB. Most of the features of this MIB are part of the proposed update to RFC 2006, but it also includes a few objects that are specific to the Cisco IOS implementation of IOS Mobile IP. The biggest feature is the ability to reference Mobile Nodes by NAI rather than just Home Address.

Support for Home Agent redundancy counters has been added, along with specific information related to the performance of the Home Agent. One key performance management statistic that was lacking from the RFC 2006 MIB was the ability to determine the number of Mobile Nodes currently using the Mobility Agent. This information could be computed by counting the number of entries in the binding and visitor tables, but for Mobility Agents with tens to hundreds of thousands of Mobile Nodes, this was a significant use of resources. The Cisco Mobile IP MIB has objects to determine the number of active bindings and visitors with just one query.

NOTE   A graphical representation of the objects available in both MIBs is available in Appendix B, "IOS Mobile IP: Supported SNMP MIBs."

Objects Matching the Call Model

The four scaling areas discussed in the section "Scaling Issues," earlier in this chapter, should be monitored closely and can be evaluated using the following management objects:

- **Total number of Mobile Nodes**—From the Cisco Mobile IP MIB, the cmiHaRegTotalMobilityBindings and the cmiFaRegTotal visitors objects give the total number of bindings on a Home Agent and visitors on the FA, respectively.

- **Frequency of Mobility**—From the RFC 2006 MIB, the haRegRequestsReceived and the faRegRequestReceived should be monitored, and the change of polling interval should compute the registration rate. You can also compare these to haRegistrationAccepted and faRegRequestsRelayed, respectively, to determine the error rate. If the received rate is not the same as or close to the accepted/relayed rate, the object for the specific error codes should be evaluated to determine where failures are.

- **Amount of data traffic**—Data traffic should be monitored using the standard IOS interface traffic objects.

- **Number of tunnels**—The number of active tunnels can be monitored using the ifNumber object from the RFC 2863 interface MIB. This includes the total number of interfaces on the box, which you can compare against the maximum number of supported IDBs.

System Log Messages

As a general practice, system messages should be logged to a remote syslog message server for offline processing. Few Mobile IP–specific error messages exist, but all of them are documented under IPMOBILE in the IOS system messages guide for the specific IOS release. The most common error message is the security violation message. Older releases of IOS generate a security violation message with type 131 when the clocks are out of sync. This is common and is a self-recovering condition, as described in Chapter 3, "Mobile IP Security." New versions of IOS no longer generate syslog error messages for type 131 errors.

Common Troubleshooting Issues

A few issues are so common to Mobile IP deployments that they are worth calling out specifically. However, these are by no means the only problems that can be encountered when deploying a Mobile IP solution. The most common problems are Path maximum transmission unit (MTU) discovery failure, packet loss because of asymmetric routing and Reverse Path Forwarding (RPF) checks, and failure to transit tunneled packets. Some of these problems are easier to solve than others, but none should be insurmountable.

Path MTU Discovery

Path MTU discovery is a common part of Internet communication that is generally not understood or accounted for. Path MTU discovery, as defined in RFC 1191, determines the largest packet size that can transit the intermediate network without fragmentation. It works by setting the "do not fragment" bit for all flows. When a packet is too large to transit a link, the router drops the packet and returns an Internet Control Message Protocol (ICMP) unreachable message to the source, indicating the largest packet size that can transit the link. When the source receives the message, it decreases the packet size and retransmits it. More discussion on how path MTU discovery works is given in Chapter 6, "Metro Mobility: Client-Based Mobile IP."

The problem that is most often seen in path MTU discovery is that when firewalls are deployed, an explicit rule is often added to drop all ICMP packets. Thus, ICMP unreachable messages are dropped and the source just assumes that a failure in the path to its peer is causing the flow to fail. Path MTU discovery does not cause problems in day-to-day connectivity because most links support a packet size of 1500 bytes, the maximum packet size on an Ethernet network. Note that path MTU discovery failure is not a problem that is specific to Mobile IP. Rather, it is seen any time an encapsulation is added to an Ethernet link. This problem is commonly seen with protocols such as Point-to-Point Protocol over Ethernet (PPPoE) and IP Security (IPSec).

A common example of path MTU discovery failure occurs when web browsing. Have you ever browsed to a web page, and it appears that the web browser is connecting to the site but the page is never displayed? Many times, the screen just appears blank. This is often because the initial request returns a small 1-packet response with the Hypertext Markup Language (HTML) portion of the page, which is safely able to traverse the path. However, larger graphics cannot download and traverse the path because of MTU issues and, thus, the page is never rendered.

Some operating systems include a feature called black-hole detection. The idea behind black-hole detection is that after half of the retransmits have failed, path MTU discovery should be disabled. Although this works well, it introduces noticeable delays. All is not lost, though; the following options can eliminate the delay.

There is no "one size fits all" solution to the problem, but a number of strategies can minimize the impact of the problem. The ideal solution would be to fix all the firewalls to allow ICMP unreachable messages to do their job. But, as we know, ideal is not always practical. In fact, a recent analysis showed that a significant portion of top Internet websites do not allow ICMP unreachable messages to get back to their web servers. Fixing every website would be an insurmountable task.

The next best option is to lower the MTU on the Mobile Node. This is a highly reliable solution but a difficult or impossible task, depending on the quantity and capabilities of the Mobile Node. Fortunately, many current Mobile Node implementations automatically lower the MTU when Mobile IP is active.

Another option is to use an IOS feature that adjusts the Maximum Segment Size (MSS) option, which is part of Transmission Control Protocol (TCP) negotiation. Using the **ip adjust-mss** *mss value* command forces the router to intercept all TCP SYN packets that exit the interface and lower the MSS value. This method can be difficult to deploy because it must occur between the Mobile Node and any peer with which it can communicate. However, in some networks, this is easy to deploy because only a few egress points exist. Other networks can have more problems.

Reverse Path Forwarding Checks

Failures due to unicast Reverse Path Forwarding, or *uRPF*, checks were covered when reverse tunneling was introduced in Chapter 6, but it is a common problem and worth a recap. The idea behind uRPF is to eliminate packets with a spoofed source address at the edge of the network.

Normal unicast forwarding is performed solely based on the destination address of a packet. When uRPF checks are enabled, the router checks its routing table to ensure that a route to the source address exists through the incoming interface. The assumption is that if a router would not send a packet out the interface to the source address, it should not receive one in the interface from that address. uRPF checks are widely deployed at the edge of service provider networks. However, it would not be surprising to scc uRPF checks deployed within an enterprise to minimize the impact of viruses and worms and to make it easier to track down infected machines.

The original design of Mobile IP used an asymmetric routing design with direct delivery from the Mobile Node to the destination. When the Mobile Node is roaming, this results in topologically incorrect source addresses. These packets are then dropped when they reach a router running uRPF. Using reverse tunneling solves this problem. With reverse tunneling, packets are tunneled from the CoA back to the Home Agent so that they can be delivered as topologically correct. Although reverse tunneling solves this problem, it creates extra overhead because twice the tunneling must occur. Although not a major problem, it is something that must be accounted for when planning a Mobile IP deployment.

Tunnel Transit

Unicast RPF checks are not the only cause for transport failure. Tunnel packet loss can also occur when traversal of a NAT device or firewall is necessary, because both IP-in-IP and generic routing encapsulation (GRE) tunnels are less common protocols than TCP and User Datagram Protocol (UDP). In other cases, other network devices are unable to forward tunnel packets because of either design or implementation flaws. This has occurred when mobile cellular networks are used for transport. When IP-in-IP packets fail to traverse a link end to end, you should attempt to use GRE tunneling followed by UDP tunneling. IP-in-IP and GRE tunneling are more efficient and more widely supported than UDP tunneling. However, some networks, firewalls, and NAT devices do not allow encapsulation to traverse. In this case, the network needs to be eliminated from the list of allowable roaming networks.

Security Association Incompatibilities

Incompatibilities in the implementation of security associations are also common for items not explicitly specified in the standards. The most common problem is the specification of the SPI value. Some clients use decimal values, whereas others use hexadecimal values. Older versions of IOS allow the specification of only hexadecimal values that can easily be converted to a binary representation for interoperability. Newer versions of IOS simplify the process even further by allowing SPI values to be specified in either syntax.

Another problem is the use of ASCII-represented keys; some implementations use padding, whereas other versions do not. Newer versions attempt key calculation, both with and without padding, but still might not be compatible with all ASCII key implementations. Given all of these factors, hexadecimal keys should be used whenever possible. Finally, some implementations of the MN-AAA extension differ when implementing PPP-style Challenge Handshake Authentication Protocol (CHAP) for use with RADIUS servers. Although the standards define specific values, 2 for keyed MD5 and 3 for MD5-HMAC, some vendors allow the specific algorithms to be configured for any SPI. Newer versions of IOS support the **ip mobile secure mn-aaa** command, which allows these algorithms to be mapped to any of the nonreserved SPI values.

Summary

To this point, we covered many facets of the Mobile IP protocol and its deployment, concluding here with management and troubleshooting. Although IOS Mobile IP can seem somewhat complex, this chapter laid out a flexible solution for address management. Furthermore, the chapter continued to help refine details for deployment and scaling factors, and it provided some guidance in developing a call model. The chapter defined network management and performance-monitoring metrics and, finally, highlighted some common troubleshooting problems.

Chapter 9, "A Look Ahead," takes a look at the future of Mobile IP. It examines the Mobile IPv6 standard and compares it to the current technology. Chapter 9 explores the implementation of Mobile IP as part of cellular network deployments. It also looks at new mobile wireless technologies, such as FLASH-OFDM. Finally, Chapter 9 introduces another host mobility protocol—Cisco Structured Wireless-Aware Network (SWAN)—and shows its relationship to Mobile IP.

Review Questions

1 What are the three modes of home addressing that Cisco Mobile IP supports?

2 How does static addressing with an NAI work?

3 A dynamic Home Address for a Mobile Node can be assigned through which of the following methods?

   a Local pool on the Home Network

   b DHCP on the Home Network

   c AAA server on the Home Network

   d All of the above

4 Describe how dynamic Home Address assignment through local pool works.

5 What role does the Home Agent assume when allocating a Home Address through DHCP? Briefly describe how it works.

6 What is fixed addressing?

7 How does a call model help in identifying scalability concerns?

8 A busy-hour profile for one or more classes of users needs to encompass which four factors?

9 What extra management does Cisco Enterprise MIB provide that RFC 2006 MIB does not?

10 What common troubleshooting issues arise in Mobile IP deployments?

CHAPTER 9

A Look Ahead

In this final chapter, Kent Leung presents current work and future directions for Mobile IP. Topics include the challenges of multiaccess technologies in public networks; wireless LAN (WLAN) mobility in the Cisco Structured Wireless-Aware Network (SWAN) architecture; authentication, authorization, and accounting (AAA)–based key generation; Mobile IP for IPv6; and finally, an introduction to nonstructured mobility.

Mobile IP and Public Access Networks

Chapter 6, "Metro Mobility: Client-Based Mobile IP," looked at many of the features necessary to deploy metropolitan mobility solutions. This chapter examines some common public-access technologies and their use or interactions with Mobile IP.

Current wireless data networks that are commonly deployed include Wireless Fidelity (WiFi), cdmaOne/cdma2000, and General Packet Radio Service (GPRS)/Universal Mobile Telephone Service (UMTS). Newcomers that arc promising include Fast Low-latency Access with Seamless Handoff–Orthogonal Frequency Division Multiplexing (FLASH-OFDM) and Worldwide Interoperability for Microwave Access (WiMAX). WiMAX is considered a wireless metropolitan-area network (MAN) technology.

The wireless wide-area network (WAN) and MAN technologies provide broad coverage up to about 5 miles, with mobility speed up to 200 mph, and data throughput from 14.4 Kbps to 2 Mbps (WAN) or 70 Mbps (MAN). The throughput numbers specified for comparison in this chapter are not theoretical limits of the technology but rather the practical rates. WiFi, although designed strictly as a wireless LAN technology, has seen deployment in metropolitan settings, but its limited coverage area limits its usefulness. A typical wireless LAN covers up to a distance of 300 feet, with data throughput capable of reaching 20+ Mbps. WLAN usage is significantly more cost effective than wireless WAN. Both wireless WAN and WLAN technologies continue to evolve, with performance increasing and cost decreasing. Not long ago, throughput for wireless WAN was considered good at 24 Kbps, and WLAN topped out at 1 Mbps. Today, commercial wireless WAN services that are available in certain cities have a bandwidth in excess of 300 Kbps, and 20-Mbps and higher throughput rates on WLAN are getting popular. For those of us who are accustomed to high-speed broadband access from the home, there's a thirst for ubiquitous wireless WAN coverage at comparable performance. Future expectation is that wireless WAN will reach tens of Mbps and WLAN will be blazing at many Gbps.

It is easy to get mesmerized by the throughput numbers of the wireless technologies, but factors such as air-link efficiency, radio access network latency, and capital and operational cost vary among them. Each technology has its strengths and weaknesses in terms of coverage area, cost, bandwidth, latency, and supported speed of movement. Maximizing the wireless data experience requires situational usage. Therefore, it is wise to have a mobility infrastructure that keeps up with the wireless evolution and takes advantage of the benefits of existing wireless technologies. Because Mobile IP provides mobility independent of the link layer, it is an ideal solution in a world of myriad types of access networks.

Public Wireless LAN

WiFi, also known as *IEEE 802.11*, is the most popular wireless LAN technology deployed for public access. Public wireless LAN deployments, typically referred to as *hot spots*, are appearing in many hotels, conference centers, coffee shops, airports, and locations where mobile workers gather or events take place. WiFi provides fast and relatively cheap (sometimes free) wireless Internet access. One major challenge to deploying Mobile IP with public wireless LAN is the integration with access control. For example, one issue is the time needed to get authorized and given access to the network. In addition, based on the method used, it would be useful to have some form of Layer 2 trigger to inform Mobile IP that access is available for expedited switchover to WiFi.

Multiple user-authentication methods exist in hot spots, and most service providers have different authentication mechanisms. The most common access method for public WLAN hot spots is Hypertext Transfer Protocol (HTTP) redirect. In this case, after a client obtains an IP address through Dynamic Host Configuration Protocol (DHCP), all traffic is blocked, with the exception of HTTP traffic, which is redirected to the service provider's portal page. When users attempt to reach a website, their browsers are directed to a sign-on web page, where users can enter their credit card or subscription information. This process poses a couple of problems. First, it requires manual user intervention, which makes the experience of switching over to WiFi not seamless. The other problem is that Mobile IP attempts to discover a Foreign Agent (FA) after WLAN association and registers to its Home Agent after obtaining an IP address from DHCP. These packets are dropped by the WLAN access point (AP) until authentication completes. But when access is granted and the client's traffic is permitted to pass through the AP, Mobile IP is not notified because the WLAN interface had already come up when DHCP completed. If previous network access (such as cellular) is unavailable during the authentication period, communication sessions that are sensitive to packet loss can suffer noticeable hangs or completely disconnect.

Many service providers are adding machine-controllable authentication service to interoperate with connection managers and allow simpler roaming services. These automated services are either based on specific well-defined URLs or based on IEEE 802.1x. IEEE 802.1x is a widely accepted standard for Layer 2 authentication that uses the Extensible Authentication Protocol, or EAP, to allow user login. Many Global System for Mobile Communications (GSM) cellular providers are using or evaluating Extensive Authentication Protocol-subscriber identity module (EAP-SIM) to authenticate subscribers. EAP-SIM leverages the GSM subscriber identity module, or SIM, to provide secure authentication using the existing GSM infrastructure. This provides a hardware token authentication system that requires no user interaction. In addition, because this is a Layer 2 method, DHCP happens after access is granted. The client's interface comes up when an IP address is obtained. This event can trigger the Mobile Node to register to its Home Agent immediately. Thus, EAP-based authentication services work well with Mobile IP to obtain access to the WiFi network and use the high-speed transport to maintain the client's sessions.

Even with automatic authentication capabilities, detecting hot spots and determining the service provider and any roaming agreements still represent challenges. This functionality is typically addressed with software referred to as a connection manager. As the public hot-spot market matures, standards will be adopted and roaming agreements will provide more capabilities. In the meantime, Mobile IP users are limited in their ability to take advantage of the hot spots they encounter.

For GSM cellular providers who want to allow their subscribers the seamless service from WiFi hotspots, one nuisance is a lack of integration of Mobile IP authentication with existing security infrastructure. Currently, accessing the network requires one type of authentication using SIM, and enabling the Mobile IP service mandates a security method that has no relationship. It would be logical to leverage the existing GSM infrastructure to generate the Mobile IP keys needed to protect the registrations. Published drafts in the Internet Engineering Task Force (IETF) have attempted to link the authentication mechanisms of both. This type of solution can simplify deployment of Mobile IP–based roaming.

Cdma2000 Technology

Code division multiple access (CDMA) is a cellular transmission method that allows multiple users to share the same radio frequency spectrum by assigning a unique code to each user. The message sent to the user appears as noise to others without the code. An analogy is the conversations in a busy restaurant. People are tuned in to the voice of the person to whom they are listening. Other loud chatter is filtered by the ear as unwelcome noise in the background.

CDMA is the access technology used in cdmaOne, a second-generation wireless communications system that was named as the first version of commercially deployed CDMA technology. This happened at the advent of the third-generation technology called cdma2000, which is an evolutionary outgrowth of cdmaOne, offering operators who have deployed a second-generation cdmaOne system a seamless migration path. The Third Generation Partnership Project 2 (3GPP2) is a standards organization that comprises North American and Asian interests on the development of cdma2000 specifications. Why is the name cdma2000 used as the successor to cdmaOne, instead of cdmaTwo or cdma3G? One reason is that the

3GPP2 forum was established in the year 2000. CDMA operators, such as Sprint and Verizon Wireless in the United States, deploy such service under the marketing brand of Sprint PCS Vision and Express Network, respectively. The throughput for a currently deployed cdma2000 network is typically about 80 Kbps, though a new rollout of services at about 300 Kbps is happening in 2005 and 2006. Few people outside of the CDMA crowd know that the Mobile IP protocol provides mobility inside the operator's cdma2000 network. Some of these operators seek to use Mobile IP for roaming to/from WiFi and other networks as well.

In cdma2000, the client, typically a phone or access card, connects to a base station (BS) on the air link. It initiates a Point-to-Point Protocol (PPP) session with the Packet Data Serving Node (PDSN). The PDSN is a network access server, providing simple IP access, meaning IP over PPP, or Mobile IP service as a FA. After the PPP session is established, the client initiates a Mobile IP session with its Home Agent through the PDSN. The Mobile Node functionality is typically embedded in the firmware of the phone and transparent to an attached portable IP device. When a client moves between BSs within the same PDSN, the same PPP session is maintained by the network. However, when a client moves between PDSNs, a new PPP session is set up at the new PDSN, and then Mobile IP reregistration maintains the IP session at the Home Agent. Figure 9-1 illustrates the handover between BSs and PDSNs in the cdma2000 network.

The signaling between Mobile Node, FA, and Home Agent is based on IETF specifications, with the exception of the dynamic Home Agent assignment feature, home Domain Name System (DNS) server configuration extension, and multiple registrations using the same Network Access Identifier (NAI). In cdma2000, the Home Agent can be dynamically assigned by the AAA server. This mechanism is valuable for anchoring the Mobile Node with geographical proximity, selecting Home Agent based on an administrative reason, and/or load balancing among available Home Agents. The Mobile Node needs to know its DNS server's IP address in the Home Network. Unfortunately, no standard method exists to learn about this address dynamically. A 3GPP2-specific extension was added to the Mobile IP registration message to pass this information to the Mobile Node. The need for supporting multiple flows (each having a unique IP address) using the same NAI has been debated. Nevertheless, 3GPP2 mandated this requirement and specified how to accomplish multiple registrations. Don't confuse this with Mobile IP simultaneous bindings, which establish multiple paths to the same Home Address and replicate each packet over the tunnels.

Besides enhancements to Mobile IP, some of the 3GPP2-specific attributes that were added to Remote Authentication Dial-In User Service (RADIUS) include the Mobile Node-Home Agent (Mobile Node–Home Agent) registration key used for the Home Agent to download from the AAA server; Internet Key Exchange (IKE), which are keys for establishing the IP Security (IPSec) tunnel between PDSN and the Home Agent; quality of service (QoS); and reverse tunneling parameters. (Source: http://www.3gpp2.com/Public_html/specs/P.S0001-B_v2.0_041004.pdf.)

Figure 9-1   *Mobile IP in cdma2000 Network*

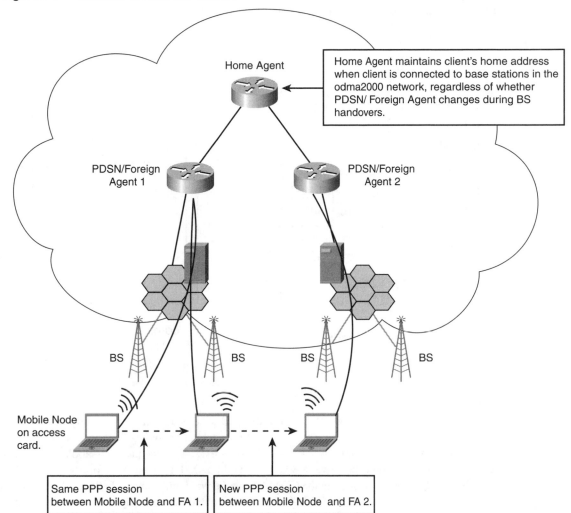

Two options are available to support roaming between a cdma2000 network and other access networks. One method is to overlay a Mobile IP session using a Mobile Node on the portable IP device. The phone or access card operates in network mode and continues to use Mobile IP for mobility service within the cdma2000 network. The Mobile Node on the IP device works in Colocated Care-of Address (CCoA) mode using the PPP session with the CDMA access device. The Home Address on the IP device is used for communications with Correspondent Nodes (CNs), while the Home Address on the access device ensures that the PPP session's IP address remains constant when attached to the cdma2000 network. The protocol stack for the data plane of the Mobile IP overlay in network mode is shown in Figure 9-2.

Figure 9-2 *Cdma2000 Network Mode*

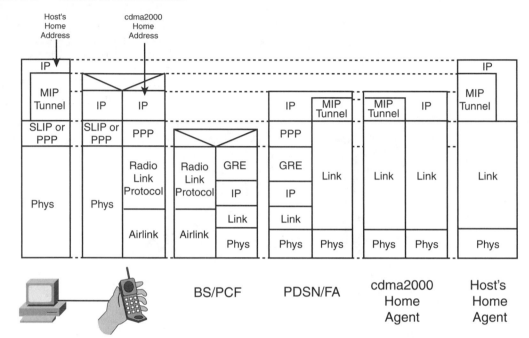

If you observed that the Mobile IP client in the IP device is unaware of mobility inside the cdma2000 network, you are right. The Mobile IP tunnel between the client and its Home Agent is clearly not the most efficient use of air-link resources. As service providers look at deploying a managed roaming service between 802.11 and cdma2000, they have the option of disabling the Mobile IP client embedded in the CDMA access device and using only the Mobile Node on the end device. In this case, the CDMA access device operates in relay mode and allows the PPP session to pass through between the client and the cdma2000 Home Agent. The responsibility for notifying the Home Agent is solely on the IP device's Mobile Node. Figure 9-3 shows the protocol stack for the data plane of Mobile IP's role in relay mode. How does the Mobile Node get the configuration such as the Home Agent's IP address and registration keys? This can no longer be provisioned over the air link as in the network mode case, so it must be either manually entered or automatically performed by some program.

Figure 9-3   *cdma2000 Relay Mode*

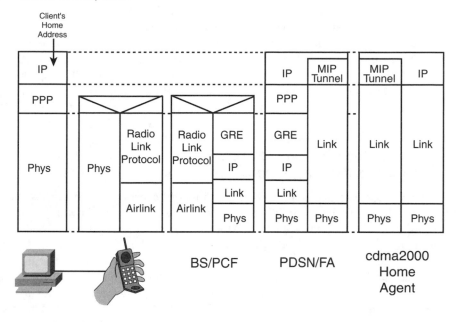

GSM Technology

GSM is a digital cellular radio standard, the most popular in the world, that uses time division multiplex access (TDMA). TDMA divides a radio frequency into time slots that are assigned to support multiple simultaneous users. For an analogy of GSM, we can bring back the overcrowded restaurant. This time, each person gets to say only one word at a time, with everyone taking a turn. Those who don't have anything to say remain silent. After the last person speaks, the next word can be conveyed, and this cycle repeats. The listener knows the sequence and therefore knows when to pay attention to gather the entire sentence and the message of the speaker.

GPRS allows GSM traffic channels to be shared by users in packet mode to support data service. Packet mode uses the air link more efficiently than circuit mode. For example, if the conversations in the restaurant are in circuit mode, each person has an allocated time to speak. The time slot is wasted when there is silence. In packet mode, the turns are taken by people who have something to say. This scheme allows the message to be conveyed more quickly and minimizes undesirable quiet periods because "talk" generates revenue for the wireless operators. GPRS represents the first packet-based technology for evolution from second-generation (2G) GSM networks to second-generation plus (2G+) networks. Cingular Wireless and T-Mobile provide this service in the United States. The throughput rate for GPRS is typically 40–60 Kbps.

The evolutionary step for GPRS to third generation (3G) is UMTS, as specified in 3GPP standards body, which should not be confused with 3GPP2, because they are different organizations working on competitive technologies. The mobility management functions for GPRS and UMTS were created within its own standards organization. A user moving in the GPRS network maintains the same IP address. This is possible because the gateway GPRS support node (GGSN) anchors the IP address and tunnels traffic to the serving GPRS support node (SGSN), which relays the packet to the client. One or more Packet Data Protocol (PDP) contexts can be activated between the client and the GGSN, which is the gateway between the GPRS network and routed IP network, as its name implies. The GPRS Tunneling Protocol, or GTP, transports packets over an IP network between the GGSN and SGSN. Conceptually, the GGSN and SGSN perform similar functions as the Home Agent and FA, respectively. Therefore, Mobile IP is not needed in the GPRS network because equivalent function already exists.

However, specifications for interworking with other access technologies have not yet been ratified in 3GPP. One possibility for multiaccess connectivity is to overlay a Mobile IP session using a Mobile Node on the host. The Mobile IP client operates in Care-of Address (CoA) mode using the IP address provided by the GGSN for network access. The Home Address on the IP device is used for communications with CNs, while the UMTS address remains constant when attached to the UMTS network. The protocol stack for the data plane of Mobile IP overlay in the UMTS network is shown in Figure 9-4. Don't get lost with the new acronyms in the diagram; the concept is that GTP anchors the UMTS Home Address and Mobile IP anchors the host's Home Address. As in the cdma2000 network mode, the Mobile IP tunnel decreases throughput over the air link. But because GPRS and UMTS don't have a FA in the network, this overhead is unavoidable. A potential remedy is adding the FA function in the GGSN to eliminate the extra tunnel encapsulation. Then handovers between GPRS, UMTS, WiFi, and others can be achieved with Mobile IP, with only the original packet over the air link.

NOTE   One challenge common to integrating Mobile IP with wireless technologies is that a radio device does not inform the Mobile Node of its signal strength and quality, or even worse, when it has lost the signal. For effective mobility, the Mobile IP clients have to come up with smart ways of gleaning Layer 2 information, when that's possible, or integrating features to query the status of the radio to determine this type of information. Knowledge of link-layer status provides the Mobile Node with an intelligent way to select the best access in a timely manner. The IEEE 802.21 Multi-media Independent Handover Group and IETF Detecting Network Attachment (DNA) Working Group are working on standardizing media-independent handover services that allow hosts to detect their IP layer configuration and connectivity status quickly.

Figure 9-4   *Mobile IP over UMTS Network*

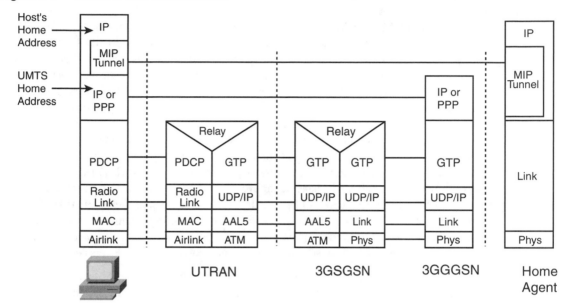

FLASH-OFDM Technology

New mobile wireless technology such as FLASH-OFDM, conceived by Flarion Technologies, is emerging as an alternative to data technologies that evolved from voice networks such as cdma2000 and UMTS. The disadvantage of the overlay approach for wireless data service is the high cost and complexity of the radio access network (RAN). Because this type of network was not designed for packet data service, the "over the air" delay, such as time needed to establish the bearer channel, is significant. For GPRS, the time it takes for the packet from the client to reach the IP gateway ranges from hundreds of milliseconds to over a second. (Source: http://www.sourceo2.com/O2_Developers/O2_technologies/GPRS/Technical _overview/gprs_latency_factors_diagram.htm.) In contrast, WiFi networks move the packet from the IEEE 802.11 air link to the gateway without much delay, usually in just a few milliseconds.

The touted benefits of FLASH-OFDM include packet-based designs, high spectral efficiency, minimal air-link latency (less than 50 msec), end-to-end quality of service, transparent multinetwork access, toll-quality packet voice service, and native multicast. It was built from the ground up with IP technologies in mind. Although this technology is not widely deployed, service providers worldwide are conducting public trials that have demonstrated some positive results. The typical throughput is about 500 Kbps with little latency. Voice over IP (VoIP) on the network had comparable call quality to wired counterparts from a user's perspective.

FLASH-OFDM was designed with a standards-based Mobile IP protocol for mobility management in an *all-IP network*. An all-IP network is common terminology with many different interpretations.

A purist's perspective on the definition is that such a network consists of an IP core network architecture, an IP RAN architecture, and an air interface that is optimized for packet data delivery. IP mobility in FLASH-OFDM has three key components involved in signaling, and two of them support tunneling of traffic. Sound similar? The Mobile Node is a function in the FLASH-OFDM access card attached to the portable IP device. Flarion's RadioRouter is a combination of a base station and an IP access router, located at the edge of the IP network, where the link layer terminates. The FA function is embedded in the RadioRouter. The Cisco Home Agent has been used for many years to maintain communication sessions by directing traffic from/to a host while in transit between base stations. The agent discovery, registration, and tunneling processes are the same as IETF's Mobile IP specifications. Unlike the cdma2000 network, which uses Mobile IP when users move between large geographical boundaries delimited by PDSNs that aggregate many base stations, the radio router's wireless coverage is in the range of only one base station. This means a motorized vehicle moving at 50 mph can be handing off every 6 minutes in the situation where base station coverage is 5 miles. The frequency of Mobile IP handovers is much greater in FLASH-OFDM compared to cdma2000. Any weakness because of high volume of signaling or unacceptable signaling latency would be exposed quickly in such a network. As mentioned previously, real-world trials have demonstrated scalable signaling capacity and low-latency handovers using Mobile IP.

How do users maintain their session switching over from FLASH-OFDM to WiFi networks at home or hot spots? The options are similar to a cdma2000 network because both use the FA and Home Agent for IP mobility. Figure 9-5 shows the protocol stack for the data plane of Mobile IP overlay in a FLASH-OFDM network. Notice that the protocol stack between the client and FLASH-OFDM Home Agent is simple and clean.

Figure 9-5   *Mobile IP over FLASH-OFDM Network*

Cisco SWAN and Mobile IP

Although most WiFi hot-spot deployments are small enough to be deployed as a single subnet, medium- to large-enterprise WLANs usually require access points to be spread across several subnets. This requirement introduced the following challenges when users move between APs in different subnets:

- Fast 802.11 reauthentication is required.
- Client's IP address must not change.
- Traffic policy for the client remains the same.

How fast does "fast" mean? Most agree that time-sensitive applications such as VoIP are a good benchmark, which is at good quality when latency is less than 150 milliseconds. When a client associates with an AP, the authentication process involves the AAA server and the client. A few message exchanges are required for the AAA server to authenticate the client (and sometimes vice versa) before the AP obtains a shared key that the client uses to pass traffic between them.

There is no value to fast reauthentication if the client has to obtain a new IP address on the new AP. Session continuity would not be possible if this happens. Therefore, the client must retain its IP address when moving to an AP that is located in a different subnet than the previous AP.

Policy, such as an access control list (ACL), QoS, and so on, should remain the same for the client that is moving about in the WLAN network. One way to imagine this is to consider that the client is always on a virtual subnet that has certain policies applied, much like a physical subnet. Regardless of which AP the client is associated with, the client's traffic is enforced with consistency based on the "home subnet" policy. Of course, an independent location-based policy can also be applied. For example, an engineer who has roamed into the Finance department's network can have certain access privileges curtailed.

The Cisco SWAN provides a framework to integrate and extend wired and wireless networks for wireless LAN deployments. The Cisco SWAN extends "wireless awareness" into important elements of the network infrastructure, providing the same level of security, scalability, reliability, ease of deployment, and management for wireless LANs that organizations have come to expect from their wired LANs. Okay, the marketing pitch is over. One aspect of SWAN is a feature that is reminiscent of Mobile IP; this is aptly named Fast Secure Roaming.

Fast Secure Roaming is a mechanism that enables a client to roam between WLAN access points in the same subnet or between subnets to support time-sensitive applications. This is achieved by taking advantage of AP-assisted channel (frequency range) scanning, expedited IEEE 802.1x rekeying, and tunneling support for Layer 3 roaming. Channel surfing to find APs can be time consuming. The 802.11 client that is ignorant to the channel layout—set up to avoid interference among APs covering an area—must scan through each channel to detect the presence of an AP. Finding neighboring APs is significantly easier if the associated AP informed the client which channels should be checked first. After the client associates with the new AP, it needs to authenticate with the network to be authorized network access. Typically IEEE 802.1x is used for authentication for WiFi. Simply put, IEEE 802.1x is a standard for passing authentication messages between a client and a AAA server over wired or wireless LAN. After successful authentication, the AAA server sends an access key to the AP for encrypting/decrypting traffic that is sent/received over the WLAN. Fast Secure Roaming caches the authentication key for local reauthentication and transfers the access key to the new AP.

Now that the client is allowed network access, its IP address would not be reachable in a new subnet. That is the point where mobility signaling and tunneling get involved. The new AP notifies the SWAN-aware switch that the client arrived. As previously mentioned, the client has an IP address on a virtual subnet where routing directs traffic to. This subnet belongs to the switch, which has the responsibility to tunnel traffic to and from the AP where the client is currently associated. Because the client's packets are anchored there, policy can be enforced at a centralized location.

Reconsider the challenges that are imposed by Layer 3 roaming. AP-assisted channel scanning and key caching and transfer provide fast 802.11 reauthentication. Tunneling allows the client to keep the same IP address. An anchor point solves the problem of consistent policy enforcement.

The Cisco SWAN Fast Secure Roaming, illustrated in Figure 9-6, currently delivers the top performance with access-point handover times of less than 50 milliseconds; these results have been independently measured. (Source: http://www.nwc.com/shared/article/printFullArticle.jhtml?articleID=59301907.) The following URLs provide more information on the solution:

- http://www.cisco.com/en/US/netsol/ns340/ns394/ns348/ns337/netbr09186a0080 184925.html

- http://www.cisco.com/en/US/netsol/ns340/ns394/ns431/ns434/networking_ solutions_implementation_guide09186a008038906c.html#wp36689

What's the difference between Fast Secure Roaming and Mobile IP? The comparison can only be based on today's solutions because both technologies continue to evolve. Each provides Layer 3 roaming capability that allows a client to roam across subnet boundaries while maintaining its communication sessions. But the fundamental difference is where in the protocol stack the support is implanted. Fast Secure Roaming is integrated with WiFi operations. It helps channel scanning, facilitates 802.1x authentication, and sets up forwarding using tunnels based on Layer 2 events. Most of the operations happen without awareness of the client's IP address. And more importantly, no new software is required on the client because the mobility signaling is provided by the network nodes. Mobile IP, however, functions at Layer 3 only. The client software is needed to detect movement learned from IP messages (agent advertisements) and to register its location (CoA) to the Home Agent. The benefit of having the Mobile Node function is that the client can select the best access link to use for connectivity.

Figure 9-6   *Fast Secure Roaming in the Cisco SWAN*

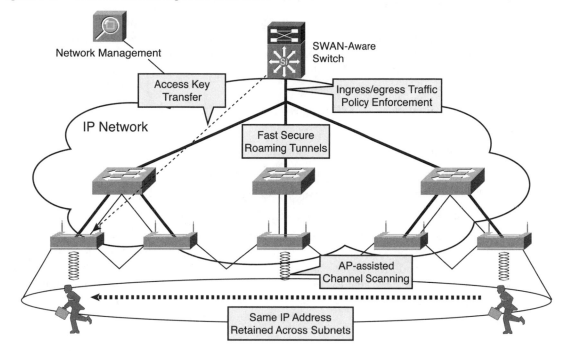

Is Fast Secure Roaming and Mobile IP competitive or complementary? The Cisco SWAN is the right mobility solution in a WLAN deployment that has clients that cannot be installed with Mobile IP software and has roaming confined to only a WLAN requiring fast Layer 2 authentication. Mobile IP, on the other hand, fits for roaming among WLAN, wired Ethernet, cellular, and other access networks. Fast Secure Roaming and Mobile IP are compatible partners when used together. An example is an employee who works in an office and attends meetings elsewhere. The user is sitting in the office watching a company broadcast on video on demand (VoD) in his docked notebook. The WLAN access card is typically already authenticated with the network and is associated to an access point. The Mobile IP client on the notebook selects the higher-speed Ethernet interface for communications, which frees the airwaves for others to consume. The user realizes that he is late to a meeting and hurries over to the conference room with his notebook. The Mobile IP client detects that the Ethernet link is down and immediately selects the WLAN interface for use. As the user heads toward the conference room, Fast Secure Roaming provides seamless handovers. The VoD session never drops or is noticeably affected during this period. Mobile IP is also unaware of any intersubnet mobility. Later, when the user returns to his office and docks his notebook, the Mobile IP client chooses the wired Ethernet again.

AAA-Based Dynamic Key Generation

The Cisco Dynamic security association and Key Distribution feature has been covered extensively, but it is not currently a standards-based solution. Chapter 3, "Mobile IP Security," mentioned that work on a standard AAA-based dynamic key-generation mechanism is under way. At the time of this writing, this work was still under way, so we are presenting a preview of the yet-to-be-accepted standard.

Mobile IPv4 provides the following extensions to protect control messages between the entities:

- **Mobile Node**—Home Agent Authentication Extension
- **Mobile Node**—FA Authentication Extension
- **FA**—Home Agent Authentication Extension
- **Mobile Node**—AAA Authentication Extension

These extensions provide authentication for Registration Requests (RRQs) and Registration Replies (RRPs) between the Mobile Node and Home Agent, Mobile Node and FA, FA and Home Agent, and Mobile Node and AAA server, respectively. Of these, only the Mobile Node–Home Agent Authentication Extension is mandatory. Authentication between the Mobile Node and FA and between the FA and Home Agent is optional. The Mobile Node–AAA Authentication Extension is required in an environment where a AAA server authenticates the Mobile Node.

The Mobile Node and Home Agent security assocation (security association) is typically based on a static preshared key, which is configured on both the Mobile Node and Home Agent. Another variant is a configuration of the key on the AAA server for the Home Agent to download before authenticating the Mobile Node. As pointed out in Chapter 3, configuring the Mobile Node can be a deployment hurdle. Having to set up another key for a client solely for Mobile IP is hard to justify for an IT department. The Zero Configuration Client (ZeCC) approach leverages the existing enterprise security infrastructure to dynamically generate the key for a Mobile IP session. However, because not all deployments use such a security infrastructure, a generic mechanism for dynamic key generation is warranted.

The generalized scheme fundamentally differs from ZeCC by specifying a new operation on the AAA server. New attributes are also needed in the RADIUS or Diameter protocol between the FA and Home Agent and the AAA server. The mobility entities communicate the authentication and key derivation method requested by the Mobile Node to the AAA server, which sends the key and keying material (targeted for the Mobile Node) to the FA and Home Agent.

The proposed IETF AAA-based key-generation mechanism creates new extensions in the RRQ and RRP messages to carry the keying material and security association parameters. In the RRQ, extensions exist to request a key between the Mobile Node and FA and/or a key between the Mobile Node and Home Agent. The extension also specifies the mechanism of how the key should be generated on the Mobile Node and AAA server. The Mobile Node adds the extension(s) in the RRQ to obtain the required key to authenticate with the mobility entities, which communicate with the AAA server using the RADIUS or Diameter protocol. At this time, the messaging has not been defined. The AAA server recognizes that key-generation request and offers the key in the reply to the FA and/or Home Agent. Also, the reply contains the key-generation material for the Mobile Node. The FA and Home Agent transfer the AAA information to extensions in the Registration Reply (RRP). Upon receiving the RRP, the Mobile Node obtains the information to generate the key to authenticate registration exchanges with the FA and Home Agent.

The new extensions are protected by the Mobile Node–AAA Server Authentication Extension in the RRQs and the Mobile Node–FA or Mobile Node–Home Agent Authentication Extension in the RRPs. The keys that authenticate the RRP are derived from the embedded keying material.

To secure its signaling, Mobile IP needs to leverage the existing security infrastructure, which is typically AAA based. Having a key-generation capability that uses an existing authentication mechanism simplifies deployment.

Mobile IPv6

As the Internet evolves from IPv4 to IPv6, mobility support in the Internet is also evolving accordingly. In the migration, seamless mobility becomes even more important because mobile users will likely account for a significant portion of the Internet population. Although the underlying principles of the Internet remain the same, IPv6 introduces mechanisms and features that should be considered by supporting protocols as they are designed. To this end, Mobile IP for IPv6 is being developed to efficiently leverage these nuances.

The aim of this section is to give you an idea of how the Mobile IP protocol is maturing. We start with an overview of Mobile IPv6 and then highlight the differences between Mobile IPv6 and Mobile IPv4. The section examines some of the issues that are arising in the design and considers the lessons that are being learned along the way.

Protocol Operation

The Mobile IPv6 base protocol is specified in IETF Request For Comment (RFC) 3775 to support communications of IPv6 hosts traversing IPv6 subnets.[1] It operates in much the same way as Mobile IPv4, with some differences pointed out in the section "Differences Between Mobile IPv4 and Mobile IPv6," later in this chapter.

When an IPv6 subnet boundary is crossed, the Mobile Node detects the network topologic movement and signals its Home Agent. The signal updates the Home Agent, which maintains the location binding of the Mobile Node's home IP address and the Mobile Node's current CoA. The home IP address is an address on the Home Network that identifies the source for the Mobile Node's communications. The CoA is the network access IP address on the Foreign Network that identifies the location of the Mobile Node. When the Home Agent receives the signal, the integrity of the information is checked, and the message source is authenticated before the mobility binding is updated. The binding sets up a forwarding entry to tunnel the Mobile Node's traffic to the CoA. At this point, the IPv6 Mobile Node can enjoy seamless mobility while roaming. You might be saying to yourself, "This sounds just like Mobile IPv4." You are right, but did you notice that there was no mention of a FA? Keep reading.

The location binding remains until the entry's lifetime expires or an explicit deletion notice from the Mobile Node is received. Given an existent binding, the Home Agent intercepts traffic destined for the Mobile Node's Home Address and encapsulates the packet to reach the Mobile Node. The encapsulated packet is destined to the CoA. Upon receiving an encap-sulated packet, the Mobile Node removes the tunnel header to obtain the original packet. Traffic from the Mobile Node is tunneled back to the Home Agent. The payloads in the tunnel can be protected by encryption. The source of the packet is the CoA that is topologically correct. The Home Agent decapsulates the packet and routes the payload containing the inner packet to the CN. The source of this packet is the Mobile Node's Home Address. Communication between the Mobile Node and CN bounces off the Home Agent in a figurative sense. Figure 9-7 shows the signaling and data flow of Mobile IPv6.

Figure 9-7   *Mobile IPv6 Signaling and Data Flow*

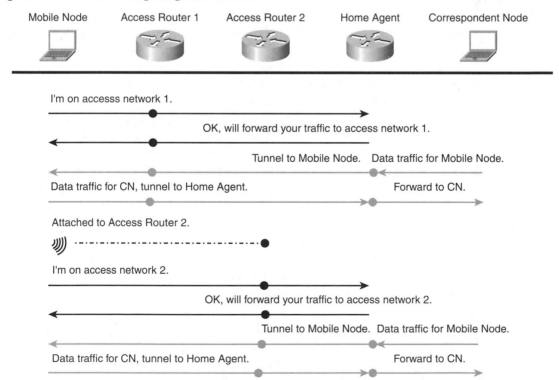

Route Optimization (Return Routability) in Mobile IPv6

The routing path for communication between a Mobile Node and CN can be optimized to allow data traffic to be exchanged directly between them. This is known as *route optimization*. Route optimization is a standard component in Mobile IPv6. As you would guess, it requires secure control signaling between the Mobile Node and CA. For traffic from the Mobile Node to the CN, the source IP address is the CoA and the destination IP address is the CN's IP address. The source and destination addresses are reversed for traffic from the CN to the Mobile Node.

Sounds great, but how does it work in the Internet? The Mobile IPv6 secret sauce is embedded in the IP header. The sender stores the Mobile Node's Home Address in the IP header of the packet to the recipient. When the packet is received on the CN, the source IP address is replaced by this Home Address so that an application believes that the peer is the Mobile Node (on its Home Network) and is unaware of the routing path taken from the CoA to reach the CN. In the other direction, when the Mobile Node receives a packet, the destination IP address is replaced by this Home Address, although the supplanted CoA ensured arrival through an optimal path.

The main challenge in route optimization is securing the control message for two hosts that do not have a preexisting security relationship. To this end, a clever, though not flawless, mechanism known as the Return Routability procedure was designed to set up the dynamic security credential between the Mobile Node and CN. The concept is based on the reasonable assurance that the Mobile Node is, in fact, reachable at both the CoA and its Home Address.

When the Mobile Node wants to set up an optimal routing, it signals to the CN through both paths: one path through the Home Network and one path directly from the Foreign Network. One message reaches the CN through the Home Agent, whereas another message arrives directly using the CoA as the source IP address. The CN responds by sending two messages, one on each path as well. Here's the first clincher: Only the receiver of both replies can formulate the security credential to signal the CN to set up the Mobile Node's Home Address and CoA association. Here's the second clincher: The solution operates with no security infrastructure or preestablished relationship between the Mobile Node and the CN. Having such a stateless functionality on the CN is a significant benefit.

Remember the previous statement in this chapter that described Return Routability: "a clever though not flawless mechanism." It is not flawless because the bad guy in the middle of both paths—a point in the Home Agent path after the IPSec tunnel—can rudely steal the security credential of the association. Also, the scheme is not efficient for mobility because the key is only for the Home Address and CoA binding. Therefore, the optimized path is maintained only if the Return Routability procedure happens each time the Mobile Node moves to a new CoA. Also, the lifetime of the key requires the procedure to run within 7 minutes. Note that the additional signaling for Return Routability takes time to set up an optimal path. While the procedure is in progress, the Mobile Node communicates with the CN through the Home Agent.

Mobile IPv6 Messaging

Mobile IPv6 introduces new messages to IPv6 and new options to extend existing IPv6 mechanisms. Numerous enhancements are found in the Mobile IP working groups, which propose more messages and options. This section covers the fundamental messages in the base protocol.

Move Detection

Because you found out that no FAs exist in Mobile IPv6, you might have wondered: "How does the Mobile Node perform move detection because there is no agent signaling?" When the Mobile Node attaches to the network, movement detection automatically happens. The IPv6 Neighbor Discovery (RFC 2461) allows the Mobile Node to learn its current subnet information and determine whether any subnet was traversed. After detecting that it is on a new subnet, the Mobile Node obtains an IP address using either DHCP or autoconfiguration, and registers with its Home Agent and/or CN. However, the RFC was not suited for the mobile environment because it had limited the minimum router advertisement interval to 3 seconds. This value would not be timely enough for a Mobile Node to learn whether the subnet had changed. Mobile IPv6 enhanced the interval to support millisecond granularity to achieve faster move detection using periodic router advertisements.

The Mobile Node does not need to passively await the router advertisements. It can send a router solicitation immediately after the link-layer state becomes active. Unfortunately, no standards exist for detecting network attachment, though Mobile Node implementations typically support this mode of operation. The solicitation/ advertisement exchange method is superior to periodic advertisements because of the asynchronous nature for better performance and reduced wireless bandwidth consumption.

Registration Messages

The premise of basic mobility starts with the following messages. Their purpose is to signal a Mobile Node's network access location to the Home Agent or CN:

- Binding Update message
- Binding Acknowledgment message

The Mobile Node sends a Binding Update to inform the Home Agent or CN of its current location when it is not on its Home Network. The location information—the mapping of the Home Address to the CoA—is stored in the binding cache entry, which sets up the routing logic on the Home Agent and CN to deliver traffic targeted for the Mobile Node's Home Address toward the Mobile Node's CoA. The traffic-flow service allows the Mobile Node to maintain communications using its Home Address while changing the network access location identified by the CoA. The Binding Acknowledgment is sent by the Home Agent or CN to confirm the reception of the Binding Update. Both messages are protected by the IPSec protocol, specified in the companion RFC 3776, between the Mobile Node and Home Agent. The binding management key, described in next set of messages, protects the messages between the Mobile

Node and CN. If you read too quickly, you might have missed that the same messages are protected differently between pairs of mobility entities. Remember that the Mobile Node and CN cannot have a preexisting security relationship? That's why the binding management key is used instead. See how this dynamic key is derived in the next section. The Binding Update and Binding Acknowledgment messages are analogous to the RRQ and RRP messages in Mobile IPv4. They perform the same roles in IP mobility operation.

An alternative method is available for authenticating the Binding Update and Binding Acknowledgment messages that is similar to Mobile IPv4. The authentication option is covered in the section "Lessons Learned," later in this chapter.

Route Optimization (Return Routability) Messages

The following messages and mobility options enable an optimized routing path for traffic between the Mobile Node and CN through the Return Routability procedure:

- Home test init (HoTI) message
- Care of test init (CoTI) message
- Home test (HoT) message
- Care of test (CoT) message
- Binding refresh request
- Binding error message
- Home address destination option
- Type 2 routing header option
- Binding authorization data option

To achieve an optimal path, the CN needs to set up a binding cache entry for the Mobile Node's Home Address/current CoA. This state requires a Binding Update message from the Mobile Node. The signaling must be authenticated by the CN. But how can this happen if the Mobile Node and CN don't share a key? The key that is known by the CN must somehow be transported to the Mobile Node. The trick lies in the relationship of the key-generation material and the two addresses.

A simplified analogy of the scheme goes like this: Jane wants to tell John something and asks him to provide a secret code. John writes "1+2" on a piece of paper and rips it in half across the plus sign. Each piece is mailed separately to Jane at address A and address B. When Jane receives both of them, she knows that the answer is 3. That value authenticates the message that Jane sends to John: "I live at both address A and address B. The answer is 3."

Specifically, the CN has a master key to use for authentication of all Binding Updates from any Mobile Node. This master key is used only to derive a pair of key-generation tokens, which combine to form the dynamic binding management key used for authentication of the Binding Update. Only one of the tokens—the one that has a relationship with the address—is delivered on each path. Derivation of the binding management key requires possession of both token values. Obtaining the tokens requires the recipient to be reached at both the Home Address and CoA. The following demonstrates how the messages derive the binding management key.

Figure 9-8 illustrates the message exchanges in the Return Routability procedure. The HoTI message is sent by the Mobile Node to request a token from the CN through the Home Agent (as shown in 1A). The purpose of the HoT message is to deliver the token to the Mobile Node on the Home Address path (as shown in 2A). The token value is calculated with the CN's master key, Home Address, and a random number. The Mobile Node sends the CoTI message to request a token from the CN through the direct path (as shown in 1B). The CoT message carries the other token to the Mobile Node on the CoA path (as shown in 2B). The token value is based on the CN's master key, CoA, and a random number. The Mobile Node derives the binding management key from the Home Address and CoA tokens. At this point, the Mobile Node can send the Binding Update with the binding authorization data option that contains a cryptographic value generated from the binding management key. The CN derives the pair of token values that are based on the fields within the Binding Update message to obtain the same binding management key. Thus, the CN can authenticate that the message is from the right Mobile Node. The Binding Acknowledgment is sent to the Mobile Node.

Figure 9-8   *Mobile IPv6 Return Routability Procedure*

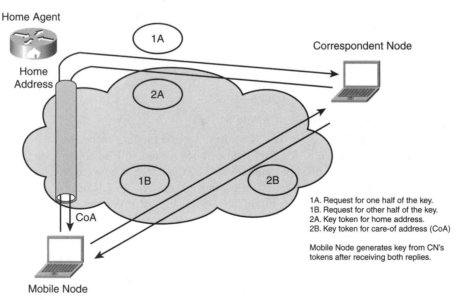

The advantage of this mechanism is that the CN is stateless. The CN is the responder and keeps no correlation between the HoT and CoT tokens it sends to the Mobile Node. CN derives the token it had sent to the Mobile Node based on the information that the Mobile Node includes in the Binding Update and then derives the binding management key. The CN responds to exactly one message with each request it receives from the Mobile Node, thus avoiding reflection attacks and packet multiplication attacks. This means that one packet sent to a destination generates multiple packets in response.

The CN sends a binding refresh request to the Mobile Node to extend the lifetime of the binding cache entry. This message requests the Mobile Node to initiate the Return Routability procedure.

After the binding cache entry is established by the exchange of Binding Update and Binding Acknowledgment messages, the traffic can flow directly, as illustrated in Figure 9-9. In Step 1, the Mobile Node sends packets to the CN using the Home Address destination option, which identifies the Mobile Node's Home Address to the recipient in the IP header. The Home Address destination option allows the Mobile Node to communicate directly to the CN using the CoA as the source IP address of packets sent out. The CN would know the IP address of the Mobile Node, regardless of where the packet came from. The Home Address is invariant, while the CoA is transient and depends on the location of the Mobile Node. In Step 2, if the CN receives a data packet with a Home Address destination option from a Mobile Node that had not performed Return Routability, the binding error message is sent to the source address of the offending packet. Otherwise, the source IP address is replaced by the Home Address in the Home Address destination option on the CN. In Step 3, the CN sends packets to the Mobile Node directly using the Type 2 routing header that contains the Home Address. The packet is destined to the CoA. In Step 4, the Mobile Node receives the packet and swaps the Home Address (in the Home Address destination option) and CoA (in the destination IP address field). The applications on the Mobile Node and CN communicate using only the Home Address, unaware that the CoA is the routing address that transports the packets between them.

Figure 9-9 *Mobile IPv6 Optimized Routing*

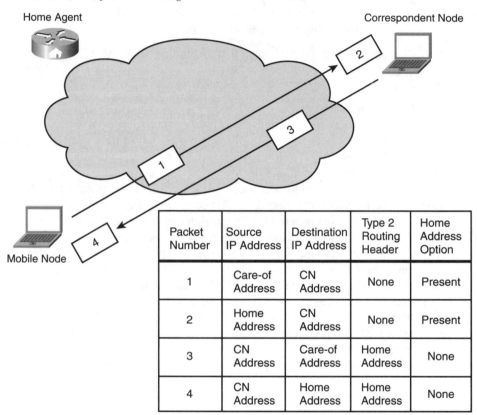

Packet Number	Source IP Address	Destination IP Address	Type 2 Routing Header	Home Address Option
1	Care-of Address	CN Address	None	Present
2	Home Address	CN Address	None	Present
3	CN Address	Care-of Address	Home Address	None
4	CN Address	Home Address	Home Address	None

ICMP Messages

Mobile IPv6 defines a dynamic Home Agent address discovery (DHAAD) mechanism that allows the Mobile Node to dynamically choose a Home Agent from a subnet. New IPv6 Internet Control Message Protocol (ICMP) messages are introduced to allow for discovering a Home Agent through this process:

- Home Agent address discovery request
- Home Agent address discovery reply

If the Mobile Node knows the home subnet prefix but not the specific Home Agent address, the Mobile Node sends a dynamic Home Agent address discovery request message to the Home Agent anycast address. The Home Agent anycast address is constructed from the prefix by appending a well-known Home Agent suffix. The Home Agent that receives the message responds with the list of available Home Agents. This information is sent in the dynamic Home Agent address discovery reply message. Each Home Agent is aware of other Home Agents on the same link based on the router advertisements received. The DHAAD request and reply messages are not protected or authenticated. If these messages are to be protected, the Mobile Node needs to know with which Home Agent to establish IPSec. Initiating IPSec requires the Mobile Node to know which peer is the Home Agent. Because the Mobile Node does not know the Home Agent and, in fact, is attempting to obtain that information, the messages cannot be protected. Unavoidably, the IPv6 addresses of all the Home Agents on the subnet are sent in the clear to the Mobile Node.

For those who are familiar with Mobile IPv4 dynamic Home Agent address resolution, the scheme sends the RRQ to a particular subnet using a subnet-directed broadcast. In this case, all Home Agents on the subnet receive the request and each sends a RRP, informing the Mobile Node of its IP address. In Mobile IPv6, only one Home Agent receives the ICMP request and sends an ICMP reply with the list of Home Agents on the subnet.

Differences Between Mobile IPv4 and Mobile IPv6

The mobility support is fundamentally the same for Mobile IPv4 and Mobile IPv6. The Home Agent and Mobile Node provide the same functional roles. The Mobile Node still selects which interface to use for communications by notifying the Home Agent where to route its traffic. The Home Agent continues to tunnel packets to the Mobile Node. The protocol remains transparent to other nodes, with the exception of route optimization, which also involves the CA.

However, Mobile IPv6 differs from an IPv4-based solution in the following ways:

- The FA is eliminated.
- Route optimization (RO) is an integral component. The Mobile Node and CN decide whether they want to enable an optimal path, and the Home Agent decides whether RO should be allowed. Traffic between a Mobile Node and CN uses a new routing header and destination option, instead of a tunnel header.
- Mobile IPv6 is a part of the IPv6 protocol itself, not a User Datagram Protocol (UDP) message.
- The control messages are required to be protected by IPSec. Authentication extension is an optional feature, as described in the section "AAA-Based Dynamic Key Generation."
- The dynamic Home Agent address discovery is based on the anycast address, not the subnet-directed broadcast.
- IPv6 autoconfiguration simplifies the Mobile Node's CoA assignment.

Some of the differences in the features offered by IPv6 are innate. We consider each of the previous points and look at the merits and tradeoffs involved.

An important difference is that no FAs exist in Mobile IPv6. One reason that Mobile IPv4 needed a FA is because of the lack of IP addresses in IPv4. Because it would be costly if each Mobile Node on the Foreign Network consumed an IP address (CoA), the FA allowed numerous Mobile Nodes to use the same CoA. On the contrary, IPv6 has an abundance of addresses. Therefore, this Foreign Network function was considered unnecessary and, in a sense, in the way for mobility in IPv6.

However, as with most things, it is not that clear cut. The time to obtain an IP address on the foreign subnet depends on the address allocation scheme involving duplicate address detection. Nevertheless, to start the registration process in the FA's case will likely take longer than the agent or router advertisement. The CoA belongs to the FA and therefore does not have the address contention issue.

An important benefit of having a FA is that only the original packet travels over the valuable air link. Without FAs, Mobile IPv6 now requires traffic to the Mobile Node to also carry a tunnel header from the Home Agent or a new IPv6 routing header from the CN. If you look closer, the number of tunnel endpoints on the Home Agent increases because no aggregation point exists on Foreign Networks; this impacts the processing and memory on the Home Agent. Furthermore, the lack of a FA means that no mobility signaling is available to enforce Foreign Network policy. Not to cry over spilled milk, but having a FA would have also helped the route optimization scenario, where the Mobile Node moves between subnets on the same FA. Specifically, the CNs need not be signaled, and traffic in transit need not be lost. It's almost like this: "Be careful what you ask for; you might just get it!"

In addition, as with most things, another solution usually exists. In this case, having a Mobility Anchor Point (MAP) in the foreign domain [described in the section "Hierarchical Mobile IPv6 (HMIPv6)," later in this chapter] provides some of the benefits of having a FA function.

Debate continues on the practical benefits of route optimization. Academically speaking, there's no doubt that reaching from one point to another in a logical straight line is better than traveling through a triangulation point. But, when you consider that routing directs packets based on various factors such as load, cost, administrative reasons, and so on, it is no longer certain. In fact, the path from the CN to the CoA can have longer transit latency than the path from the CN to Home Agent to CoA. Regardless, route optimization is commonly believed to be a "good thing." But good things don't come free.

Bypassing the Home Network means a lack of centralized policy enforcement and accounting for billing on the Mobile Node's traffic, and new dependency on the Foreign Network to provide these critical functions.

Additional signaling is incurred between the Mobile Node and the CN to set up the optimal path. Signaling introduces more processing on both ends and more consumption of air-link bandwidth. Also, a trust relationship is required between peers to update the routing entry. Mobile IPv6 route optimization uses the Return Routability procedure to set up the keys to protect the signaling between the Mobile Node and the CN. If the CN can exchange signaling with the Mobile Node using both addresses, one can assume that the Mobile Node is legitimate, especially because the request is to bind the addresses. As discussed previously, one known weakness in the Return Routability scheme is interception by a bad guy in the middle, when messages from both addresses are in the clear.

Location privacy is an issue when route optimization is used. Even though the Mobile Node's CoA does not provide adequate physical location, nevertheless the network access location is known to the CN. This can be enough detail to warrant reasons for nondisclosure.

Some Mobile IPv4 deployments support Voice over IP without a noticeable quality issues. VoIP traffic is highly susceptible to loss, latency, and jitter. *Loss* is when a packet is dropped in the network. *Latency* is the one-way trip time from one end to the other side. *Jitter* is the variance in time interval between the incoming packets. Various techniques are used, such as buffering and repeating on the receiving node, to improve the perception of the voice quality. Although the traffic in this network is always routed through the Home Agent, users could not detect that their conversations were Mobile IP–enabled VoIP.

Another common IPv4 application is the enterprise virtual private network (VPN), a secure pipeline between the users and their corporate network. This virtual link is set up to allow employees to access their services at work through a VPN gateway. At this point, it's unclear how this model will be adopted in IPv6. If a similar technique is used, the VPN gateway becomes the triangulation point between the Mobile Node and CN. Thus, the route optimization cannot be applied because the traffic is secured by the VPN gateway where it is routed through.

Despite the cost of additional states for the peers, some additional messaging, and roundtrip delays, proponents of route optimization argue that the benefits include the following:

- Reduction of traffic load on the Home Network
- Less network load on the entire Internet
- Less jitter and latency in communications
- Robustness against network problems because of fewer routing path traversals
- Avoidance of tunneling overhead

Traffic from the CN to the Mobile Node uses a new routing header instead of a tunnel header.

Tunneling places a new IP header in front of a packet, allowing traffic to be directed to another location. The cost is that the packet "grows" by the size of the additional IP header(s). One side effect of an increased packet size is that fragmentation might be needed, as discussed for Mobile IPv4. Regardless of whether fragmentation occurs before or after encapsulation, the packet requires reassembly, which adds latency to the traffic. Another side effect of encapsulation is that the increased-size packet is sent over the air link to reach the Mobile Node, reducing the effective bandwidth of the air link.

With route optimization in Mobile IPv6, a new IPv6 routing header trims the overhead by replacing the tunneling method. Instead of an entire IPv6 header being added to a packet from a CN, only the Mobile Node's Home Address information is added through the routing header, and the packet is destined to the CoA instead. As a comparison point, an IPv6 header using the Advanced Encryption Standard (AES) for encryption is 52 bytes while the Home Address option is 18 bytes. The typical Mobile IPv4 tunnel header is 20 bytes.

The routing header allows the packet to traverse a path leading to the CoA, and thus, enables the CN to send directly to the Mobile Node.

The signaling used in Mobile IPv6 is a part of the IPv6 protocol itself. In Mobile IPv4, UDP messages perform the registration. In addition, the control messages are protected differently.

The IPSec Authentication Header (AH) or Encapsulating Security Payload (ESP) protects the signaling between the Mobile Node and Home Agent, as specified in RFC 3776. The integrity of the message can be confirmed by authentication. In Mobile IPv4, IPSec might not be supported on the Mobile Node and Home Agent and, thus, could not be used as the standard security mechanism.

In contrast, all IPv6 nodes are required to support IPSec. As you have seen before, theory is not always reality. Thus, the nodes might not always support IPSec. Moreover, many protocols, including IPSec, were designed and implemented without mobility in mind, and thus do not lend themselves seamlessly to integration with mobility.

Is there a need then to support IPv6 nodes without IPSec or with only static IPSec functionality? The section "Authentication Option," later in this chapter, covers this topic.

The dynamic Home Agent resolution method in Mobile IPv6 allows the Mobile Node to choose the Home Agent on a particular subnet. If the Mobile Node knows the home subnet prefix but not the specific Home Agent, the Mobile Node can send an ICMP message destined to the anycast address on the home subnet. Normal routing takes the message to the nearest Home Agent, which responds with the list of available Home Agents. The Home Agent updates the list based on reception of router advertisements on the subnet.

In Mobile IPv4, the Mobile Node sends the RRQ to the subnet-directed broadcast address. This is a special address that is routed normally to a particular subnet. The router on that subnet broadcasts this message on the targeted subnet. All the Home Agents on the subnet receive the RRQ and send a RRP, informing the Mobile Node of their IP addresses.

In IPv6, a device can autoconfigure its IP address after receiving the router advertisement. This is possible because the Mobile Node can learn the subnet prefix and append its message authentication code (MAC) address, which is typically unique, to obtain a routable IP address on the subnet. Of course, duplicate address detection must be used to avoid collision with other nodes. This mechanism is simple and quick, allowing the Mobile Node to get the CoA for home registration. In IPv4, a common procedure is using DHCP, which takes four message exchanges between the client and the DHCP server.

In IPv4, Address Resolution Protocol (ARP) finds the MAC address for a particular IP address. The IP address–to–MAC address association is stored in the ARP entry so that the sender knows which MAC address to use to send a packet destined to that IP address. For Mobile IPv4, the Home Agent sends gratuitous ARP messages on the home subnet after the Mobile Node registers to update devices that already have an ARP entry for the Mobile Node. In addition, the Home Agent performs proxy ARP by responding to an ARP request on the home subnet. Both methods ensure that packets destined for the Mobile Node are received by the Home Agent, which tunnels them to the Mobile Node.

In Mobile IPv6, these Home Agent functions are provided by the IPv6 neighbor discovery mechanism. ARP is an Ethernet-based protocol, whereas neighbor discovery is an IP-based protocol. Both mechanisms provide the same end functionality.

Transition to Mobile IPv6

Mobile IPv4 deployments are not switching over to Mobile IPv6 overnight. Is there a need to leverage existing Mobile IPv4 infrastructure to support IPv6 clients? Or would it be better to build a future-proof Mobile IPv6 infrastructure for IPv6 clients and legacy IPv4 clients? Should there be coexisting Mobile IPv4 and Mobile IPv6 infrastructures?

As a reference point, cdma2000 is expected to support both Mobile IPv4 and Mobile IPv6. IETF has proposals that support each of these cases. The answer will depend on the network that is used for IPv6 services. If an existing Mobile IPv4 network is already in place, an overlay of the IPv6 data traffic would suffice. Most likely, we will see new Mobile IPv6 networks built for these new services. The following section explains how the Mobile IPv4 clients can upgrade to Mobile IPv6 to reap the benefits.

Lessons Learned

Mobile IPv6 has a clear advantage in that it is the successor to Mobile IPv4. This might be stating the obvious, but because Mobile IPv4 has been deployed and tested in the field, much can be learn from the experience. So, what was learned from Mobile IPv4 that can be applied to Mobile IPv6?

A major eyeopener was that service-provider deployments use the AAA infrastructure. Although the Mobile IPv6 protocol defined in RFC 3775 is designed using a security association between a Mobile Node and a Home Agent, the relationship between the Mobile Node and AAA is mandatory in these deployments. And, the NAI is the common identifier for the AAA infrastructure. Thus, it seems that using an authentication mechanism for the NAI is prudent, because the standard IPSec is between the IP endpoints. Another point to consider is that the network would like to use the same security key with the Mobile Node, regardless of whether it is using Mobile IPv4 or Mobile IPv6.

Deployment of Mobile IPv4 struggled because of the configuration needed on the client. It was then easy to realize that Mobile IPv6 needed a method to bootstrap the Mobile Node configurations, such as the Home Agent address, security association with the Home Agent, and so on, using the AAA infrastructure.

Not all lessons learned need to stem from deployment experience. Just analyzing the situation and behavior that would ensue gives rise to clever solutions. To this end, Hierarchical Mobile

IP and Fast Mobile IP (described in the sections that follow) are enhancements to Mobile IPv6 that make the protocol more efficient.

Network Access Identifier

In Mobile IP deployments—whether IPv4 or IPv6—a Mobile Node is typically identified by an NAI for authentication purposes. Recall that a Mobile Node using an NAI can be dynamically assigned a Home Address, and even its Home Agent. Although the Mobile Node is identified by the NAI, the Home Address remains the routing identifier, and the Home Agent serves as the Home Address routing anchor.[2]

The authentication identifier (NAI) and routing identifier (Home Address) provide different functions but are linked in the control message processing. The control message is authenticated based on the NAI and then updates the routing for the Mobile Node. Identifying a Mobile Node by an NAI allows integration with the AAA infrastructure.

Because many Mobile IPv4 deployments already use NAI to authenticate the Mobile Nodes, this sets precedence for Mobile IPv6. Thus, a service provider can use the same AAA infrastructure, regardless of the IP version used by the Mobile Nodes.

Authentication Option

The Mobile IPv6 control messages require integrity, authentication, and antireplay protection. No doubt, IPSec in conjunction with IKE surely provides these functions. However, as pointed out previously, IPSec might not always be a viable and practical method. For example, consider the following:

- IKE and IPSec are general-purpose protocols that can be heavyweight for simple fast authentication in a mobility environment.

- No standard method exists for integrating IKE/IPSec with the AAA infrastructure.

- Mobile IPv4 deployment migration to Mobile IPv6 requires the same security infrastructure.

One key proponent for an alternative authentication method is the 3GPP2 standards organization, which is chartered to develop the specifications for cdma2000 wireless communications systems. Cdma2000 operators have deployed some of the largest Mobile IPv4 customer base.

In IETF, this issue has been heatedly debated. A majority, although not an overwhelming percentage, of participants in the Mobile IPv6 Working Group favors the introduction of a new destination option to provide authentication between the Mobile Node and Home Agent. Here are the practical rationales behind IPSec-less authentication:[3]

- IPSec might not be required or feasible in all cases in which Mobile IPv6 can be used. For small price-sensitive devices, the use of IPSec can consume too much battery life and too many processing cycles. Although this type of Mobile Node is not IPv6 compliant because IPSec is a mandatory component, it is still a reality.

- The Common Enterprise VPN solution has another IPSec to encrypt traffic between the Mobile Node and the VPN gateway. Mobile IPv6 needs encryption between the Mobile Node and Home Agent for the Return Routability procedure used for route optimization. Two layers of encryption are redundant and reduce the throughput rate.

- The multiple round trips needed to perform IKE to establish the IPSec security association increase the delay during initial setup and handoffs.

- No standard mechanism currently exists for IKE/IPSec to use the AAA infrastructure to authenticate a Mobile Node. Support for this method in existing implementations is vendor specific. AAA-based authentication is a common practice in Mobile IPv4 service provider networks. It would make sense to use the same AAA mechanism, or specifically the Mobile Node-AAA key, to authenticate Mobile IPv6 or dual-stack clients.

- Some IPSec implementations can require significant modifications to support Mobile IPv6.

- The change needed to support Mobile IPv6 in IPSec hardware accelerators is problematic because the development cycle is expensive and occurs over a period of time.

- IPSec is security critical. In some systems, it might have been through a formal security evaluation. Changes to IPSec risk potential breakage that can compromise security.

- Some implementations support AH and ESP, but not IKE. Even if the implementation supports IKE, major changes to IKE might be needed to support Mobile IPv6.

- The use of a manual IPSec security association in service-provider deployment suffers from scalability issues and creates a provisioning nightmare. In addition, this method lacks replay protection.

- Because the IPSec security association is linked to the Home Address, manual IPSec would prohibit the flexibility of a dynamic Home Address or home prefix assignment.

- Configuration of IPSec by users is challenging. How are users supposed to configure the security policy database? If IPSec is being used for other purposes at the same time (for example, corporate VPN access), how can you make sure that no conflict exists with Mobile IPv6?

- Some user feedback suggests the need to make IPSec easier to configure or to have an alternative for Mobile IPv6 authentication.

Opponents to the alternative authentication option[4] offer the following arguments:

- IPSec is part of a standards-based IPv6 node. Why should Mobile IPv6 be modified to satisfy deviants? The authentication option might be promoting IPv6 noncompliance in regard to IPSec.

- Having multiple authentication methods complicates implementation and deployment.

- Why not keep IPSec but use the AAA infrastructure to set up a security association between the Mobile Node and Home Agent?

- A better solution is to use IKEv2 with EAP for addressing the problem of a standardized integration with AAA-based credentials. This means that EAP is carried in the IKEv2 messages and authenticates the Mobile Node with the AAA server. Then IKEv2 dynamically sets up the IPSec security association between the Mobile Node and Home Agent. Note that IKEv2 is a work in progress in IETF, and it will be some time before standards-based commercial implementations are available.

- Route optimization is not supported in the alternative authentication method.

Technical merits can be found on both sides. Having the option of a built-in Mobile IPv6 authentication method allows the real world to decide what works. And deployments will likely use the timely solution that provides the most benefit.

Bootstrap

In Mobile IPv6, the IPSec security association protects the Binding Update between the Mobile Node's Home Address and the Home Agent's IP address. The Mobile Node must know its Home Address, its Home Agent address, and the IPSec security association with that Home Agent. In deployment scenarios, the Mobile Node can be dynamically assigned a Home Address by the Home Agent or AAA server, and moreover, the Home Agent can be dynamically assigned by the AAA server. These deployment issues challenge the simple security relationship between the Home Address and Home Agent.

The question is then "How do you seed the Mobile Node with the Home Address, Home Agent address, and IPSec security association when the addresses are dynamic in nature?" Commonly, a AAA server authenticates users of the network and grants access and service authorization, as well as providing accounting. The Mobile Node and AAA server have a security relationship in this type of network infrastructure. Thus, logically, the Mobile Node can be bootstrapped with the required Mobile IPv6 information by integrating with the AAA server.[5]

The benefit of integrating with a AAA infrastructure is that it allows the Home Address and Home Agent to be dynamically assigned. Besides not having to be preconfigured with these parameters, dynamic assignment has several other benefits. On the dynamic Home Address assignment front, benefits include DHCP-based address management, duplicate address collision recovery, randomly generated addresses for privacy, and address autoconfiguration. Dynamic Home Agent assignment is desirable for the following reasons:

- The Home Agent discovery mechanism on a subnet
- Load balancing among multiple Home Agents
- Locating the nearest Home Agent to the Mobile Node

By having the ability to bootstrap the Mobile Node through the AAA server, all of these benefits can be gained.

The solution for integration with the AAA infrastructure is in the standardization process. One approach is using EAP,[6] which has the following steps:

1 The Mobile Node boots up and initiates network access authentication using EAP.

2 Optionally, a protected channel [for example, a Transport Layer Security (TLS) tunnel] is set up for delivery of subsequent EAP signaling. This step is necessary when sensitive information is exchanged between the Mobile Node and the AAA server.

3 Authentication between the Mobile Node and the AAA server happens. The procedure and its security properties depend on the selected EAP method.

4 After authentication, the AAA server authorizes Mobile IPv6 service and downloads host configuration information within EAP payloads to the Mobile Node. At this point, the Mobile Node knows its Home Address, the assigned Home Agent address, the peer authentication method (that is, certificates or a preshared key), and the cryptographic material (for example, a preshared key) needed to set up an IPSec security association with IKE. The IKE preshared key can be either constructed by the AAA server and then delivered to the Mobile Node or independently derived by each side.

5 After successful authentication and Mobile IPv6 service authorization, the EAP session is terminated.

6 The bootstrap has completed, which allows the Mobile Node to register with the assigned Home Agent using the IKE security association obtained in Step 4.

As with most proposals in the IETF, technical debates will continue on the various aspects of the design.

In cdma2000 deployments, a Mobile Node–Home Agent authentication option protects the Mobile IP signaling. Specifically, the Mobile Node–Home Agent key is dynamically generated by the Mobile Node and AAA server at the beginning of a mobility session. The AAA then delivers the shared key to the Home Agent so that the Home Agent can use the key to protect the Mobile IP messages between itself and the Mobile Node. Cdma2000 networks have the PDSN that participates in the bootstrapping scheme.

In the 3GPP2 specification, the PDSN is the network access server that authenticates the Mobile Node during PPP session setup. During the authentication phase, the PDSN downloads the Home Agent address and Home Address/home subnet prefix information from the home AAA server. Note that the NAI identifies the Mobile Node for authentication purposes and the Home Address is only a routing identifier. This means that any IP address can be assigned to the Mobile Node, regardless of whether it was provisioned statically or dynamically generated by the network, or derived by the Mobile Node, as in the case of IPv6 autoconfiguration using the home subnet prefix.

After the PPP session comes up, the Mobile Node learns about its Home Address and the assigned Home Agent from the PDSN during DHCPv6. Then the Mobile Node sends a Binding Update to the Home Agent. The message contains the NAI option and is protected by the Mobile Node–AAA server authentication option. The Home Agent processes the Binding

Update by sending a AAA request with the extracted authentication credentials (for example, NAI, authentication option fields) to the home AAA server. The home AAA server authenticates the Mobile Node and generates the Mobile Node–Home Agent key by executing a defined formula with the Mobile Node–AAA server key, random number, Home Agent address, and Home Address. The Mobile Node–Home Agent key is included in the AAA reply that is sent to the Home Agent, which stores the key to authenticate the Mobile Node–Home Agent authentication option.

The Home Agent performs duplicate address detection on the Home Address in the Binding Update before sending the Binding Acknowledgment to the Mobile Node. The message contains the NAI option and the Mobile Node–Home Agent authentication option. When the Mobile Node receives the Binding Acknowledgment, it generates the same Mobile Node–Home Agent key derived from the same formula to validate the message. Further reregistrations use NAI to identify the Mobile Node and Mobile Node–Home Agent authentication option to protect the message exchanges.

The proposed solution provides a bootstrapping mechanism, dynamic Home Address and Home Agent assignment, and a method for Mobile Node–Home Agent key generation.

Hierarchical Mobile IPv6 (HMIPv6)

When the Mobile Node moves to a new location, control messages are exchanged between the Mobile Node and Home Agent to update routing for the Mobile Node's traffic. Until the update is processed, a period exists when traffic to the Mobile Node is forwarded by the Home Agent to the previous location. The number of packets lost during this time directly depends on the latency of the update. Adding some fuel to the fire, if route optimization is being used, the Mobile Node must send updates to all the CNs after a move. The latency between the Mobile Node and CN is another factor that contributes to packet loss. Looking from a different angle, it is not hard to see that the number of update messages required increases with the number of CNs involved. Thus, a move by the Mobile Node consumes precious air-link bandwidth because of the update signaling.

The solution that addresses this issue is to confine the signaling locally and hide the movements from CNs. The MAP is introduced to anchor the CoA of the Mobile Node in the region of the visited network.[7] The MAP operates as a Home Agent serving the regional CoA. The Home Agent and CNs send traffic to the regional CoA to reach the Mobile Node. When the Mobile Node moves inside the region, only the MAP is aware. The movements are hidden from the Home Agent and CN because the MAP directs traffic to the location of the Mobile Node. The result is signaling with reduced latency because the MAP is topologically proximate to the Mobile Node. In addition, air-link usage for updates to CNs is eliminated. Another benefit is location privacy, because the exact visited subnet is unknown for the CN and Home Agent. One disadvantage is that the MAP encapsulates traffic to the Mobile Node, increasing the size of packets over the air. Figure 9-10 illustrates handovers within the region of an MAP.

The Mobile Node learns whether the visited network supports HMIPv6 and activates local mobility management with the MAP accordingly. If it is using HMIPv6, the Mobile Node communicates with the Home Agent and CN using the MAP's CoA. The Home Agent and CN perform normal operation using the CoA provided by Mobile Node.

The goal of Hierarchical Mobile IP is to localize the signaling when the Mobile Node moves within a region. Achieving this goal makes practical sense. Generally, micromobility is essential within the access network to provide fast handoffs with minimal packet loss. However, such a function is usually "home-brewed" by each access technology. For example, the Cisco SWAN and Lightweight WLAN Access Point Protocol (LWAAP) support this type of function for WLAN, and cdma2000 has the A.10/A.11 (also known as the *RP interface*). An MAP might not be necessary depending on the topologic coverage of the Layer 2 micromobility scheme. If the footprint is relatively small, having an MAP would be effective in reducing signaling latency, eliminating Return Routability messages, and reducing the number of packets in transit that can end up being dropped.

Figure 9-10   *Hierarchical Mobile IPv6*

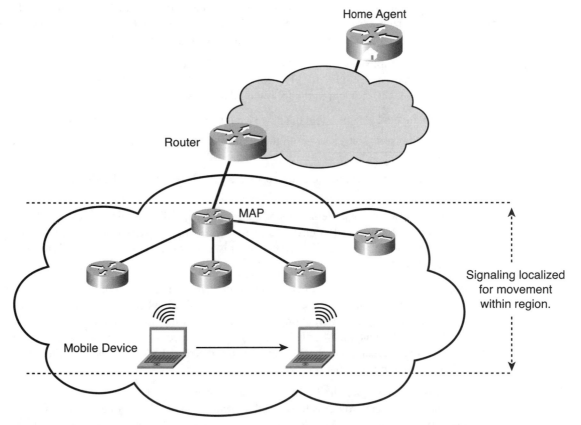

Fast Mobile IP

Latency in a network arises from both the network layer and link layer. *Network layer hand-over latency* is the total time for network prefix detection and location update signaling. *Link-layer latency* includes scanning for base stations or access points; obtaining signal information such as strength and quality for handover determination, attachment, or association; and network access authentication and authorization.

While Mobile IPv6 can control network layer latency, each link-layer technology addresses its own handover latency. To this end, a fast handover mechanism is introduced for Mobile IPv6.

We now look into some details of the latency issue. After link-layer indication that a Mobile Node has a new network attachment, the Mobile Node must figure out whether it has changed subnets. If it has not, the foreign subnet remains the same and no location update signaling is needed. On the other hand, if the Mobile Node learns about a new subnet, it must first use the duplicate address-detection mechanism before it can use the new CoA on the foreign subnet. Also, the Mobile Node needs to announce itself on the subnet through neighbor discovery message exchange. Then the Mobile Node can signal its Home Agent and optionally any CN(s) to direct traffic to the new CoA. Each of these steps increases the latency for the handover. Real-time applications such as Voice over IP are sensitive to packet loss, latency, and jitter. Therefore, it would be beneficial to reduce these types of problems in the network layer.

The goal is to accomplish as many of the steps a priori to the handover because the purpose of each operation cannot be eliminated. The solution offered in the Fast Handovers for Mobile IPv6 draft[8] tackles the problem in the following three ways:

- The Mobile Node learns about the new Foreign Network while still at its current location.
- The Mobile Node signals to set up tunneling from the previous access router to the new access router.
- The Mobile Node then immediately uses the new CoA to update the Home Agent and CN(s).

The solution has two flavors: predictive and reactive. The predictive fast handover is the scenario when the Mobile Node signals the current access router (AR) to set up for handover to the new foreign subnet. The reactive fast handover is when the Mobile Node signals to the new AR after the handover.

How does the Mobile Node know whether the current AR can provide predictive fast handover? The Mobile Node can signal to the current AR on a direct link whenever "anticipation" of a handover is feasible. When anticipation is not feasible or if the Mobile Node has not received a signal acknowledgment, the Mobile Node can signal immediately after attaching to the new AR's link. Note the assumption that the round-trip time from the Mobile Node to the previous AR is typically much faster than to the Home Agent.

For predictive fast handover, the Mobile Node notifies the current access router, before it moves, which new access router is to be used. How does the Mobile Node know about other Foreign Networks? When the Mobile Node hears a new base station or access point at the link layer, the Mobile Node requests the network prefix mapping from the current access router. The routers are expected know the AP-to-subnet mappings of neighboring routers, though the method is not specified. After the Mobile Node knows the new subnet, it signals the current access router to notify the new access router and tunnel traffic to the new location.

The Mobile Node announces itself on the new subnet and starts using the new CoA immediately to update the Home Agent. In the slight chance that a duplicate address exists, a recovery scheme is in place to select a new CoA for the Mobile Node to use. Figure 9-11 shows the signaling flow of predictive fast handover.

Figure 9-11   *Predictive Fast Handover*

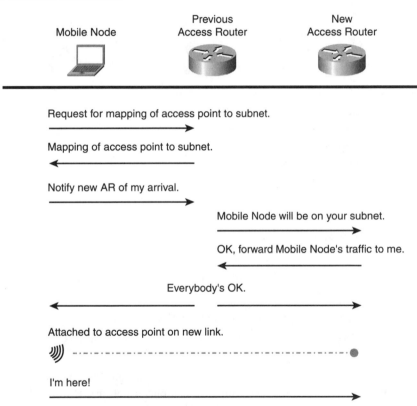

For reactive fast handover, when the Mobile Node moves to a new AR, it already knows that the new location is a different subnet. Thus, it immediately signals to the new AR to notify the previous AR. The previous AR then tunnels the Mobile Node's traffic to the new AR. In the meantime, the Mobile Node notifies its Home Agent and any CN(s) of its new location. The previous AR's binding of Home Address to new CoA is removed by signaling from the

Mobile Node after the location update to the Home Agent and the CN has completed. Figure 9-12 shows the signaling flow of reactive fast handover.

Note that the fast handover schemes operate independently from normal signaling between the Mobile Node and Home Agent or CN. The signaling is between the Mobile Node and the latest two ARs to reduce packet loss until the location update to the Home Agent and CN completes. If you are waiting to hear how the security relationship between the Mobile Node and current AR, or even between ARs, is established, it is not specified in the draft. One can assume, however, that AR-to-AR communication is secured within the network.

Figure 9-12 *Reactive Fast Handover*

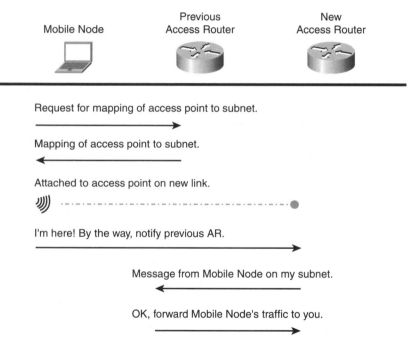

Request for mapping of access point to subnet.

Mapping of access point to subnet.

Attached to access point on new link.

I'm here! By the way, notify previous AR.

Message from Mobile Node on my subnet.

OK, forward Mobile Node's traffic to you.

Another point is that some link-layer handover takes a significant amount of time. The signaling needed to improve performance requires intersubnet capability. How much integration between link layer and network layer is needed for fast handover is still under debate. Seemingly, more interaction and cohesiveness between the layers would produce better performance. However, the gain in latency reduction comes at the cost of layer independence.

MANET

Thus far, the book has discussed mobility in the context of a structured and "centralized" network. While the Mobile Node is away from home, it registers back to an infrastructure or central location, namely, the Home Network, with its Home Agent. Moreover, it can use the infrastructure on the foreign domain through a FA or access router. Thus, not only does the Mobile Node have the freedom to roam, but it also has the luxury of a structured network for support.

Now imagine a mobile environment in which a central infrastructure does not exist. The Mobile Nodes would have to determine and manage their own routing as they and their peers move. This is quite a nontrivial task and has been the focus of much research over the years. The term for such a network is a Mobile Ad Hoc Network (MANET). You might already be familiar with such networks under the term *packet radio networks*, which have been around since the 1960s in a limited military capacity. The terms are synonymous. With the boom of mobile devices, MANETs are finding broader scope in commercial and military environments. And, as wireless technology advances, users desire even more freedom as they roam.

The aim of these networks is to support robust and efficient communication in a mobile wireless decentralized network by incorporating routing functionality into Mobile Nodes. An MANET has characteristics that make it fundamentally different from most wireline and centralized wireless networks.

An MANET is an autonomous set of nodes distributed over a geographical area that communicate over bandwidth-constrained wireless links. This sounds like a loaded sentence, but basically it means a group of Mobile Nodes that want to communicate with no existing infrastructure. This could be an army battalion, a mobile sensor network, participants in a conference, or even mobile users at a rock concert. Each node in an MANET can represent a transmitter, receiver, or relay station with varying physical capabilities. Typically, a discriminating and valuable capability is the power source because many nodes can operate on a limited battery supply. In such a network, packets usually traverse several intermediate (relay) nodes before reaching their destinations. These networks typically lack infrastructure: Nodes are mobile, no central hub or controller exists, and thus no fixed network topology exists. Although this can place more responsibility on the nodes, it allows mobile networks to be deployed without a priori planning or structure in place.

MANETs must also contend with a difficult and variable communication environment. Packet transmissions are plagued by the usual problems of radio communication, which include propagation path loss, signal multipath and fading, and thermal noise. These effects vary with terminal movement, which also induces Doppler spreading in the frequency of the transmitted signal. Finally, transmissions from neighboring terminals, known as multiaccess interference, hostile jammers, and impulsive interference (for example, ignition systems, generators, and other nonsimilar in-band communications) can contribute additional interference. Sounds a bit chaotic and messy!

Given this nature of MANETs, whether two nodes can directly communicate with one another is a function of their variable link quality, including signal strength and bandwidth. Thus, end-to-end routing paths vary based on environment and resulting network topology. In such networks, the topology can be stable for periods of time and then suddenly become unpredictable. Because MANETs are typically decentralized systems, no central controllers or specially designated routers exist to facilitate routing as the topology changes. All the routing decisions and forwarding (relaying) of packets must be done by the nodes themselves, and communication is on a peer-to-peer basis.

Mobile ad-hoc networking covers a broad spectrum of networking scenarios, ranging from a tactical battlefield to personal peer-to-peer communications. As you could guess, numerous variants of MANETs exist, depending on network size, network density, nodal mobility, and communication environment. The optimal routing approach depends on these various factors, and thus, a notion of the best MANET routing protocol does not exist. For example, an MANET network with high nodal mobility in a hostile environment has different routing requirements than an MANET network with a low rate of topological change.

Regardless of the network scenario, we can draw a few conclusions on the behavior of an MANET. Figure 9-13 shows a three-dimensional plot that characterizes MANET routing. Essentially, this plot shows that the "amount of data" successfully transmitted in the network, the "number of nodes" in the network, and the "frequency of movement" of the nodes are all intimately related. If you think about it for a minute, it is all intuitive. For example, if a network supports many nodes that are moving around often, the amount of data that can be transferred is far less than a network supporting few nodes that are relatively stationary.

Figure 9-13　*State of the Art for MANET Routing Protocols*

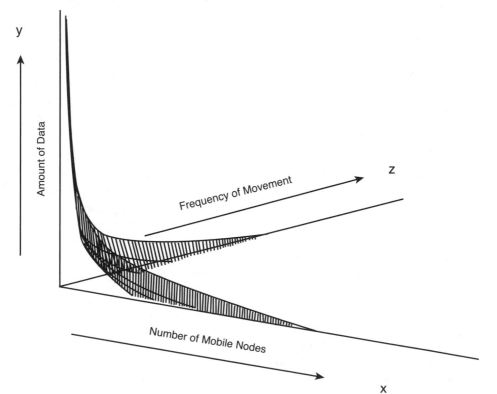

Any routing protocol deployed in an MANET should be able to perform as the network characteristics change, keeping the inferences of the previously described plot in mind. You already know that no notion of a best MANET routing protocol exists because it is not possible to be optimal in all scenarios. The MANET Working Group in the IETF has investigated this problem for several years. During this time, numerous MANET routing protocols have been proposed in the MANET Working Group. In a broad sense, the protocols can be categorized into two groups: reactive (on-demand) protocols and proactive protocols. Proactive protocols incur latency initially when determining all routes, even though they might never be used. Conversely, reactive protocols incur latency during the route discovery phase when a route is needed and also when using an obsolete route in a routing cache. After much technical debate and performance evaluations in the research community, three MANET protocols, as follows, were moved to experimental RFC status, with one on the way:

- Ad Hoc On Demand Distance Vector Routing (reactive)[9]
- Dynamic Source Routing Protocol (reactive)[10]
- Optimized Link State Routing (proactive)[11]
- Topology Broadcast based on Reverse Path Forwarding (proactive)[12]

Not to belabor the point, but no "winner" exists among these protocols. In fact, the performance of a protocol highly depends on the network environment and traffic pattern. For example, proactive protocols perform better in networks with higher mobility, because the protocol overhead to keep routes alive as the topology changes is warranted. On-demand protocols perform better in relatively stable networks with set source-destination communication pairs. Although several research implementations of the protocols can exist, the protocols are still considered to be in an infancy stage. No real-world deployments of the protocols exist, and performance evaluations have been based on testing studies.

Cisco Engineering is taking its own approach by leveraging existing IOS routing protocols, with initial efforts focusing on the Open Shortest Path First (OSPF) protocol.[13] Besides the fact that no winning MANET routing protocol exists, there are several other advantages for this approach, including easier integration of MANETs with existing networks. This would allow mobility devices to more easily migrate between an MANET and an infrastructure network. At the time of this writing, a special design team has been tasked in the IETF to standardize an OSPF-MANET routing protocol. (Cisco is a key participant in the design team.)

Besides routing within the MANET, it is necessary to route across the MANET. An MANET can be a stand-alone network in which the nodes communicate just among themselves. This can be the case in a sensor network, for example. Or, the MANET network might need to communicate across the global Internet. For such cases, integration between the MANET routing protocol and Mobile IP seems imminent. The two can already coexist, with the MANET protocol providing the backend peer-to-peer communications and Mobile IP providing global communication through a gateway node on the MANET registering back to a Home Agent. However, because direct link-layer connectivity between the gateway(s) in the MANET and a

FA on the visiting network is likely not always possible, modifications are necessary for viable integration.

Needless to say, the future of MANET routing is still in the works, and research continues. Stay tuned for coming attractions!

References

1 Johnson, D., et al., "Mobility Support in IPv6," IETF RFC 3775, June 2004.

2 Patel, A., et al., "Mobile Node Identifier Option for Mobile IPv6," draft-ietf-mip6-mn-ident-option-02.txt, Feb. 2005.

3 Roe, M., [Mip6] Justifications forstandardizingdraft-ietf-mip6-auth-protocol-00.txt, at 5:13 PM +0100, Sept. 20, 2004.

4 Patel, A., et al., "Authentication Protocol for Mobile IPv6," draft-ietf-mip6-auth-protocol-04.txt, Feb. 2005.

5 Patel, A., "Problem Statement for Bootstrapping Mobile IPv6," draft-ietf-mip6-bootstrap-ps-01.txt, Oct. 2004.

6 Giaretta, G., et al., "MIPv6 Authorization and Configuration Based on EAP," draft-giaretta-mip6-authorization-eap-02.txt, Oct. 2004.

7 Soliman, H., et al., "Hierarchical Mobile IPv6 Mobility Management (HMIPv6)," draft-ietf-mipshop-hmipv6-04.txt, Dec. 2004.

8 Koodli, R., "Fast Handovers for Mobile IPv6," draft-ietf-mipshop-fast-mipv6-03.txt, Oct. 2004.

9 Perkins, C., et al., "Ad-Hoc On Demand Distance Vector Routing," RFC 3561, July 2003.

10 Johnson, D., et al., "The Dynamic Source Routing Protocol," draft-ietf-manet-dsr-10.txt, July 2004.

11 Clausen, T., et al., "Optimized Link State Routing," RFC 3626, Oct. 2003.

12 Ogier, R., et al., "Topology Information Based on Reverse Path Forwarding," RFC 3684, Feb. 2004.

13 Coltun, R., D. Ferguson, and J. Moy, "OSPF for IPv6," RFC 2740, Dec. 1999.

Review Questions

1 How are Cisco SWAN and Mobile IP complementary?

2 The AAA-based key-generation mechanism delivers keys to which mobility entities?

3 What is a major hurdle to route optimization?

4 Name the message that conveys the location of the Mobile Node to the Home Agent or CN?

5 What is the benefit of Hierarchical Mobile IP?

6 Identify the fundamental difference between MANET and Mobile IP?

Answers to Review Questions

Now that you've read this book, you should be an expert on the basics of Cisco Mobile IP and network mobility solutions. Just to be sure, in each chapter, we've provided some review questions to help you gauge your understanding. This appendix offers you the answers, just in case you need them.

NOTE A friendly suggestion: Read each question carefully before answering—and beware of any sly tricks!

Chapter 1

1. You would use a Mobile IP solution, rather than DHCP or a simple WLAN, when you are interested in which of the following?

   a Nomadic mobility

   b Intrasubnet mobility

   c Always-on IP mobility

   d Stationary IP communication

   e Link-layer mobility

   Answer: c. Mobile IP allows the user to remain in active communication as the user moves. Thus, the user can maintain TCP/UDP connections while moving, because the home IP address of the Mobile Node does not change. DHCP, on the other hand, is a nomadic solution. The user obtains a new address in the foreign/new network and must close all communication before moving again. WLAN provides mobility within one IP subnet.

2. What is the difference between nomadicity and mobility in the context of Mobile IP?

   Answer: *Nomadicity* refers to the ability to move from one location to another and start communications. The user must terminate and restart sessions and applications as a result of the move. By contrast, *mobility* refers to the ability to move and maintain communication in the process.

3. What are the four requirements that a mobility solution must address?

   Answer: A mobility solution must address four requirements: location discovery, move detection, update signaling, and path (re)establishment.

4. Link-layer mobility protocols by themselves are capable of handling interaccess technology handovers.

   a True

   b False

   Answer: False. By definition, link-layer mobility is associated only with a specific access link technology.

5. IP layer mobility allows all IP-enabled applications, whether they use TCP, UDP, or another transport protocol, to seamlessly inherit full mobility across a diverse range of access link types.

   a True

   b False

   Answer: True.

Chapter 2

1. List the major entities in a Mobile IP deployment.

   Answer: The major entities in a Mobile IP deployment are Mobile Node, Home Agent, and Foreign Agent (or Care-of Address).

2. Mobile IP provides which of the following features? (Select two.)

   a A dynamic security association between the Mobile Node and Home Agent that changes as the Mobile Node roams across different subnets

   b Seamless roaming across IP subnets

   c Redirection routing to the Mobile Node based on the distance to the Mobile Node's new location

   d Mobility transparent to Correspondent Nodes

   e Host-specific routing to the Mobile Node

   Answer: b and d. Mobile IP provides seamless roaming across different IP subnets. The Mobile Node maintains communication through its home IP address. Thus, communication is transparent to Correspondent Nodes. A tunnel entry is included in the routing table at the Home Agent to tunnel packets to the Mobile Node.

3. In Mobile IP, when a Mobile Node moves to another domain, how do the Correspondent Nodes (CNs) now communicate with the Mobile Node?

a The Mobile Node informs the Correspondent Node of its movement, and thus a dynamic tunnel is created between the Correspondent Node and the Mobile Node's Care-of Address. The Correspondent Node sends packets for the Mobile Node through the tunnel.

b The Correspondent Nodes communicate as normal with the Mobile Node, sending packets to the Mobile Node's home IP address. The Home Agent intercepts the packets and forwards them to the Mobile Node through a dynamic tunnel established between the Home Agent and Care-of Address.

c The Correspondent Node sends packets to the home network and requests the Home Agent to tunnel the packets to the Mobile Node through the Mobile Node's Care-of Address.

d The Correspondent Node suspends communication with the Mobile Node until the Mobile Node returns home.

Answer: b. Mobility of the Mobile Node is transparent to the CN. The CN communicates with the Mobile Node as normal.

4. Which two features of a mobility protocol are facilitated by agent advertisements in Mobile IP?

a Location discovery

b Move detection

c Update signaling

d Path (re)establishment

Answer: a and b. The agent advertisement can be used for move detection and contains the Care-of Address, which is the location used by Mobile IP.

5. Which of the following is not used for move detection?

a The router address and prefix length extension portion of the agent advertisement

b The Care-of Address portion of the agent advertisement

c Link-state information

d RRQ message

Answer: d. The Mobile Node uses the RRQ message to communicate with its Home Agent after it detects movement.

6. Mobile IP handover occurs at Layer 2.

a True

b False

Answer: False. Mobile IP handover occurs at Layer 3 and is independent of Layer 2 handover. Mobile IP handover is the update of the routing table at the Home Agent.

7. Name three different types of Mobile IP handover policy algorithms. Briefly describe each one.

   Answer:

   - **Steady-state algorithm**—In this algorithm, the Mobile Node holds on to its current Foreign Agent as long as it can. After the Mobile Node establishes a valid registration with a Foreign Agent, it continues to listen for advertisements from other Foreign Agents. However, the Mobile Node cannot register with a new Foreign Agent until the current Foreign Agent's advertisement lifetime has expired.

   - **New network algorithm**—Using the Mobile IP agent advertisement and the prefix length extension, the Mobile Node knows exactly which subnets are available on the current link. When a Mobile Node hears an advertisement on that link, it compares the network prefix(es) of its current Mobility Agent's advertisement against any newly received agent advertisements. If they differ, the Mobile Node can assume that it has roamed and needs to initiate a Mobile IP handover.

   - **Link-state triggers**—Using Layer 2 information along with Mobile IP agent solicitations, the Mobile Node can determine even more quickly whether it has moved.

8. How does a Mobile Node know whether it is on its Home Network or a Foreign Network?

   a By comparing the lifetime granted in its current Mobile IP registration against that advertised in Mobile IP agent advertisements

   b By comparing the Foreign Agent address configured on the Mobile Node against that advertised in the Mobile IP agent advertisements

   c By comparing its Care-of Address against the Home Agent address advertised in Mobile IP agent advertisements

   d By comparing its Home Address and network prefix against those advertised in Mobile IP agent advertisements

   Answer: d. Upon hearing a Mobile IP agent advertisement, the Mobile Node can compare its network prefix against that advertised. It can thus discern whether it is at home or roaming.

9. A Mobile Node finds itself away from home on a network with a Foreign Agent. Describe the Mobile IP registration process, starting with how the Mobile Node learns that it is not home.

   Answer: The Mobile Node hears an agent advertisement from a Foreign Agent and determines that it is roaming by comparing its Home Network prefix against that in the advertisement. The Mobile Node learns the Care-of Address from the advertisement. It sends a RRQ to the Home Agent through the Foreign Agent. The Home Agent authenticates the RRQ and processes the request. It sends a RRP to the Mobile Node through the Foreign Agent. In the RRP, the Home Agent grants the registration lifetime for the Mobile Node.

10. What types of Care-of Addresses can a Mobile Node use on a Foreign Network?

    Answer: A Mobile Node can use a Foreign Agent–based Care-of Address and a Colocated Care-of Address on a Foreign Network.

11. Which of the following are advantages of a Mobile Node using a Foreign Agent Care-of Address? (Select two.)

    a Many Mobile Nodes can roam off of the same Care-of Address, which saves address space in IPv4.

    b The Mobile Node can retain the same Foreign Agent Care-of Address as it moves across different foreign domains.

    c The Mobile Node can be preconfigured with the Foreign Agent Care-of Address.

    d The same tunnel between the Home Agent and Foreign Agent can support numerous Mobile Nodes.

    e The Mobile Node does not need to reregister with its Home Agent when it moves to a different foreign domain.

    Answer: a and d. As the Mobile Node roams across different foreign domains, it can obtain a different Care-of Address.

12. Which of the following indicate situations when the Mobile Node would use a Colocated Care-of Address? (Select two.)

    a If the Mobile Node is statically configured with a Colocated Care-of Address

    b If the Mobile Node doesn't hear an agent advertisement from a Foreign Agent on the foreign domain

    c If the Mobile Node doesn't hear an agent advertisement from its Home Agent on the foreign domain

    d If the Mobile Node cannot detunnel its own packets

    e If the Foreign Agent is not providing services that the Mobile Node would like

    Answer: b and e.

13. How does a Mobile Node signify to the Home Agent that it would like a dynamic Home Address to be assigned?

    Answer: The Mobile Node sets the Home Address field in the RRQ to 0.0.0.0.

14. Describe the steps that a Foreign Agent follows during the registration process.

    Answer: When a Foreign Agent receives an RRQ, it first verifies any necessary security associations. If the Foreign Agent cannot or will not provide the requested services, it generates an RRP with an appropriate failure code. If the Foreign Agent is willing and able to provide all the requested services, it creates an entry in the pending registration table. A pending registration is held by the Foreign Agent for a maximum of 7 seconds before assuming that the Home Agent is unavailable. If an RRP is not received from the Home Agent, the Foreign Agent generates an RRP with a "registration timeout" error code. If the Foreign Agent receives the RRP from the Home Agent and deems the reply valid, it moves the pending registration entry into the visitor table.

15. Describe the steps that the Home Agent follows upon receiving a RRQ from a Mobile Node.

Answer: When the Home Agent receives the RRQ, it begins by verifying all security associations. After the authenticity of the RRQ has been verified, the Home Agent either updates the Mobile Node's binding, if it already exists in the binding table, or creates a new binding for the Mobile Node in the binding table. If a Mobile Node is requesting that a Home Address be dynamically assigned, the Home Agent receives an RRQ with a Home Address of 0.0.0.0. Before the binding is created, the Home Agent allocates an address to the Mobile Node that the Mobile Node retains for as long as its binding is active. The Home Agent includes the dynamically assigned address in the Home Address field of the RRP. When the registration has been accepted, the Mobile IP tunnel created, and the routing table updated, the Home Agent sends a gratuitous ARP on the Home Network to ensure that all traffic for the Mobile Node is delivered to the Home Agent. Finally, the Home Agent builds the HA-MN authenticator and sends an RRP to the CoA.

16. What is triangle routing?

Answer: Traffic for the Mobile Node goes from the Correspondent Node to the Home Agent to the Mobile Node, and return traffic goes directly from the Mobile Node to the Correspondent Node, bypassing the Home Agent, thus forming a triangular path.

17. What does a Mobile Node do upon returning home?

Answer: Upon returning home, a Mobile Node sends a deregistration message to the Home Agent, allowing the Home Agent to delete the mobility binding.

Chapter 3

1. What are the two key features that secure the Mobile IP registration messages?

Answer: Replay protection and authentication extensions secure the Mobile IP registration messages.

2. What prevents a rogue node from setting up the mobility binding for the Mobile Node on the Home Agent?

  a All Mobile IP control packets traverse the home AAA server, where the packet is authenticated.

  b The Home Agent discards any Mobile IP control packet if the IP source address does not equal that of the Mobile Node's Home Address.

    c The Mobile Node and Home Agent share a security association, and all Mobile IP control packets must be authenticated between the Mobile Node and Home Agent.

    d The FA performs egress filtering and drops any Mobile IP control packets that do not emanate from the Mobile Node's Care-of Address.

Answer: c. The communication between the Mobile Node and Home Agent *must be secure!* The Mobile Node and Home Agent must share a security association, and all Mobile IP control packets must be authenticated.

3. List the different types of Mobile IP authentication extensions, and describe their purpose.

Answer:

- **Mobile Node–Home Agent Authentication Extension (MHAE)**—Provides secure messaging between the Home Agent and Mobile Node. It is mandatory.

- **Foreign Agent–Home Agent Authentication Extension (FHAE)**—Provides secure messaging between the Foreign Agent and Home Agent. It is optional.

- **Mobile Node–Foreign Agent Authentication Extension (MFAE)**—Provides secure messaging between the Mobile Node and Foreign Agent. It is optional.

- **Mobile Node–AAA Authentication Extension**—Provides secure messaging between the Mobile Node and AAA server. It is optional.

4. Describe how the MHAE and FHAE can secure the same RRQ.

Answer: A Mobile Node secures its RRQ with an MHAE and forwards the request to its Foreign Agent. The Foreign Agent can append an extension to the RRQ and secure the extension with an FHAE. The two extensions secure different parts of the message and are between different Mobile IP entity pairs, namely, the base RRQ is secured between the Mobile Node and Home Agent, and the appended extension is secured between the Foreign Agent and Home Agent.

5. What elements comprise a security context? How is a security context identified?

Answer: A security context is comprised of an algorithm and mode, a key, and a replay protection method. A specific security context is identified in the authentication extension by the security parameter index, or SPI, value.

6. What is the standard hash algorithm that must be supported in a Mobile IPv4 deployment?

Answer: HMAC-MD5 must be supported in a Mobile IPv4 deployment. HMAC is a method of computing a hash of a hash of the message and is cryptographically stronger.

7. To verify the integrity of a message that has an authentication extension appended, the recipient does which of the following?

    a The recipient compares the authenticator value in the appended extension to that stored in the security association for the sender.

    b The recipient computes a cryptographic hash on the authenticator value and compares it to the value stored in the security context.

  c The recipient indexes the security association with the SPI and finds the authenticator value to compare to the value in the extension.

  d The recipient computes a cryptographic hash of the message and compares it to the authenticator value in the appended extension.

  Answer: d. The recipient uses the SPI in the authenticator to identify the security association being used and then uses that security association to compute its own cryptographic hash, which it compares with that contained in the authenticator. If the computed value matches the authenticator value in the message, the recipient knows that the message is as the sender intended. However, if the values do not match, the recipient can deduce that the message has been tampered with in transit.

8. Replay protection in registration messages is needed for which of the following reasons?

  a To thwart off reflection and replay attacks, where the message is retransmitted at a later time

  b To ensure that data flow is not disrupted and traffic is not redirected by the attacker

  c To guarantee that a unique field exists in the registration messages

  d A and B only

  e A and C only

  f A, B, and C

  Answer: f.

9. Briefly describe the timestamp replay protection method.

  Answer: The Mobile Node sends its timestamp in the identification field of a RRQ. When the Home Agent receives the registration, it verifies the timestamp to ensure that the time in the identification field is within a configured interval of its current timestamp. If the Home Agent finds that the difference between the timestamp and the current time is greater than the allowed interval, it rejects the registration. The Home Agent also updates the first 32 bits with the current timestamp in the RRP. Upon receipt of the RRP, the Mobile Node matches the sent RRQ message to the received reply by comparing the lower 32 bits and then updating its time by computing an offset. The Mobile Node then attempts to reregister with this updated timestamp.

10. Briefly describe the nonces replay protection method.

  Answer: Nonces are a concept in which the identification field is split into two 32-bit values, where the lower-order values are allocated by the Mobile Node and the high-order values are allocated by the Home Agent. For every RRQ, the Mobile Node generates a new lower-order value. The Home Agent copies that value into the lower-order portion of the identification field in the reply and generates a new random value for the high-order portion. The values generated by the Home Agent are then saved and used as the high-order portion of the identification field in the next RRQ sent by the Mobile Node. Because the Home Agent always knows what the next high-order portion of the identification field is supposed to be, it can easily determine whether a message is being replayed.

11. How does the Mobile Node secure registration messages using the FA Challenge mechanism?

   a The Mobile Node appends a valid challenge value to a registration message that it learns from the Foreign Agent's advertisements.

   b The Mobile Node appends a valid challenge value that it learns from its Home Agent in a reply message secured with the MHAE.

   c The Mobile Node appends a valid challenge value from a pool of challenge values with which it is preconfigured.

   d The Mobile Node appends a valid challenge value that it learns from the Foreign Agent through link-layer signaling.

   Answer: a. The Foreign Agent advertises challenge values in its agent advertisements. It maintains a pool of challenge values that are time sensitive. When a Mobile Node sends a RRQ, it must be secured with a valid challenge value.

12. What is the challenge window?

   Answer: The Foreign Agent often offers multiple challenge values that are valid for a specified amount of time, known as the *challenge window.*

13. The MN-AAA Authentication Extension can secure RRQs and RRPs.

   a True

   b False

   Answer: False. Because the AAA server does not sit in the registration path, this extension must only be generated by the Mobile Node. Thus, it can authenticate RRQs, but it cannot be used in the RRP because the reply is generated by an HA—or perhaps even an FA, which has no access to the AAA server.

14. Why is the Session Identifier used in Cisco dynamic security association and key distribution?

   Answer: The session identifier differentiates among multiple devices being used by the same user.

Chapter 4

1. Draw a basic Mobile IP topology.

   Answer:

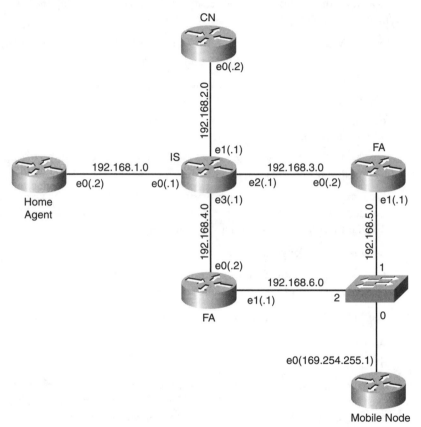

2. Which command enables the Mobile IP process on a router?

   Answer: The **router mobile** command enables the Mobile IP process on a router.

3. What are virtual networks and why are they used?

   Answer: Virtual networks commonly support nodes that never physically come home. Virtual networks are expressed as a network number and mask. Similar to a loopback interface, a virtual network is always up and not susceptible to physical failures, thereby ensuring higher availability.

4. Give an example of a basic Home Agent configuration with the following features: Home Agent address 192.168.1.2, virtual network 192.168.100.0/24, and Mobile Node 192.168.100.10 residing on the virtual network. Don't forget to include the Mobile Node-Home Agent security association.

Answer:

```
hostname HA
!
interface Ethernet0/0
 ip address 192.168.1.2 255.255.255.0
!
router mobile
!
ip mobile home-agent
ip mobile virtual-network 192.168.100.0 255.255.255.0
ip mobile host 192.168.100.10 virtual-network 192.168.100.0 255.255.255.0
ip mobile secure host 192.168.100.10 spi 100 key hex
1234567890abcdef1234567890abcdef
!
end
```

5. Give an example of a Foreign Agent configuration with the following features: Foreign Agent address 192.168.3.2 and Care-of Address 192.168.5.1 on Ethernet 1/0.

Answer:

```
hostname FA1
!
interface Ethernet0/0
 ip address 192.168.3.2 255.255.255.0
!
interface Ethernet1/0
 ip address 192.168.5.1 255.255.255.0
 ip mobile foreign-service
!
router mobile
!
ip mobile foreign-agent care-of Ethernet1/0
!
end
```

6. Give an example of an IOS Mobile Networks configuration with Home Agent 192.168.1.2 and Home Address 169.254.255.1.

Answer:

```
hostname MN
!
interface Loopback0
 ip address 192.168.100.10 255.255.255.255
!
interface Ethernet0/0
 ip address 169.254.255.1 255.255.255.0
 ip mobile router-service roam
```

```
!
router mobile
!
ip mobile secure home-agent 192.168.1.2 spi 100 key hex
1234567890abcdef1234567890abcdef
!
end
```

7. A router can serve as a Home Agent and Foreign Agent at the same time.

   a True

   b False

   Answer: True. One Mobile Node's Home Network can often be another node's visited network. In this case, you would want a single router to run both Home Agent and FA services.

8. Configuration of security associations for IOS Mobile IP is always done from the perspective of the agent that is to use that security association.

   a True

   b False

   Answer: True. For example, the **ip mobile secure foreign-agent...** command configures an HA-FA security association on the Home Agent. If the same command were configured on the Mobile Node, it would imply an MN-FA security association.

9. List two commands that are useful for troubleshooting on the Home Agent.

   Answer: The **show ip mobile binding** and **show ip mobile host** commands are useful for troubleshooting on the Home Agent.

10. Name a command that is useful for troubleshooting on the Foreign Agent.

    Answer: The **show ip mobile visitor** command is useful for troubleshooting on the Foreign Agent.

Chapter 5

1. What does campus mobility mean?

   Answer: Campus mobility refers to mobility within a single administrative domain. The main assumption in this model is that communication is within the campus (intranet), and no roaming exists across global Internet connectivity.

2. What is a AAA server? How does it help in a Mobile IP deployment?

   Answer: A AAA server is a centralized database that can store and maintain security associations, and manage network function. It is helpful to incorporate a AAA server into the network architecture for scalability reasons. If a Home Agent is supporting hundreds or thousands of Mobile Nodes, these MN-HA security associations can be stored on the AAA server instead of the Home Agent, freeing memory on the Home Agent.

3. When using a AAA server in the Home Network, which of the following statements is true?

   a The Mobile Node shares a security association with the AAA and not the Home Agent, and thus the AAA server authenticates the RRQ and informs the Home Agent whether the request should be accepted or denied.

   b The AAA server allows administrative functions to be streamlined.

   c The MHAEs are stored on the AAA, and the Home Agent consults the AAA server to retrieve a security association upon receiving a RRQ.

   d The AAA server and Home Agent must share a security relationship.

   Answer: b, c, and d. The AAA server is a centralized database that can store security associations and is efficient in streamlining administrative functions. The AAA server does not authenticate a Mobile Node per se, but rather it provides the requesting Home Agent with the security association through a AAA protocol, for example, RADIUS or TACACS+. Because the AAA server and Home Agent exchange critical information, they must share a security association.

4. What is RADIUS? Why is RADIUS recommended over TACACS+ for use in a Mobile IP deployment?

   Answer: RADIUS is a AAA protocol that provides authentication and accounting services in a client/server model. RADIUS uses UDP as the transport mechanism and only encrypts the password portion of packets, with the remainder of the packet sent in the clear. Thus, RADIUS is considered lighter-weight than TACACS+.

5. Describe the Cisco IOS feature that mitigates the latency involved in processing a Mobile Node's RRQ when the Home Agent must consult the AAA server for the Mobile Node's security association.

   Answer: Security association caching is a mechanism that allows the security association to be locally stored on the Home Agent after it has been retrieved from the AAA server. The next time the Home Agent has to authenticate the Mobile Node, it only needs to consult its local cache. Depending on configuration, the security association can either be deleted from cache automatically after a binding terminates or can be kept permanently on the Home Agent. The security associations can also be manually cleared.

6. What is ZeCC?

   Answer: ZeCC stands for Zero Configuration Client. It is designed to provide dynamic MN-HA key generation by integrating with a commonly deployed authentication infrastructure.

7. What are the two Home Agent formations in the Cisco Home Agent Redundancy feature?

   Answer: The two Home Agent formations in the Cisco Home Agent Redundancy feature are the active-standby formation and peer-peer formation.

8. Briefly describe the Updating function in the Cisco Home Agent Redundancy feature.

   Answer: When an RRQ is accepted by the active/peer Home Agent, the binding is updated/created on the standby/peer Home Agent. This process keeps the mobility binding table synchronized between the Home Agents. Note that an active Home Agent assumes the lead Home Agent role and receives all the RRQs from Mobile Nodes. It then updates the standby Home Agent with the necessary binding information. In the case of the peer configuration model, the peer Home Agents share the lead Home Agent role and either of them can receive the RRQs from the Mobile Nodes. They update each other accordingly.

9. Briefly describe the Downloading function in the Cisco Home Agent Redundancy feature.

   Answer: A Home Agent downloads the mobility binding table from the active/peer Home Agent immediately upon assuming the standby/peer Home Agent role. The standby/peer Home Agent ensures that it has downloaded the entire mobility binding table through a reliability mechanism. This process ensures that the standby/peer Home Agent has a copy of the current mobility binding table before providing backup Home Agent service.

10. Which of the following statements are true about the Cisco Home Agent Redundancy feature?

    a The active Home Agent and standby Home Agent both receive an incoming RRQ and set up the mobility binding. Only the active Home Agent responds with the RRP.

    b One of the Home Agents in the redundancy group receives the incoming RRQ and updates the standby Home Agent with the mobility binding.

    c All Home Agents in the redundancy group must share a security association.

    d The standby Home Agent keeps track of all active mobility bindings, but it only sets up the Mobile IP tunnels upon becoming the active Home Agent.

    Answer: b and c. Only one Home Agent can receive an incoming RRQ—the active Home Agent if the RRQ is addressed to the redundancy group address or either Home Agent if the RRQ is addressed to the loopback address configured similarly on all Home Agents in the redundancy group. The standby/peer Home Agent also sets up the Mobile IP tunnels upon being updated with mobility bindings.

Chapter 6

1. What does the term metro mobility mean?

   Answer: Metro mobility means mobility across multiple public and private networks.

2. What are the challenges or concerns for Mobile IP in the metro mobility model?

   Answer: Many of the challenges stem from the security implications of Internet routing. When crossing AS boundaries and traversing public networks, as in the metro mobility model, traffic from the Mobile Node is difficult to distinguish from spoofed traffic.

3. What feature is necessary for a network to overcome ingress filtering?

   a GRE tunneling

   b Reverse tunneling

   c Mobile Agent–Foreign Agent security association

   d Firewall on the home network

   e IP-in-IP encapsulation

   Answer: b. Reverse tunneling also allows multicast support and private addressing.

4. Draw a diagram showing how packets travel when using reverse tunneling.

   Answer:

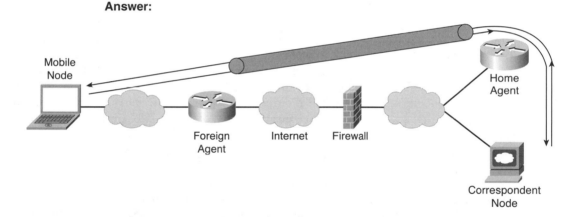

5. What is tunnel path MTU, and why is it sometimes an issue when using Mobile IP?

   Answer: Tunnel path MTU is the upper limit on the size of a packet that can be sent over a tunnel. It represents the largest amount of data that can be sent along the entire path without having to be fragmented. Because Mobile IP adds another IP header to a packet, it increases the size of the packet. This is especially significant in the metro mobility model, because the tunnel path can traverse multiple autonomous systems with varying MTU capabilities.

6. Describe the Path MTU Discovery mechanism.

   Answer: The Path MTU Discovery mechanism works as follows:

   - The sender sets the DF (don't fragment) bit in the IP header for all IP packets to a destination, and initially assumes the path MTU to be the outgoing link MTU.

   - Any router along the path that cannot forward the packet on the next outgoing link, because the link MTU is less than the total length of the packet, instead sends an ICMP destination unreachable message with code conveying that "fragmentation is needed, but the DF bit is set" back to the sender. This message usually includes an extension specifying the MTU of the link requiring fragmentation. The packet is then dropped.

   - Upon receipt of such an ICMP destination unreachable message, the sender decreases the path MTU estimate to the destination and sends smaller IP packets along the path.

   - Discovery is complete when the sender receives no more such ICMP destination unreachable messages.

   When using tunnel encapsulation, the DF bit must be copied onto the outer tunnel header. This ensures that the path MTU discovery can still be used.

7. What is NAT and why is it a challenge when using Mobile IP?

   Answer: NAT is Network Address Translation. An NAT box translates the address used by the node in the private network to an address that is valid in the global network. When the Care-of Address tunnel endpoint is behind an NAT, the IP-in-IP tunneling cannot pass through the NAT gateway. The IP layer encapsulations do not carry transport layer (TCP/UDP) port numbers to permit unique translation of the private Care-of Address into the public address.

8. How is the coexistence of NAT with Mobile IP achieved?

   Answer: Coexistence of NAT with Mobile IP is achieved through a UDP tunneling protocol. The IETF Mobile IP Working Group standardized RFC 3519, which defines a UDP tunneling protocol to be used for both the forward and reverse Mobile IP tunnels. The new protocol defines extensions to the registration and agent advertisement portions of the Mobile IP protocol. A key feature of this NAT–Mobile IP solution is that data packets are now also sent to the UDP ports that set up the Mobile IP registration, that is, UDP port 434 on the Home Agent and the UDP source port used for the RRQ on the Mobile Node.

9. How does the Home Agent infer that a Mobile Node is roaming behind an NAT gateway?

   Answer: The Home Agent evaluates the RRQ and compares the source IP address of the packet to the Care-of Address inside the request. If the two addresses differ, the Home Agent deduces that an NAT gateway exists in the middle and enables the use of UDP tunneling.

10. Mobile IP and IPSec can coexist with proper configuration and placement of the devices. Draw a diagram that shows Mobile IP over IPSec and IPSec over Mobile IP.

Answer:

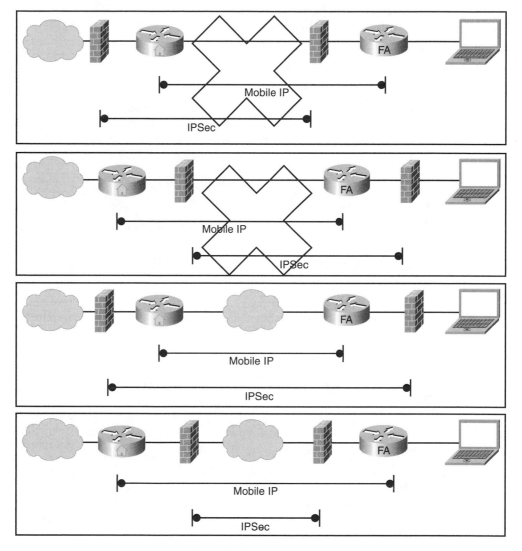

11. In the previous question, a particular protocol tunnel is contained within the other, that is, Mobile IP over IPSec or IPSec over Mobile IP. In these cases, in what order is the encapsulation removed?

Answer: Encapsulation is always removed in the opposite order in which it was added.

12. What are the advantages and disadvantages of IPSec over Mobile IP?

Answer: Running IPSec over Mobile IP allows the user to roam without needing to reestablish the VPN after each access-link change. However, this configuration only allows the Mobile Node to roam outside the private network. This solution works well for users that never roam into the private network.

13. What are the advantages and disadvantages of Mobile IP over IPSec?

Answer: For users that need to roam into the private network, running Mobile IP over IPSec can allow sessions to be maintained within the private network. Unfortunately, with Mobile IP over IPSec, the IPSec session must be reestablished every time the access link changes. This can be acceptable in configurations where the Mobile Node has only one single public network connection and the IP address does not change, such as with a cellular network.

14. Registration Revocation allows for which of the following?

a Timely release of Mobile IP resources

b Early adoption of domain policy changes with regard to services offered/required of a Mobile IP binding

c Timely notification to a Mobile Node that it is no longer receiving mobility services, thereby significantly shortening any black-hole periods to facilitate a more robust recovery.

d Accurate Mobile IP and resource accounting

e All of the above

Answer: e.

15. What are the four main components of resource revocation?

Answer:

- The Mobility Agents advertise support for the revocation feature by setting a newly defined X bit in the Mobile IP agent advertisement.

- The Mobility Agents convey to one another that they are interested in receiving revocation messages by appending the Revocation Support Extension to registration messages. In this extension, the mobility agent can also express whether it wants the Mobile Node to be notified upon revocation (or early termination) of the binding through the I bit in the extension.

- After negotiating and establishing use of the revocation mechanism for mobility binding(s), the Mobility Agents send reliable revocation messages to one another upon revocation (or early termination) of a mobility binding.

- If it is determined that the Mobile Node should be notified that its binding has been revoked, the Foreign Agent simply unicasts an agent advertisement to the Mobile Node with a [re]set sequence number of 0. The Mobile Node understands that its mobility binding has been reset and that it must reregister.

Chapter 7

1   Cisco Mobile Networks is a mobility solution that provides which of the following? (Select three.)

   a   Dynamic host routing propagation to clients on the mobile router.

   b   The devices connected to the mobile router do not need to be Mobile IP aware because the MR is providing the roaming capabilities.

   c   Foreign Agent redundancy for transparent Foreign Agent failure between the mobile router and Foreign Agent.

   d   Packets destined to the mobile router are double encapsulated. The Home Agent forwards packets destined to the mobile networks to the Foreign Agent, which then forwards the packets to the mobile router, which then forwards to the devices on its networks.

   e   It allows entire network(s) to roam.

   Answer: b, d, and e: Cisco Mobile Networks allows entire networks to roam. It is ideal for airplanes, ships, and trains, that is, any architecture where the entire network is in motion.

2.   In network mobility, how does the Home Agent know which mobile networks are connected to a mobile router?

   Answer: This can either be done through static configuration of the mobile networks or through dynamic updates during the Mobile IP registration process.

3.   What is the roaming interface?

   Answer: Roaming interfaces are used as the gateway between the mobile networks and the rest of the network.

4.   What is the preferred path feature, and why is it needed?

   Answer: The mobile router can obtain Layer 2 connections on different interfaces and therefore must decide on which interface to roam and register. Preferred path allows the mobile router to select the best interface on which to roam and register based on a priority.

5.   What is the hold down period? Describe its purpose.

   Answer: After hearing a Foreign Agent's advertisement, the mobile router waits the hold down period before deciding to use the agent. The hold down period allows the mobile router to be sure that a link is reliable enough to hear the agent for a period of time before committing to use the agent. The mobile router avoids prematurely registering with a Foreign Agent on a lossy wireless link.

6. Draw a diagram showing routing to and from a mobile router.

Answer:

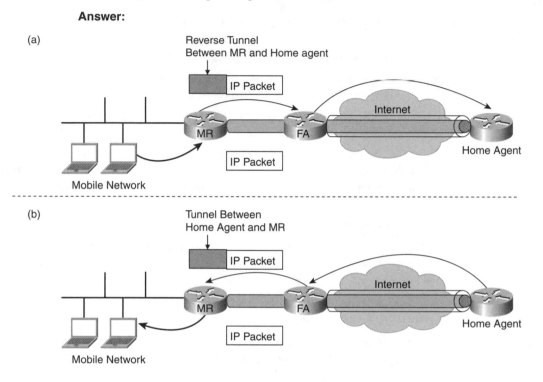

(a)

Reverse Tunnel
Between MR and Home agent

IP Packet

Internet

MR

FA

Home Agent

IP Packet

Mobile Network

(b)

Tunnel Between
Home Agent and MR

IP Packet

Internet

MR

FA

Home Agent

IP Packet

Mobile Network

7. What additional processing over standard Mobile IP must the Home Agent do to support network mobility?

Answer: The Home Agent must inject the mobile networks into its forwarding table so that routing protocols configured on it can redistribute these mobile routes. The mobile router must also create an additional tunnel to the mobile router's Home Address and add routes to the mobile networks through this tunnel. The Home Agent then advertises reachability to these mobile networks through the Interior Gateway Routing Protocol (IGRP), thereby attracting packets that are destined to nodes on the mobile networks.

8. Draw a diagram depicting the dual tunnels used in network mobility.

   Answer:

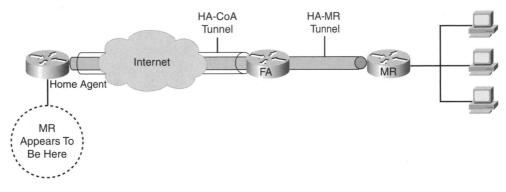

9. For IOS Mobile Networks, why is another tunnel needed inside the standard Home Agent Care-of Address tunnel?

   Answer: This second tunnel is required because if a Foreign Agent is in use, it only has a route to the Home Address. Packets destined to the mobile networks would follow the standard routing back to the Home Agent and end up in a routing loop.

10. What is the Priority Home Agent Assignment feature?

    Answer: The Cisco Mobile Networks–Priority Home Agent Assignment feature allows a mobile router to select a closer Home Agent when it is roaming. The mobile router can select a preferred Home Agent from a set of configured Home Agents based on a combination of existing Home Agent priority configurations on the mobile router and Care-of Address access lists configured on the Home Agent.

11. What caveats are involved with using the Priority Home Agent Assignment feature?

    Answer: If the Mobile Node changes the preferred Home Agent, the IGP must converge before the forwarding path is optimized. While the IGP is reconverging, packets can bounce around the network following stale routes. In some cases, these packets can be lost.

    Answer: The same Home Network needs to be configured on all Home Agents. You cannot make the Home Address reachable through the Home Agent that is in use without injecting host routes into the network. Host routing would defeat the purpose of Mobile IP. You should use a route map to prevent the Home Network from even being redistributed into the IGP and use an address from the mobile network for management of the mobile router.

12. By using the Cisco Foreign Agent Optimized Routing for Mobile Networks, the Foreign Agent can do which of the following?

a It can directly set up a visitor entry between a node on a visiting mobile router and a Correspondent Node, and tunnel traffic to the Correspondent Node.

b It can directly receive traffic from a Correspondent Node and tunnel the traffic to a visiting mobile router.

c It can directly send traffic from a Correspondent Node that is directly connected to it, to a node on a mobile network of one of its visiting mobile routers.

d It can directly send traffic from a node on one of its visiting mobile routers to a node on another visiting mobile router.

Answer: c. Traffic from a Correspondent Node that is directly connected to a Foreign Agent can be sent to a node on a visiting mobile network without having to traverse the Home Agent.

13. Briefly describe the Mobile Router Redundancy feature.

Answer: The Mobile Router Redundancy feature leverages HSRP and provides a backup mechanism in case the mobile router fails. One mobile router in the redundancy group is deemed the active mobile router, with the other mobile routers in passive mode. The active mobile router is the router responsible for registering with the Home Agent and for maintaining an active mobility binding. If the active mobile router fails, one of the passive mobile routers is selected as the new active mobile router based on a priority selection algorithm. Upon becoming the new active mobile router, a mobile router sends an agent solicitation out of its roaming interfaces to learn about the existing Foreign Agents and registers back with its Home Agent.

14. Mobile IP traffic is sent on one link and received on another link in which of the following?

a Nested Mobile IP tunnels

b Asymmetric links

c Bidirectional links

d Simultaneous bindings

Answer: b. If a mobile router and Foreign Agent communicate through asymmetric links, the Foreign Agent receives the mobile router's RRQ on an interface different from the one on which it sent its agent advertisement. Also, the Foreign Agent forwards the RRP to the mobile router on an interface different from the one on which it received the RRQ.

15. How are QoS features added to the dynamic tunnels established in network mobility, that is, the tunnel between the Home Agent and Foreign Agent, and the tunnel between the Home Agent and mobile router?

Answer: Tunnel interface templates are used. Using a tunnel template, QoS preclassification (the **qos-preclassify** command) can be applied to the tunnel, allowing the original packet header to classify the packet on the outbound interface instead of the Mobile IP tunnel header. It lets the router peek into the original packet and use the QoS credentials of that packet, allowing certain traffic types to receive preferential treatment over the Mobile IP tunnel.

Chapter 8

1. What are the three modes of home addressing that Cisco Mobile IP supports?

Answer: The three modes of home addressing that Cisco Mobile IP supports are static addressing, static addressing with NAI, and dynamic addressing with NAI.

2. How does static addressing with an NAI work?

Answer: When used together, the NAI serves as the unique identifier for the Mobile Node, and the static Home Address is verified for use by that particular NAI. The Mobile Node proposes the configured Home Address as a nonzero Home Address in the RRQ message, and the Home Agent verifies that the Mobile Node can indeed use the Home Address based on its NAI. The Home Agent can accept this address or return another address in the RRP message.

3. A dynamic Home Address for a Mobile Node can be assigned through which of the following methods?

   a Local pool on the Home Network

   b DHCP on the Home Network

   c AAA server on the Home Network

   d All of the above

Answer: d.

4. Describe how dynamic Home Address assignment through local pool works.

Answer: One or more address pools are configured on the Home Agent. The Home Agent then allocates addresses from the pool on a first come, first served basis. The Mobile Node keeps the address as long as it has an active mobility binding on the Home Agent. The Mobile Node can update its binding by sending a RRQ with either the allocated address or 0.0.0.0 as its Home Address. When the binding expires, the address is immediately returned to the local pool so that it can be assigned again.

5. What role does the Home Agent assume when allocating a Home Address through DHCP? Briefly describe how it works.

   Answer: The Home Agent assumes the role of a DHCP proxy client. IOS Mobile IP leverages the existing DHCP proxy client in IOS to allow the Home Address to be allocated by a DHCP server. The Home Agent obtains an address through DHCP on behalf of the Mobile Node. The DHCP proxy client allows the Home Agent to maintain the DHCP lease by tracking the lease time for each Mobile Node and renewing the lease while that Mobile Node still has an active binding. The NAI is sent in the Client-ID option of the DHCP request and can be used by the server to provide dynamic DNS services.

6. What is fixed addressing?

   Answer: Dynamic addressing can be truly dynamic where the Mobile Node gets a random address upon initial registration. Dynamic addressing can also allocate the Mobile Node the same IP address all the time, commonly referred to as *fixed addressing.*

7. How does a call model help in identifying scalability concerns?

   Answer: Call models are generally built toward the busy hour. The idea is that humans are creatures of habit, and in many cases, our habits are similar to those around us. The hour when all users are their most active is referred to as the *busy hour.* From a network engineering perspective, if enough capacity exists in the busy hour, enough capacity will be available all day long.

8. A busy-hour profile for one or more classes of users needs to encompass which four factors?

   Answer: A busy-hour profile for one or more classes of users needs to encompass number of nodes, frequency of mobility, amount of data traffic, and number of tunnels.

9. What extra management does Cisco Enterprise MIB provide that RFC 2006 MIB does not?

   Answer: Cisco Enterprise MIB provides management of Mobile Nodes with NAI, Home Agent redundancy, and number of Mobile Nodes currently using the Mobility Agent.

10. What common troubleshooting issues arise in Mobile IP deployments?

    Answer: Troubleshooting issues include path MTU discovery when firewalls are deployed, transport failure because of reverse path forwarding checks, traversal of NATs or firewalls, and incompatibility in implementation of security associations.

Chapter 9

1. How are Cisco SWAN and Mobile IP complementary?

   Answer: A Mobile Node benefits from Cisco SWAN's Fast Secure Roaming when accessing a WLAN network and maintains its communication when moving to other access networks, such as cellular or fixed Ethernet using Mobile IP.

2. The AAA-based key-generation mechanism delivers keys to which mobility entities?

   Answer: The AAA server generates the MN-FA authentication key to the Foreign Agent and/or the MN-HA authentication key to the Home Agent. The message from the AAA server also contains the information for the Mobile Node to generate the same key, derived from the MN-AAA shared key.

3. What is a major hurdle to route optimization?

   Answer: A major hurdle is a method to secure the signaling between the Mobile Node and CN, which are strangers. The Return Routability procedure is the standard method of obtaining the key to protect the control message.

4. Name the message that conveys the location of the Mobile Node to the Home Agent or CN.

   Answer: The Binding Update message is sent by the Mobile Node to inform the Home Agent and CN of its location. This creates a binding cache entry that directs packets to the registered Care-of Address to reach the Mobile Node.

5. What is the benefit of Hierarchical Mobile IP?

   Answer: The benefit is that the minimized signaling is confined within the region between the Mobility Anchor Point (MAP) and Mobile Node. The data traffic is redirected to the new location by the MAP, thereby reducing packet loss that might have been incurred by the additional latency if the RRQ had to traverse the distance to the HA.

6. Identify the fundamental difference between MANET and Mobile IP.

7. Mobile IP is based on the premise of having a network infrastructure to support Layer 3 mobility. MANET deals with setting up the routing fabric that is made up by Mobile Nodes that enter or exit in ad-hoc mode.

IOS Mobile IP: Supported SNMP MIBs

This appendix contains graphical representations of the Simple Network Management Protocol (SNMP) Management Information Base (MIB) objects, which are available in Cisco IOS (see Figures B-1 and B-2).

NOTE   To view Figure B-1 and Figure B-2 in a complete, unbroken format, visit http://www.ciscopress.com/title/158705132X. These figures, which are available in both JPEG and PDF format, are located under the section "Appendix."

Figure B-1 *RFC 2006 MIB Tree*

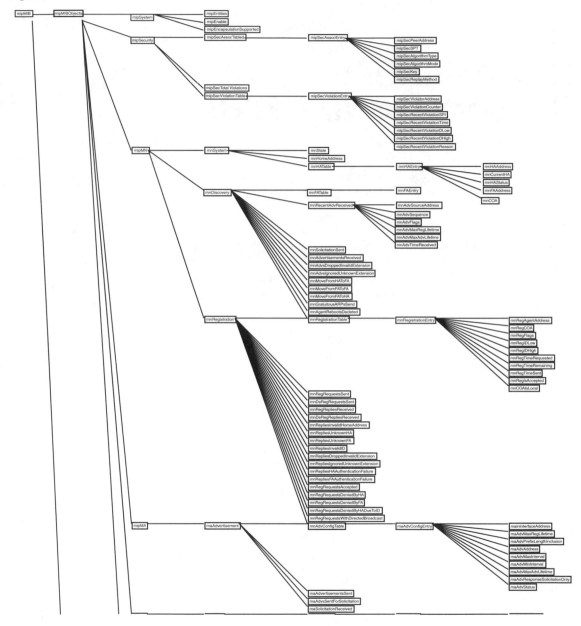

Figure B-1 *RFC 2006 MIB Tree (continued)*

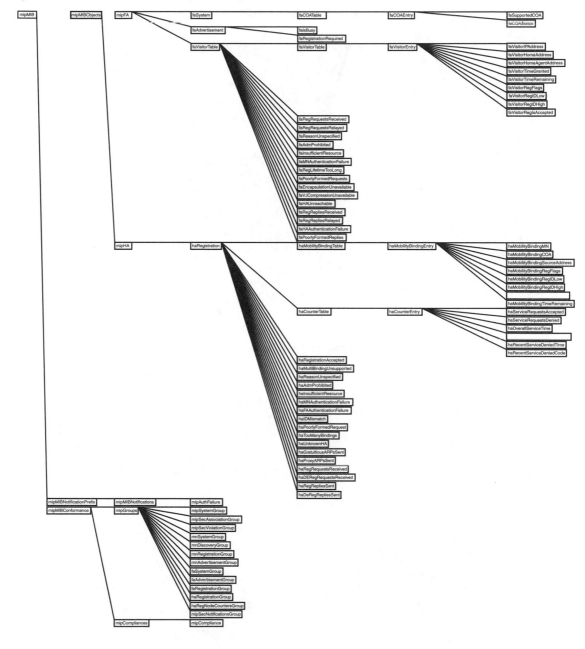

Figure B-2 *Cisco Mobile IP MIB Tree*

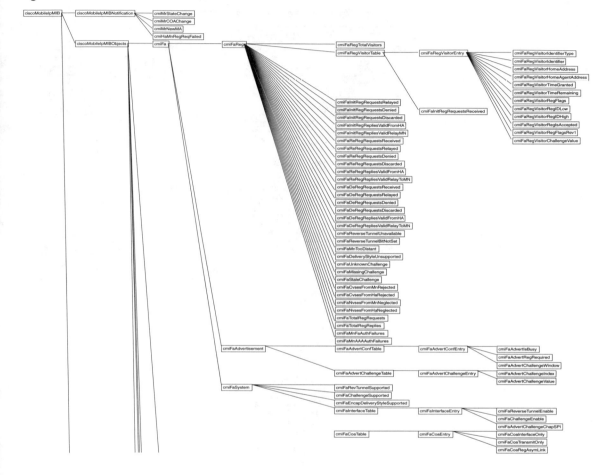

Figure B-2 *Cisco Mobile IP MIB Tree (continued)*

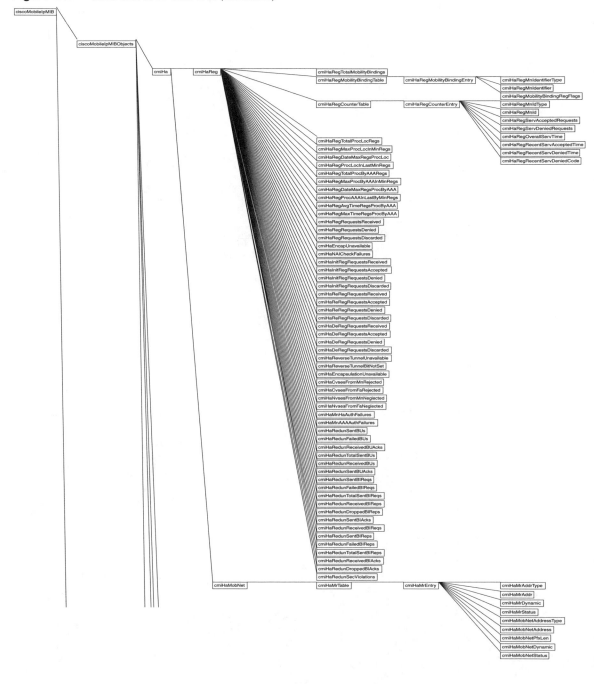

Figure B-2 *Cisco Mobile IP MIB Tree (continued)*

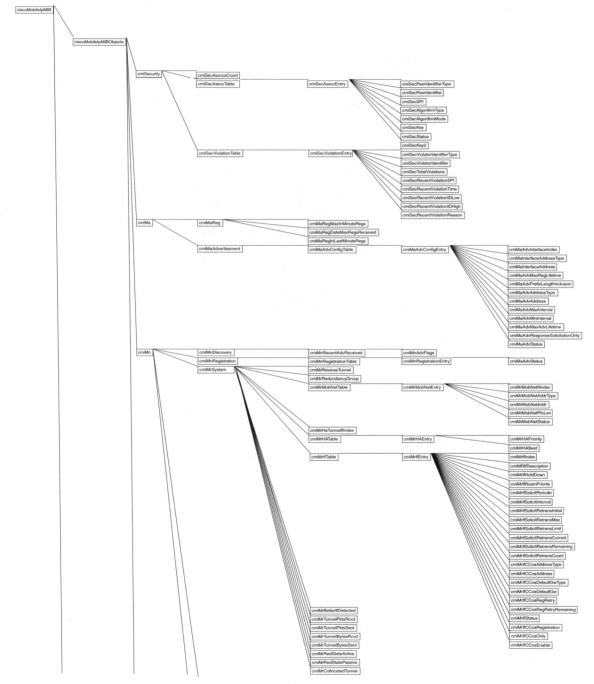

Figure B-2 *Cisco Mobile IP MIB Tree (continued)*

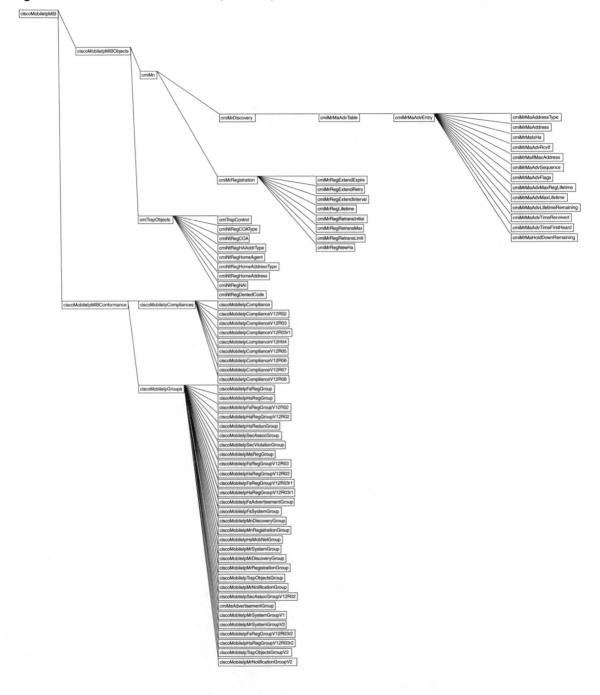

INDEX

A

aaa option, 100
AAA server
    aaa option, 100
    address assignment, 190
    assigned DHCP server, 191
    authorization of static home addresses, 193
    home addressing, 190
    load-sa option, 100
    local pool selection, 191
    overview, 96, 98–100
    permanent option, 100
    RADIUS, 100–101
    TACACS+, 101
AAA-based dynamic key generation, 220–221
access links, 29
active-standby home agent configuration, 108
address assignment, 190
address fields, 42, 44–45
agent advertisements
    handover, 28–33
    location discovery, 28
    move detection, 28–33
    overview, 24–27
    router advertisement, 24
    router solicitation, 24
agent selection, 154–155
algorithm security, 61–62
asymmetric links
    configuration, 167–168
    example, 168–169
    overview, 166–167
authentication, 41
authentication options, 234–236
authentication response extension, 72

B

baseline topology
    IOS Mobile IP
        correspondent node configuration, 79
        foreign agent configuration, 83–85
        home agent configuration, 80–81, 83
        intermediate system configuration, 79
        mobile node configuration, 85–86
        overview, 77, 79
bootstrap, 236–238
broadcast support, 38

C

call model, 194–195
    example, 197–198
    objects matching, 199–200
campus mobility
    AAA server
        overview, 96, 98–100
        RADIUS, 100–101
        TACACS+, 101
    Cisco Zero Configuration Client, 102–103
    Home Agent Redundancy
        configuration commands,
            107–108, 110–113, 115
        overview, 104–106
    overview, 95–96
Care-of Address (CoA)
    collocated CoA (CCoA), 22
    foreign agent CoA, 22
    overview, 21
cdma2000 technology, 209–210, 212
challenge extension, 71
Cisco Dynamic Security Association and Key
  Distribution, 70
    authentication response extension, 72
    challenge extension, 71
    configuration extensions, 72
    domain extension, 71
    security association setup extension, 71
    session index extension, 71
Cisco Enterprise MIB, 199
Cisco Mobile Networks
    asymmetric links
        configuration, 167–168
        example, 168–169
        overview, 166–167
    Colocated Care-of Address support, 170
        dynamic Colocated Care-of Address,
            171–172

N

O

P

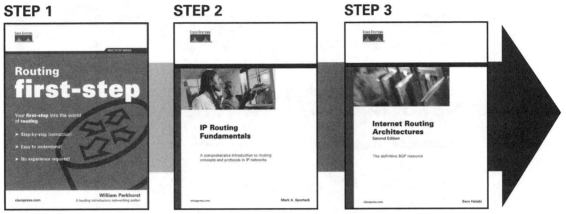

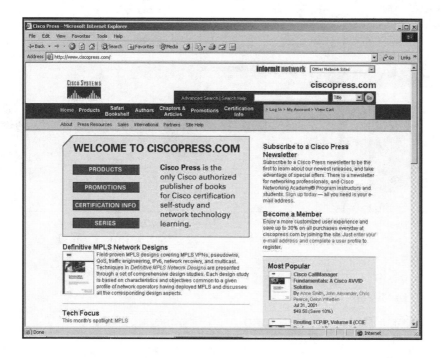

SEARCH THOUSANDS OF BOOKS FROM LEADING PUBLISHERS

Safari® Bookshelf

Safari® Bookshelf is a searchable electronic reference library for IT professionals that features thousands of titles from technical publishers, including Cisco Press.

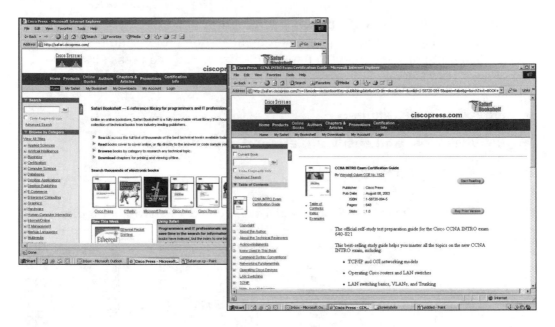

With Safari Bookshelf you can

- **Search** the full text of thousands of technical books, including more than 130 Cisco Press titles from authors such as Wendell Odom, Jeff Doyle, Bill Parkhurst, Sam Halabi, and Dave Hucaby.

- **Read** the books on My Bookshelf from cover to cover, or just flip to the information you need.

- **Browse** books by category to research any technical topic.

- **Download** chapters for printing and viewing offline.

With a customized library, you'll have access to your books when and where you need them—and all you need is a user name and password.

TRY SAFARI BOOKSHELF FREE FOR 14 DAYS!

You can sign up to get a 10-slot Bookshelf free for the first 14 days. Visit **http://safari.ciscopress.com** to register.

☐ **YES!** I'm requesting a **free** subscription to *Packet*™ magazine.

☐ No. I'm not interested at this time.

☐ Mr.
☐ Ms.

First Name (Please Print) | Last Name

Title/Position (Required)

Company (Required)

Address

City | State/Province

Zip/Postal Code | Country

Telephone (Include country and area codes) | Fax

E-mail

Signature (Required) | Date

☐ I would like to receive additional information on Cisco's services and products by e-mail.

1. Do you or your company:
A ☐ Use Cisco products   C ☐ Both
B ☐ Resell Cisco products D ☐ Neither

2. Your organization's relationship to Cisco Systems:
A ☐ Customer/End User   E ☐ Integrator   J ☐ Consultant
B ☐ Prospective Customer   F ☐ Non-Authorized Reseller K ☐ Other (specify):
C ☐ Cisco Reseller   G ☐ Cisco Training Partner
D ☐ Cisco Distributor   I ☐ Cisco OEM

3. How many people does your entire company employ?
A ☐ More than 10,000   D ☐ 500 to 999   G ☐ Fewer than 100
B ☐ 5,000 to 9,999   E ☐ 250 to 499
c ☐ 1,000 to 4,999   f ☐ 100 to 249

4. Is your company a Service Provider?
A ☐ Yes   B ☐ No

5. Your involvement in network equipment purchases:
A ☐ Recommend   B ☐ Approve   C ☐ Neither

6. Your personal involvement in networking:
A ☐ Entire enterprise at all sites   F ☐ Public network
B ☐ Departments or network segments at more than one site   D ☐ No involvement
C ☐ Single department or network segment   E ☐ Other (specify):

7. Your Industry:
A ☐ Aerospace   G ☐ Education (K–12)   K ☐ Health Care
B ☐ Agriculture/Mining/Construction U ☐ Education (College/Univ.) L ☐ Telecommunications
C ☐ Banking/Finance   H ☐ Government—Federal   M ☐ Utilities/Transportation
D ☐ Chemical/Pharmaceutical   I ☐ Government—State   N ☐ Other (specify):
E ☐ Consultant   J ☐ Government—Local
F ☐ Computer/Systems/Electronics

CPRESS

Packet magazine serves as the premier publication linking customers to Cisco Systems, Inc. Delivering complete coverage of cutting-edge networking trends and innovations, *Packet* is a magazine for technical, hands-on users. It delivers industry-specific information for enterprise, service provider, and small and midsized business market segments. A toolchest for planners and decision makers, *Packet* contains a vast array of practical information, boasting sample configurations, real-life customer examples, and tips on getting the most from your Cisco Systems' investments. Simply put, *Packet* magazine is straight talk straight from the worldwide leader in networking for the Internet, Cisco Systems, Inc.

We hope you'll take advantage of this useful resource. I look forward to hearing from you!

Cecelia Glover
Packet Circulation Manager
packet@external.cisco.com
www.cisco.com/go/packet